Power at Bay

Bridget Gubbins

Earthright Publications

British Library Cataloguing in Publication Data

A catalogue record for this book is available from the British Library

Earthright Publications
7 Tiverton Way
CAMBRIDGE
CB1 3TU

ISBN 0 907367 11 9

Disclaimer

The author and publisher believe that this account of the actions of the Druridge Bay Campaign and the events in which they were involved is fair and accurate. It is largely the perspective of one person and it is recognised that other participants may have different views of what happened. Great effort has been taken to ensure that there is no misrepresentation, and the author and publisher apologise to any person or organisation who feels that they have not been fairly treated or described.

Set in Century Schoolbook
Printed on Fineblade Cartridge

Design and layout by Green Dog Creations, Newcastle upon Tyne
Pre-press by Digiset, Gateshead
Printed by J W Arrowsmiths, Bristol

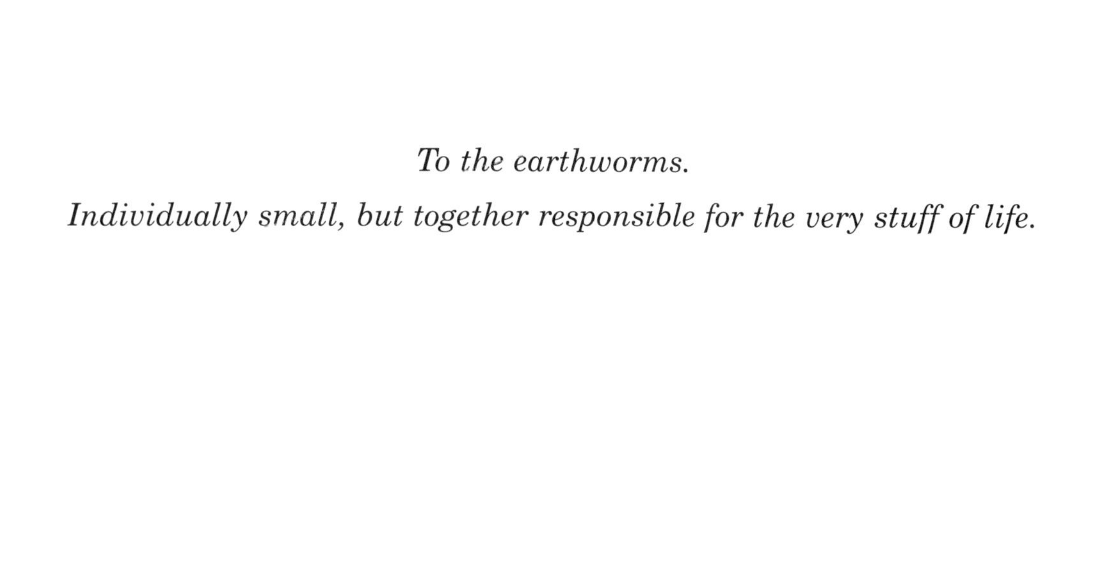

To the earthworms.

Individually small, but together responsible for the very stuff of life.

Contents

Our Campaign - Your Campaign

In these boxed sections the Druridge Bay Campaign addresses other campaigners directly, and offers help, support and encouragement.

The Location of Druridge Bay

Location of north-east England

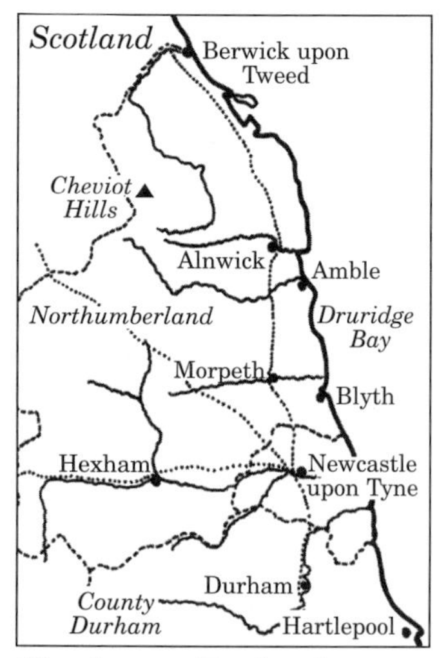

North-east England

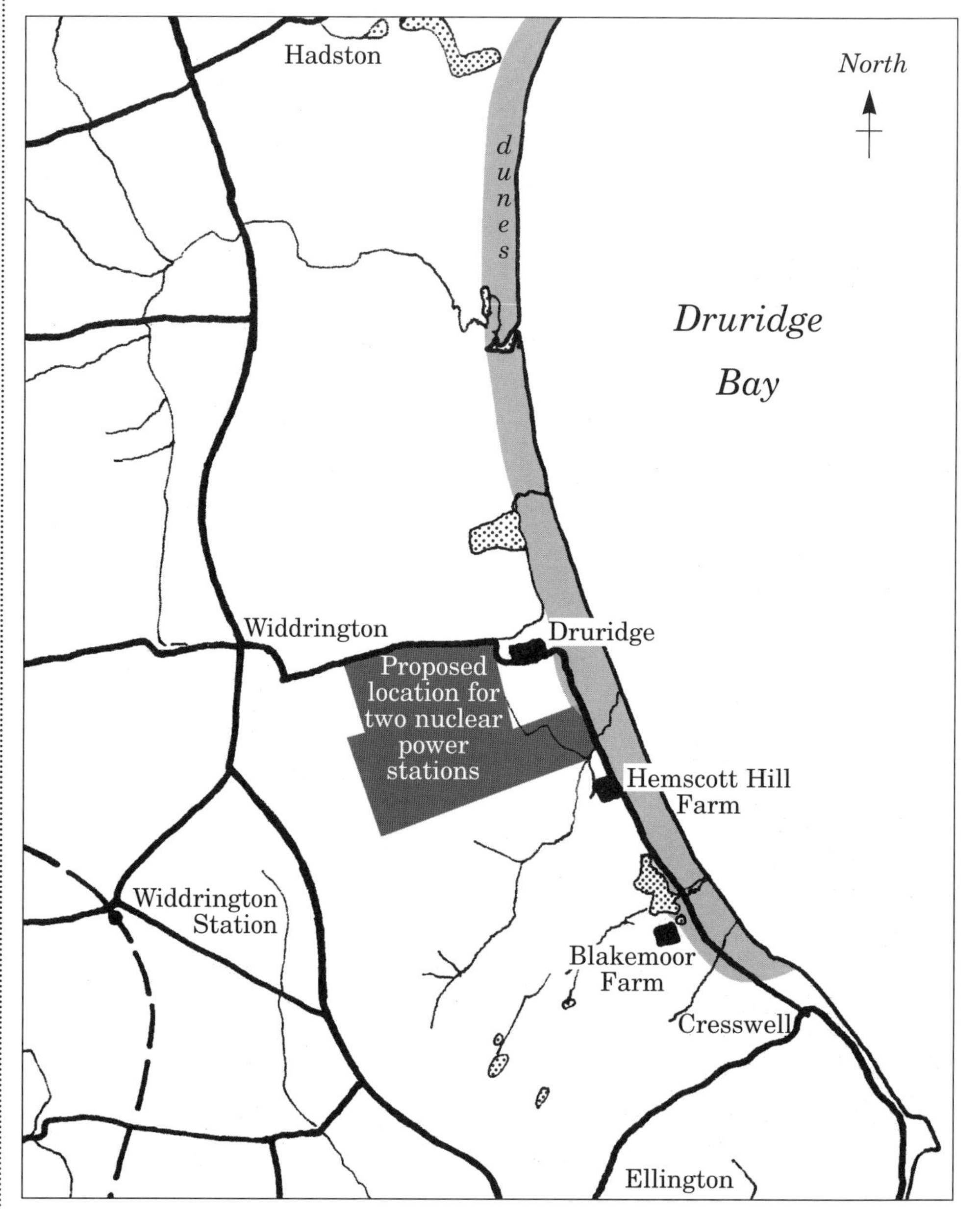

Introducing the Story

In all good fairy stories, we know when we start reading that however awful the adventures of the luckless heroes and heroines, they will win in the end. The ogres, the giants, the thunderous powerful enemies will be overcome.

The Druridge story has a happy ending. When you start reading the first chapter, you do it with the knowledge that in the end the Druridge Bay Campaign overcame the opposition. The nuclear power station builders were finally driven away, after eighteen years of resistance; the multi-national company abandoned its legal rights to take away the beach, after a six year struggle.

However the heroes and heroines of the story, when they were tussling with the giants during those years, did not know they would win. At times, the work was heartbreaking, especially when the nuclear industry drilled and purchased the land, or when people had to watch yet another lorry-load of beach sand being driven away, and the storm-surging sea rushing through the dunes.

The first three chapters of this book describe the activities of the Druridge Bay Campaigners, the generally unapplauded little people. The first chapter is about the developing threat posed by the nuclear industry to this beach fifteen miles north of Tyneside. It sets the threat in context, and describes how local people tackled it from a base of very little knowledge. The third chapter tells how the campaigners eventually persuaded the declining nuclear industry and the fading Conservative government to abandon for ever any idea of nuclear power stations at Druridge Bay. In between, the second chapter is about sand extraction, which had been taking place, with increasing impact, for decades. For more than five years, Druridge campaigners relentlessly focused public attention on the Ready Mixed Concrete group, until they changed their policy.

The second part of the book looks at how and why the campaigners succeeded. Now that its spontaneous work is over, there is time for a little reflection. The account is my own, as the Druridge Bay Campaign's publicity officer, and as one who has been closely involved with all its phases. It is not academic, and it is not the last word. Other objective observers, students and teachers will surely see things which I do not see, or disagree with aspects of my interpretation. I briefly survey books by academics about pressure groups. Were we a pressure group? If so, what kind? Our interactions with the parliamentary process are outlined, producing a picture of local pressure group activities in a now-ended era of Conservative government.

There are chapters about the people themselves, and the internal organisation of a campaign, which grew organically in response to perceived needs. The characters of those involved created the Druridge Bay Campaign's style and flavour. They speak for themselves through interviews. The next chapter turns the tables on the media people, as I interview them rather than the other way round. Reporters from local newspapers, radio and TV give detailed descriptions of what we did well. They offer advice which should be uniquely useful to other campaigners.

Finally, there is an honest analysis of the true role of our campaigns. Were we responsible for what is seen locally as two great environmental successes, or would the changes have happened anyway? The fallen giants are given a chance to put their points of view, which does not usually happen in fairy stories.

Running throughout the main text are two other themes. The story of the decline of the coal mines, in parallel to that of the developing nuclear industry, is told through the words of a local member of the National Union of Mineworkers. And there are eighteen 'Our Campaign Your Campaign' boxes. In these I address other campaigners directly, offering help, support and encouragement on topics such as how we made friends with our MP, or kept going at moments of despair, or built up really good contacts with the media. These sections are intended to encourage and share experience, rather than to tell others how to do things. Each campaign is bound to be entirely individual.

I realised as I wrote this book that the very act of doing it was creating a myth. By putting down this story in words, by gathering together the pictures, I am immortalising a story that would otherwise fade away gradually from people's memories. It would be almost as though the struggles had never happened.

I am glad therefore that Monica Frisch of Earthright Publications asked me to write *Power at Bay*. I have tried to make it easy to read, lighthearted in style, dotted with comments and poetry, interviews and anecdotes. I hope it will be of use to other campaigners and of interest to students. Then eventually, as copies gather dust on bookshelves in years to come, I would like to think that young people of the next generations may pick it up from time to time; that they may think about what their forefathers and mothers did, and what might have been.

Bridget Gubbins

October 1997

Acknowledgments

I gratefully acknowledge help in producing this book from the following.

Dr Rob Baggott of De Montfort University, William Walton of Aberdeen University and Stuart Hall of the Open University for encouragement in the early planning stage.

Ian Lavery of the National Union of Mineworkers for providing information.

Interviewees and respondents to letters, named in the text.

Liz Carruthers, the Druridge Bay Campaign's Administrative Officer, for checking references.

Monica Frisch, Libby Paxton and Fiona Hall for editing and general support.

Steve Allcroft for proof reading.

All those who have supplied photographs and other illustrations, who are credited in the list of illustrations. Special thanks to the Newcastle Chronicle and Journal Ltd for waiving their usual copyright fees.

Druridge Bay Campaign Chairs & Staff

Chairs

Nov '84 - Oct '86	Gary Craig
Nov '86 - Oct '87	Jim Wright
Nov '87 - Oct '89	Jonatha Robinson
Nov '89 - Mar '90	Betty Greenwell
Mar '90 - Oct '92	Jane Gifford
Nov '92 - Oct '94	Jonathan Nicholson
Nov '94 - Oct '96	Fiona Hall
Nov '96 -	Libby Paxton

Administrative Officers

Sept '86 - Dec '93	Wendy Scott
Feb '94 - May '95	Sarah Nuttall
Sept '95 - June '97	Liz Carruthers

Publicity & Information Officer

Apr '86 - June '97	Bridget Gubbins

Alan Beith MP lays the first stone of the Cairn at Druridge Bay.

Against All Odds
Chapter 1

A stone pile to beat a nuclear pile

Druridge Bay is a bleak windswept place much of the time. On the landward side of the dunes, on a cold March day in 1983 a few people were bracing themselves against the wind and hammering wooden stakes into the corner of a field. They made a small fenced enclosure. A few days later, a council dumper dropped a ton of stones over the wall, into the space.

Early one Saturday shortly afterwards, a group of people wrapped against the elements, came to the field, and made a little circle with the stones, about eight metres in diameter. Other people began to arrive, and one of them was obviously someone important. The people began to position themselves behind the stones. The important person stood in the centre of the circle, and spoke to the group. When he had finished speaking, he went to the outer stone circle and carried one of the larger ones to the centre. Then others in the group did the same, and when they had finished there was a pyramid of stones, about a metre high. Some of the children played on the stones, and had their photographs taken.

* * *

Each stone on the pile expressed visibly someone's opposition to nuclear power stations at Druridge. Member of Parliament Alan Beith had laid the foundation stone, Friends of the Earth and the others attending added their own. That event took place fourteen years ago. Life has moved on for those who were present. Little children are young adults, and some of us who were young parents are now grandparents. Two head teachers and one college principal have retired. Roland Bibby, the local historian, and Councillor George Green both lived to hear that Druridge was saved, dying shortly afterwards. Marjorie Mowlam, then a University of Newcastle lecturer, who nonchalantly chewed gum at the founding of the Cairn, is now a member of the Cabinet.

What started in that field, fourteen years ago, was the beginning of an unstoppable movement, the dogged expression of the feelings of relatively powerless individual people. The Cairn, as we called it, grew higher and higher over the years as opposition mounted, people clambering over the stile to add their own stone. A stone pile to beat a nuclear one*.

* *The phrase "A stone pile to beat a nuclear pile" comes from the Evening Chronicle headline reporting on this event. The word pile is a name for a nuclear reactor. It comes from the pile of graphite bricks in the first nuclear reactor in the University of Chicago in 1942.*

The innocent bay

A lovely beach has no longer a right to exist simply for the sake of its loveliness. Its materials may be coveted. Its sand can be sold. Its waters can cool power stations. Those in power, over the hills and far away, endlessly wheeling and dealing, scheming, designing, can make plans which will disturb it. Those nearby can abuse it too, water companies allowing sewage waste to pour onto the beach, family picnickers leaving plastic junk among the dunes.

For generations people have visited Druridge Bay on summer picnics, for wild winter walks, for exercise, birdwatching, sandcastle building, the pursuits that add joy to lives. Before the end of the 1970s, there was some mining on farmland behind the dunes, and some opencast coal workings. The beach was still wild, undamaged. But in the background, the emerging nuclear electricity generating industry was needing new sites for power stations. Discussions, leading to decisions, were taking place far from the bay, which would eventually lead to outrageous proposals for its use.

Although this book is the story of Druridge Bay, and the people who fought to save it, the same story is happening at thousands of other places all the time. Nowhere is safe. Our story is about the nuclear industry, with its huge dominating strength in the 70s and 80s, which wanted our bay, and which had every power it needed to get it. It is about people who were totally unprepared for such a threat, but who somehow summoned the strength to fight it. Gradually, the powerful industry backed off. We tackled other threats to the bay, and we saved it. We played out our drama on our local stage, a small act in the push for what seemed cheap, limitless power.

Wonderful atomic power

The 1950s

Queen Elizabeth opened Calder Hall atomic power station in 1956. Although principally a reactor producing plutonium for the military bomb programme, it generated electricity as a by-product, and sold it to the grid for civil use. It was hailed as a world-leading new industry for our country. Coal mines in Cumbria were closing down. The new industry would provide employment.

There was a flurry of worry caused by the Windscale fire of 1957. The fire occurred in one of the smaller military plutonium reactors. 20,000 curies of radioactive iodine was released to the atmosphere. I was a thirteen year old navy-uniformed schoolgirl. I can still see the newspaper photos of white-coated men pouring churns of radiation-contaminated milk down drains. The milk was carried to the rivers and on to the sea.

The young, emerging nuclear industry had nothing to do with Northumberland. Druridge Bay in the 50s is mistily receding in the memories of living people. There were coal mines behind the sand dunes, and miners' families from the villages of Chevington, Amble, Widdrington and Ellington might walk to the beach for Sunday picnics, down narrow country roads. People from Tyneside might go for a family caravan holiday. My mother took my brothers and sisters and me for a one-week holiday in a converted double-decker bus at Ellington caravan site. Only better-off people with cars could drive to remote, rural, Druridge for an afternoon walk. My friend's father was a doctor, and sometimes I was invited to go along.

A poem by U A Fanthorpe after talking to an old lady captures the atmosphere. It was written for a Druridge Bay Campaign poetry collection, *Tide Lines*.

Druridge Bay: the old lady remembers as she falls asleep

It never rained there then,
(It would do, of course
But I can't remember it raining on us.)

The friendly farm where the children fetched
Milk and hot water. The wide beach.
Over an hour to get there from home.
Widdrington the nearest place.
And the peace. The peace.

Lots of us went, car-loads,
Deebanks, Crawshaws, Mother, all of us,
Children in troupes. Someone took a picture.
And Mother there in black (<u>You look like the teacher</u>)

The day Betty Deebank (crying) lost
Her new-for-her-birthday watch.
When we went back next Saturday
We found it. Such joy!

All the way going home we sang
(<u>Rimington</u> the new hymn-tune then).

It wasn't dark till ten, the summer moon
Came up as we were going home singing …
Blackcurrant tarts freshly made …

Rain
    milk and hot water
                        the peace, the peace,
                                    children
                                        such joy

And Mother there in black.

Rain … water … children ...

Mothers in black.

More pretty beaches needed

The 1960s

After Calder Hall, other early Magnox* nuclear power stations, were built around the country. Central government decided that twelve should be built within a decade. By 1962, the twin reactors at Berkeley and Bradwell were up, followed by Hunterston A in Scotland in 1964, Trawsfynydd and Hinkley A in 1965, Oldbury, Dungeness A and Sizewell A in 1966, and the last to be built was going up at Wylfa in the mid-60s. There was not a lot of fuss about them. They were just there.

Because of its Magnox stations, Britain was generating a higher percentage of its electricity from nuclear power than any other country in the world. But more compact new power station designs were appearing. New sites would be needed...

...while the winds and waves battled over Druridge Bay as they always had done.

By the end of 1964 the nationalised Central Electricity Generating Board, which ran the country's electricity generating and supply industry, was getting ready to order a new generation of nuclear power stations.

There was a difference of opinion among industrial consortia preparing to tender for the new nuclear power station about which was the best of the new designs. In May 1965, the Minister for Energy told the House of Commons that the second generation of nuclear power stations would be of the advanced gas cooled reactor, or AGR, design.

The consequence of this choice was a humiliation for the nuclear power industry. First to be started was Dungeness B, in 1965. After that came Hinkley B and Hunterston B, Hartlepool and Heysham stations. They were constantly hindered by construction delays and technical problems. By the mid 70s, none of them were fully operational.

The Hartlepool nuclear power station was only 60 miles south of Druridge. Durham miners had protested to prime minister Harold Wilson without success. The contest between nuclear- and coal-generated electricity had begun.

The Northumberland Coast Area of Outstanding Natural Beauty was given its protective designation in 1958. The AONB extended south from Berwick to Amble, stopping just north of Druridge. Perhaps the coal mining behind the dunes was the reason. Perhaps even then, Druridge was a dot on a map in remote board-rooms.

In 1971, I dandled the toes of my baby son, Patrick, in the runnels of water at Druridge Bay, a few days before leaving to live in the United States.

The Miners

"There was lots of work. Thousands and thousands of miners employed in the pits. Blyth Power Station was being built. Some lads I know worked there for ten years. When that finished, they could go elsewhere, to the coal workshops or to factories. The engineering workers were a very practical workforce. They could move from job to job. The men had so many choices.

"But there was unrest in the pits. Because of the choices, men and boys would think 'Why the hell should I go down the pit, if I can go to a factory, or get a job somewhere else?' The wages were low. That's what caused the unrest in the mining industry, why the strikes came about."

George Ferrigon,
Wansbeck Councillor.
NUM Mechanics member.

1960 - miners employed in Northumberland 34,200

Thirty two new nuclear power stations

The 1970s

Because of the problems with the AGRs, the CEGB announced in 1973 that it would like to go for Pressurised Water Reactors, after all. Not modest in their ambitions, their original plan was for thirty two massive 1200 Megawatt nuclear power stations to be ordered between 1974 and 1984.

Just think now of all those beaches round Britain, with people unaware ... and what might have been. On sunlit summer days, their loveliness ... and what could have happened if the techno-dreamers had succeeded.

It was a nuclear planners' daydream. It never happened. Instead, the Wilson government which came to power in 1974 chose to go for six smaller 660MW steam-generating heavy water reactors, one of which was actually constructed at Winfrith in Dorset. Then in 1974, the UK Atomic Energy Authority declared that Britain should have twenty five 1000MW fast reactors by the year 2000.

It takes the breath away. What madness. What optimism. What greed. And what about the beaches?

In 1973, the South of Scotland Electricity Board applied for outline planning permission to build two nuclear power stations at Torness, a bleak windswept headland just north of the border with England. Eighty miles north of Druridge. Each of the nuclear power stations, the type of which was not at that time decided, would contain four reactors. The public inquiry which followed in 1974 took a mere eight days.

By 1977, my husband and I were living in the North East again. Back to the beach we would go, with our two growing boys and our new baby girl. Digging down to Australia, seaweed-walled sandcastles, boy dreamings over the horizon, Viking longboats, wave-leaping legs, soggy sand-laden corduroys, shivering blue-cold bodies. A family day out, in the wind-whipped air of Druridge. Just like every other family. And dog walkers. Race-horse trainers. Football kicking short-sleeve-shirted lads indifferent to the penetrating chill.

In May 1978, Torness was granted consent by the Secretary of State for Scotland. A rugged rocky promontory, beaten by the same harsh winds and tides as our coastline.

In the summer of 1978, the UK Atomic Energy Authority declared that the Cheviot Hills in the Northumberland National Park were a possible site for high level nuclear waste. No longer could people in Northumberland think this was someone else's problem. Farmers, landowners and country dwellers, and conservation groups from the suburbs became agitated. They set up the Cheviot Defence Action Group. My husband and I were busy with our young family. We were shocked. We sent £15 to the Cheviot Defence Action Group.

* *Further details about the different kinds of nuclear power stations mentioned in this and following chapters can be found in the Glossary.*

The Miners

The strikes

1960 - miners employed in Northumberland 34,200

"After the oil crisis, new pits opened, and new seams were opened. Some of the old miners that had left, experienced men, came back. Others who had gone to work in factories and other places didn't want to return. Their new jobs weren't so hard.

"The miners' wages were at the bottom of the parity levels, and the coal was needed. We were in a good bargaining position. So there were two strikes, in 1972 and 1974. We got a good settlement, good wages, better working conditions and a pension scheme.

"I don't think many men loved working down the pits. It was a job. The attraction was the good wage. And they deserved it.

"Mrs Thatcher became opposition leader after Ted Heath's government collapsed after the strikes. She never forgave the miners for bringing down the government."

George Ferrigon

1970 - miners employed in Northumberland 21,200

In November 1978, four hundred demonstrators blocked access to Torness Point, to prevent site clearance. Photographs appeared in our local papers. Nuclear power was becoming a local issue. Long-haired woolly hatted protesters, squatting in a derelict hut, scrambling up into digger trucks. I cheered them silently. I was very unpolitical.

Our two big boys were in school then, age seven and five, and our one-year old daughter was toddling. The age when waiting for Christmas is so tantalising, and the decorated tree lights up the living room.

On 22 December 1978, this was the front page story in the *Morpeth Herald.*

DRURIDGE MAY BE SITE FOR A-POWER STATION

C.E.G.B. considering area for test bores

The Central Electricity Generating Board are looking at beautiful Druridge Bay as a possible site for an atomic-powered power station.

They are understood to be considering test bores in the area.

The CEGB believe there is a need for additional power generation in the North East, and that it ought to be nuclear powered. Northumberland County Council are very concerned at the proposal and will be pressing the CEGB for as much information as possible...

Immediately after the announcement, Alan Beith MP for Berwick upon Tweed declared his opposition. In January 1979, the local Liberals, the National Union of Mineworkers and Castle Morpeth councillors followed. In March, Wansbeck MP George Grant told Tony Benn he would oppose anything like this at Druridge. By March 1979, the Druridge Bay Association was set up, a group of local residents, vocal, articulate, finding their way round a new and technical issue. By August Wansbeck District Council came out against.

And what about me, my husband, and our family? And all the other inarticulate people who lived in the area? Miserable at the idea, confused by the huge, featureless power of the nuclear authorities, not even imagining there was any way that their feelings could be expressed.

Why Druridge?

The North East needs more electricity, stated the CEGB in a July 1979 document produced in response to questions from Northumberland County Council.

Our Campaign - Your Campaign

The Odds are Overwhelmingly Against You

The power of the state, of a multinational company or a determined local authority is ranged against you, a few inexperienced individuals. It's too exhausting to contemplate challenging them, and easier to turn a blind eye.

How well we all know that feeling. We are all bombarded with problems about which we could or should actively do something.

In 1979, there was almost no hope that we local protesters could stop nuclear power stations being built at Druridge Bay. People acted without any sense that they had a realistic chance of winning. Yet the bay has been saved.

The particular problem facing you seems unbearable, overwhelmingly difficult to do something about, yet seems to call you to do something.

Remember

You've nothing to lose, and you may surprise yourselves and win.

You'll feel better doing something than turning away.

You may tackle the huge problem, and yet be unsuccessful. Your effort is a part of the process, and may result in the next group winning.

Circumstances change, and what once seemed impossible may yet be achieved.

> "Electricity demand on the North East coast is already met in part by imports from elsewhere. By the early 1990s it is anticipated that these imports could reach about the limits of the capability of the existing transmission system."

> "It takes at least six years to build and put to work a power station which therefore requires construction to start in 1983/84 for 1990 commissioning."

The site has the required characteristics.

> "There is access to the sea for cooling water,

> "It is away from built-up areas,

> "It is outside the Area of Outstanding Natural Beauty that commences at Amble."

If not at Druridge, the choice may be even worse.

> "Should Druridge not prove to have the right combination of factors, it is probable that a suitable nuclear site in the North East would have to be within a more environmentally sensitive area."

There was always an intention to build two nuclear stations.

> "An initial power station development would be of about 1200 MW, and allow for a possible second phase of development."

They did not know how the site would be restored after the power station had finished its useful life.

> "The reactor itself, which is internally radioactive, cannot be dismantled for some time. It would be advantageous to delay this for 50 years or more. Studies are being carried out to determine when and how final dismantling might take place."

Ten new nuclear power stations

1979

In May, Mrs Thatcher's government came to power. In December 1979, her energy minister David Howell announced the following.

> "The electricity supply industry have advised that even on cautious assumptions they would need to order at least one new nuclear power station a year in the decade from 1982 ... We consider this a reasonable prospect against which the nuclear and power plant industries can plan."

The CEGB wanted to look very closely at the PWR design, the same which had nearly caused a disaster at Three Mile Island earlier in the year.

* * *

You could no longer go to Druridge Bay and simply see its blustery sands and rolling waves. The silver sea-grassed dunes were waiting to be dug away. There were vague uncertain shapes hovering, chimneys and domes, wires and pylons, fleeting radioactive shadows. The bay was no longer innocent.

The Miners

The Druridge nuclear power station

1970 - miners employed in Northumberland 21,200

"Quite a few lads who worked in the pits at the time would say 'Oh well, it's going to happen. If they build a nuclear power station, it's jobs'. Not thinking of the consequences.

"Gradually, they realised. Blyth power station was the main customer for coal in this area. Blyth was getting on in years. If a nuclear power station is coming, Blyth would be run down. People began to put two and two together. The nuclear power station was part of Thatcher's plan to close the pits."

George Ferrigon

1980 - miners employed in Northumberland 18,000

The early protesters

Were they NIMBYs?

The Druridge Bay Association was Druridge Bay's first pressure group*. They lobbied, wrote, organised meetings, attended public meetings, and enlisted a couple of thousand subscriptions, took a 30,000 signature petition to 10 Downing Street.

The question arose which faces all protesters. Is it possible to protest against one proposal, without being against the principle? Should the Druridge Bay Association be against the Government's nuclear power plans as a whole, or simply against the choice of Druridge Bay? Did the Druridge Bay Association members only care about Druridge, and think nuclear power stations are alright somewhere else, somewhere already spoiled?

Our Campaign - Your Campaign

Not-In-My-Back-Yardism or NIMBYism

A decision you may need to make is whether you are campaigning against the wider implications of a proposal, or only against a particular example. Are you against out-of-town shopping centres, or just opposed to this badly-sited proposal which will damage a Site of Special Scientific Interest? Are you against building any new roads in the UK, or just this bypass?

We had to decide if we were against nuclear power, or only against a nuclear power station at Druridge Bay.

It's a hard decision, and there may be long discussions and differences of opinion. Generally, the simpler and more local the remit, the more people you will bring in.

The Druridge Bay Campaign united very diverse political and temperamental groups round "opposition to nuclear power stations at Druridge Bay". Thus between 1984 and 1990 we were not technically opposed to nuclear power, and were not an anti-nuclear group.

This made some difficulties, especially for people like me who are totally opposed to nuclear power, even though it was sensible from the point of view of bringing a wide range of groups into the organisation. We used a fair amount of verbal juggling to get round practical difficulties when writing documents or making public statements.

After 1990, we widened our remit, and attacked nuclear power more openly. However, many of our members remained only concerned about Druridge Bay.

Remember

There is no easy answer to the NIMBY problem, so don't expect one.

People's views can often change as they learn more about an issue.

It is natural that people are more concerned about problems on their doorstep, about which they can see the direct consequences. Don't let your opponents make you feel guilty.

The acronym NIMBY stands for Not In My Back Yard. We like our cars. We don't want our countryside spoiled by a new road. We like flying abroad for holidays. We don't want our woods ruined by a new airport. We like convenient out-of-town shopping centres. We don't want our green pastures built on. We need electricity. We don't want to face how it is produced.

In all the phases of opposition, the Druridge Bay campaigners had to find a way of dealing with this dilemma.

The Cheviot Defence Action Group had managed to oppose nuclear dumping in the Cheviots and at the same time declare that they were not opposed to nuclear power. They decided

> *to oppose the burying of nuclear waste in rock, in the present state of knowledge as to its safety, without opposing nuclear power as a source of energy.*

* *The Druridge Bay Association is completely separate from the Druridge Bay Campaign which was formed later, in 1984.*

The Druridge Bay Association decided that they would have opposed any power station or industrial type of proposal at Druridge Bay. They were not against nuclear power, though some of the members gradually became so. Perhaps some came to realise that with a technology as potentially dangerous as nuclear power, the whole world is its back yard.

There are no easy answers to the NIMBY question. People will defend their own area where they will only sympathise with the troubles of those further away. There is only so much strength and energy in people's lives to spare for good works. But it may happen that when people become involved in a local issue their eyes get opened to the larger picture, and this creates a momentum for change.

The Conservative/Independent controlled county council took a tentative opposing stance in February 1980. A nuclear power station at Druridge would be "contrary to local planning policy concerning the environment, agriculture and recreational activity ... The Planning Committee are not convinced that a case has been established by the CEGB to cause them to depart from their planning policy."

Heavily pregnant, I took notice. In March, our fourth child was born.

Three Mile Island nuclear power station, in Pennsylvania, USA, which had a near-meltdown in 1979.

The campaigners get worn out

In July 1980, test drilling started at Druridge. There was sabotage. Local people reported that pipes had been cut on the drilling rigs, and *The Journal* and *Evening Chronicle* reported that sand and soil had been added to the fuel and hydraulic tanks, lights on the rigs smashed, and sugar added to the fuel tank. The Druridge Bay Association disclaimed any involvement.

In December 1980 the CEGB announced that test drilling showed one of the two possible areas of Druridge Bay to be suitable for nuclear power stations. Hope disappeared. I wondered if we could bear to bring up our children here, with a nuclear power station at our bay, spreading its influences over the area.

The county council had taken its position. The miners had had a rally. The district council, Castle Morpeth, had stated a clear "No". After two years of exhausting action, the Druridge Bay Association was worn out.

The CEGB then went quiet about Druridge because their target for the first PWR was Sizewell.

Sizewell will be first

Sizewell in Suffolk had a Magnox reactor, constructed in the mid 1960s. It was a rural site, next to a shingle beach, chalky cliffs, meres and fens, heathery mosses. A site that had once been just as lovely as Druridge.

Northumberland County Council came under the control of a Labour adminstration in May 1981. Its leader was Jack Thompson. Instead of a nuclear power station at Druridge, the new county council wanted a further coal fired power station at Blyth. This would help the pits stay open, maintaining local employment.

By August 1982, Druridge was on the shortlist of sites for the PWR. First was to be Sizewell, second Hinkley in Somerset, and after that the list of four other named sites included Druridge. By September 1982, Jack Thompson and the council agreed to put aside £100,000 for their case at the Sizewell Inquiry.

The Sizewell planning inquiry eventually started in February 1983. It would decide if the Suffolk site was suitable, and on the principle of building PWRs in the UK.

Both Northumberland County Council and Wansbeck District Council presented their cases. The county council wanted a guarantee that issues of principle should not be determined once and for all at Sizewell, and that all these matters could be fully discussed at a future planning inquiry in Northumberland. Wansbeck District Council took part in a consortium organised by the Town & Country Planning Association, which enabled them to make a full statement concentrating on the future of the coal industry. By presenting written evidence, both councils were able to cross examine CEGB witnesses.

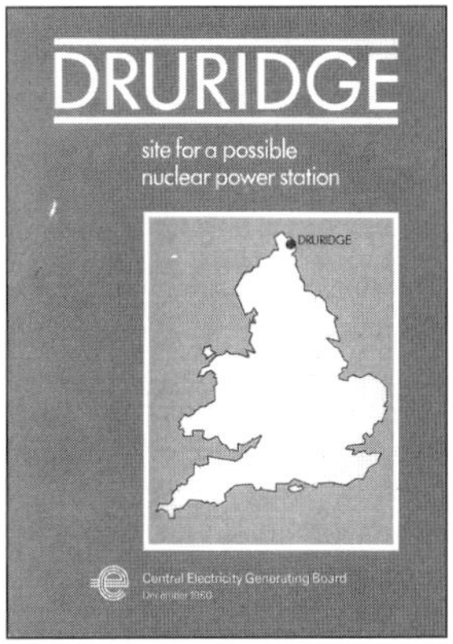

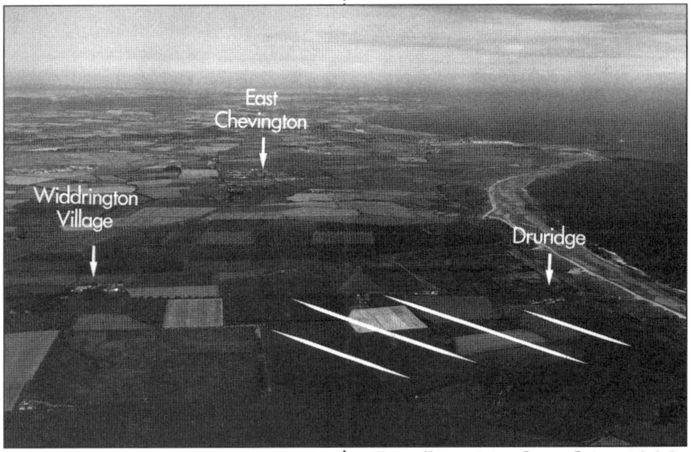

Leaflet circulated in 1980, after the CEGB completed test drilling. It included the aerial photograph of Druridge Bay showing, hatched, the prospective site for at least two nuclear power stations.

One group fades, another emerges

Our children were growing bigger. In 1983, they were aged twelve, nine, five and three. The Sizewell Inquiry was beginning, and it had the effect of stirring some of us out of the doldrums. My husband and I read a tiny article in the *Morpeth Herald* saying that Friends of the Earth were drawing a raffle at Druridge, to raise money for the cost of their presentation to the Sizewell Inquiry. We tucked our four children in our van, on the spur of the moment. Don Kent and a few members of Tyneside Friends of the Earth were there at the Widdrington Inn. Two other families from Morpeth were there with their children, curious like us, unsure what to expect. Don encouraged us to start a Friends of the Earth group in Morpeth, to get the Druridge issue back on the agenda.

That was the beginning of fourteen years of non-stop protest for me. We started a new group after putting notices in shop windows, and sending an announcement to the papers.

"DRURIDGE BAY BATTLE LINES" stated the *Evening Chronicle*. I was described as a Morpeth housewife, and I supposedly said: "The branch was formed because of the CEGB's plans for Druridge Bay. I was not a member of Friends of the Earth two weeks ago, but I was worried about what was happening, and so I went on a rally to Druridge. After that a few of us decided to form our own branch."

Our first significant action was the founding of the Cairn, the symbolic event I described in the opening of this chapter. We followed it with a gathering at the bay, to which we invited musicians and politicians.

Most of us had never done any protesting in our lives. We learned by trial and error, and with the initial support of Don Kent. Lindy Conway became group co-ordinator, Paddy Conway the treasurer. They had been at the raffle at Widdrington. Hilda Helling, a retired secretary who lived in Morpeth, organised a petition. Ed Metcalfe, a chemistry lecturer, was our scientific person. I became the group's press officer.

I learned the great strength that comes from working in a group. The mutual support. The way each individual's skills contribute to the whole. It was satisfying to be actively working for the bay, rather than passively, fearfully, doing nothing. Druridge Bay, with its stirring beauty, its golden spaces, was only a few miles from our homes. Its spirit was always with us, bringing forth ideas and creativity.

The Generating Board is confident

In December 1983, the Newcastle newspaper, the *Sunday Sun*, interviewed George Johnston, the CEGB's station planning engineer for the north of England. He was cool and calm, as he always was in the many public appearances where we confronted him. Ice cool on the surface perhaps, but warmly confident inside. Here are some extracts from the interview.

> *Reporter: The CEGB eventually found a piece of "undisturbed ground" which met nearly all its requirements. And it happened to be just a few yards inland from the magnificent Druridge Bay.*
>
> George Johnston: When we look for a nuclear power station site, we try to avoid national parks, areas of outstanding beauty, the green belt, areas of historical interest, protected coastline…
>
> …And then for reasons relating to the distribution of population around power stations and the application of an emergency plan on the basis that it is easier to apply it to a few people than many, we try to avoid populated areas…

Our Campaign - Your Campaign

Starting Absolutely from Scratch

You've decided to start your campaign. That's the first big step. But what on earth do you do next?

Lindy, Denise and I sat amid the remains of the family breakfast table, while our children played at our feet. We decided to call a meeting. We agreed who would make and put up notices around town, and who would contact the newspapers. We agreed at whose house the meeting would be, and who among our friends we would encourage to come. Your campaign will probably have a humble start something like that.

At your first meeting, you'll need to decide a name, and a clear aim for your group. You'll discuss your first action. You'll certainly find that the knowledge, contacts, ideas and experiences of those who come to your first meeting will give you a good start.

Gradually, you'll develop your strategy.

This book will stimulate your own ideas for actions - what works well with government, how to raise public awareness and inform your opponents of your objections. There are handbooks you can buy, or borrow from the library, which will give you step by step guidance.

Remember

We started completely from scratch too. Most of us lacked experience of campaigning. We had no special talents, but we were a fairly mixed bunch of local people. We gained skills by doing things.

Your campaign is new and unique. Every well-known group probably started with a discussion in a kitchen, in a pub or in a field.

Your members have all sorts of skills and resources. Cooking and childcaring, hammering and nailing, placard-making and singing, writing and painting, typing and using a computer. You have a treasure trove in your midst.

...We know what the land is like at the Druridge site. We've drilled it. And we will drill it again...

Reporter: We put it to Mr Johnston that the Central Electricity Generating Board, apparently backed by the Government, is now at loggerheads with the local rulers who represent people in this area.

George Johnston: First of all central government is not involved in this. It is entirely within the remit of the CEGB to decide when and where it investigates sites. It is entirely independent of the Department of Energy. They do not influence us in any way. This is our decision. We are not at all influenced by the political complexions of the councils.

We will work with whichever local authorities there are. They are the legally elected representatives of the people. Yes, it's true that Northumberland and the district council have declined to co-operate with us. And their view, which we do not share, is that our investigations are premature, and that we have not proved a need.

> We have to work a long time ahead - 12 or 14 years. That's the minimum. We cannot wait until the last moment.
>
> We haven't proved a need. That is perfectly true. We prove the need, we demonstrate it, when we make an application…
>
> …At the end of the day, it is the Board's decision, not a county council or a district authority's decision. It is the Board which is responsible for ensuring that people get an electric light when they put a switch on.
>
> And therefore the Board must take the ultimate decision, as to whether or not to go ahead with an application, or investigations.
>
> Local authorities have manifold responsibilities but they are not responsible for ensuring the supplies of electricity to their constituents.
>
> *Reporter: To whom is the CEGB ultimately responsible?*
>
> George Johnston: To the Minister, the Secretary of State for Energy…
>
> …So if the Board should decide it wants to go ahead, having decided that there is a need, then it can go ahead with a high degree of confidence of success.

Political and temperamental opposites unite

Our Friends of the Earth group was completely inexperienced in pressure group activity. What therefore could we usefully do? It was out of the question that we should try to do anything as high-powered as present evidence to a public inquiry like that of Sizewell. In any case, Northumberland County Council was doing that.

We could raise awareness. We could stimulate our councils to further action. We could make a fuss, go to meetings where CEGB men were present, write to the papers, raise money, organise fairs and concerts. We did all of these, in our tiny amounts of spare time.

The most important thing we achieved in the long term was the bringing together of groups which were politically completely different, finding a mechanism where they could work comfortably and creatively together.

There were the miners. Fearing for their jobs, preparing for a strike. Feared by others for the disruption they had caused to the nation with strikes in the 70s. There were various trades unions who supported the miners.

There was the Northumberland and Newcastle Society, concerned about conserving historic buildings and countryside. Its membership was very middle class, retired university lecturers, planners, architects. They were worried about the choice of Druridge Bay for any kind of development.

Our Campaign - Your Campaign

Bringing the Powerful Opponents Down to Size

You have to stand face to face with your opponents, on a platform, for a radio programme, on TV.

They are rich, powerful, clever, smartly dressed, and have the backing of big organisations. You are not at all rich, probably don't feel very clever, and are one of a small group. You have prepared your arguments as well as you can, but you're still nervous.

Imagine your opponents without their trappings. Imagine their wife/husband nagging at them; their teenage son/daughter being insolent to them; their lover abandoning them. Any of this is likely in their private lives.

Imagine them in undignified postures as they satisfy the calls of nature. Strip away their facades and they're frail human beings just like you.

Remember

You are right. You know you are, or you wouldn't be campaigning.

It may not seem like it at the time, but you are part of local history, of the great human story.

Ordinary people are likely to identify with you, the little hero or heroine, rather than the big adversary. You will make friends in return for your courage.

There was Tyneside Anti-Nuclear Campaign, very left-wing experienced activists. They were opposed to nuclear weapons, close to the miners and other unions, already involved with Torness and the Cheviots protests.

There was the National Trust with its mile of dunes at Druridge. It certainly wasn't an anti-nuclear organisation, but it didn't want a nuclear power station near its property.

There was CND, at the height of its powers owing to the Cruise missile crisis. Closely allied to the Labour Party at the time, and seen to be outrageously anti-patriotic by conservative bodies.

There was Northumberland Wildlife Trust, with nature reserves at Druridge. Some of its organising committee had links with local engineering firms like Parsons, which made turbines for nuclear power stations, and who favoured nuclear power. Many of their members however were opposed to anything which might spoil Druridge.

There was the dedicatedly anti-nuclear Green Party.

There were the fairly anti-nuclear Labour Party branches. Northumberland is industrial in the south east, round the mining towns of Blyth, Ashington, Bedlington.

There were some of the local Liberal branches and one Conservative group. Much of Northumberland is very rural. The north of the county had a Liberal MP, Alan Beith, and the south and west was Conservative.

All these varied viewpoints could squabble over the Druridge issue, or they could be brought together.

The Druridge Bay Campaign was established in January 1984. Our Friends of the Earth group encouraged the conservative, countryside and green groups to belong. Tyneside Anti-Nuclear Campaign was linked in with the unions.

Without the work of our Friends of the Earth group, it is very likely that the Druridge Bay Campaign would have been made up of groups only with strong anti-nuclear left-of-centre views. It would not have represented the total regional community if this had happened.

The National Union of Mineworkers took a leading role, and the first meeting of the new federal organisation was held in Burt Hall, the red-brick Victorian headquarters of the NUM in Newcastle. In those days, the NUM was strong, and the banners of the collieries hung from the rafters of the hall.

A simple, unifying principle

The only way such a truly different set of organizations could unite was round one simple principle. That was - *opposition to nuclear power at Druridge Bay.* Whatever was the position of each group on the nuclear power issue, everyone was bound together in this way. They were prepared to ignore differences in other spheres while working together to save Druridge Bay.

By March 1984, there were 47 signed up affiliated groups to the Druridge Bay Campaign federation, in four sections: trades unions, environmental groups, councils and political party branches. There were many Labour party branches, several Liberal branches, all the half dozen Green branches, and one Conservative. Thus we could say the Druridge Bay Campaign represented the whole political spectrum.

Causing delays

If the CEGB had had their way, ordering 32 reactors between 1974 and 1984, there could have been many new ones up and running by this time. Instead, the public inquiry into the first one was just starting.

Every action which had delayed the CEGB's ambitions was important in saving Druridge and countless other beaches round the country.

In January 1980, when Northumberland County Council had come out against the Druridge proposal, a newspaper report had the headline "DELAY". It reads: "If planning permission is sought towards the end of the year (1980), as expected, there will probably be a public inquiry. And there is confidence among the anti-Druridge Bay lobby that in such an event the Government would be sensitive to local opinion. 'The more we can delay, the more chance we have. There are options for a site other than Druridge Bay' said Mr Alan Brown of the Druridge Bay Association."

Our Campaign - Your Campaign

Representing the Whole Community

Our campaign had a wide spectrum of support, from left to right politically, from conventional to radical in temperament. This whole-community support was one of our greatest strengths.

You may need the same wide support. How do you get it?

You need to match the characteristics of your members with those you are trying to influence, and you need to be practical about encouraging all kinds of people to join your campaign.

We had to convince the National Trust's regional director that they should join the Druridge Bay Campaign, which included the National Union of Mineworkers and colourful anti-nuclear organizations. We chose one of our members who was a social worker and church goer, conventional in dress and style, mother of two young children, to meet him. Her calm, reasoned approach resulted in success.

Another time, I had the job of convincing the Mayor that he should come to our event. He was a conservative-leaning independent. "I don't want to go to something with all those lefties waving banners around," he said. "If you don't come, that's what it will be," I said. "We need you." He came, and remained one of our strongest supporters.

We needed at least some support from the Conservative Party if we were to be truly representative of all political viewpoints. There was one green Tory in our county. We encouraged her, cossetted her, appreciated her. She kept her local association paying its annual membership dues. Thus we could show we were non-party political.

Remember

Whatever the political group controlling your district, or ruling the country, it can change at the next election. You need friends in power, and in opposition.

In any political group there will be varying opinions, and you may find unexpected allies.

In October 1981, an *Evening Chronicle* headline was "DRURIDGE BAY PLANT DELAY". A planning application will be delayed by three to four years, CEGB officials had told the county council. The recession and a slump in demand for electricity were given as the main reasons, as well as a need to replace expensive oil-fired power stations in the south of England. Also, the expected public inquiry at Sizewell, due to start he said in the second half of 1982, would further delay Druridge plans.

In 1983, our Friends of the Earth group effected a one-year delay at Druridge. The drilling rigs were expected for the second, detailed test drilling, in June 1983. A friendly neighbouring councillor told us that our district council, Castle Morpeth, could issue an Article 4 Direction to the Secretary of State for the Environment requiring the CEGB to obtain planning permission before test drilling.

We wrote to all members of the council, asking them to do this. Castle Morpeth decided to pass the responsibility to Northumberland County Council. We wrote to MPs asking them to lobby the Secretary of State, who could have had the last word. He decided against us. The effect of our action meant however that the CEGB could not start drilling in 1983, as the extra couple of months' delay did not give time for the six months' work to be completed before the winter season.

The greatest delay of all was the Sizewell Inquiry itself. The huge and detailed range of objections, including those from our councils and the other national anti-nuclear campaigns, dragged the inquiry out for over two years, from its start in February 1983 to March 1985.

When all seemed lost

1984/85

Early in 1984 the CEGB were ready to do detailed test drilling. They had the power and authority of the Government behind them, and they fully expected to get planning permission at the ongoing Sizewell Inquiry.

The drilling rigs arrived at Druridge at 7am on 17 May 1984, after a secret overnight journey. There they were. Big transporter trucks with drilling equipment ready to get to work. A reporter rang me before breakfast. My friend Rosie Stacy and I went there the morning they arrived, with our four-year-old daughters. We walked the last mile from the bus stop, on a May morning with hawthorn blossom in the hedges, and made our token protest. The media photographed and interviewed us. For me, it was the lowest moment of the whole campaign. We seemed so pathetically powerless.

The CEGB had taken special legal powers to make a criminal offence of a civil trespass on to the site, and the area was policed by security men and guard dogs. They didn't want sabotage like last time.

The newly formed Druridge Bay Campaign had prepared to have a demonstration at the bay on the Saturday after the drilling rigs arrived. As none of us knew when this would be, other than at some time in the early summer so as to enable the six month job to be completed in good weather, all the groups had to be alerted quickly.

We told the papers, expecting that people would come in their thousands. Three hundred or so came, along with MPs Alan Beith, Frank Cook from Stockton North, Bob Clay from Sunderland North and Jack Thompson who now represented Wansbeck. At the last minute, two full bus loads of striking miners arrived, boosting the numbers. We had speeches by the Cairn, with press and TV presence. Ellington Colliery brass band led us along the narrow country lane to the site entrance. We made a good show with our boards, saying STAND UP FOR DRURIDGE.

For six months, the drilling rigs were there at the bay. On the other side of the dunes, the tides flowed in and out, the summer picnickers came and went, dogs splashed into the foaming waves, fishermen stood by their rods. Thus the days passed.

The Miners

The strike

1980 - miners employed in Northumberland 18,000

"March 1984 to March 1985. That was the year of the strike. Heseltine was energy secretary. There was going to be a programme of pit closures. That's when we said 'Look that's enough'. Twenty pits were to close, 20,000 men in the country. It was then that Arthur Scargill said that the plan he had seen was for a lot more than that. Which turned out to be right.

"Mrs Thatcher manoeuvred into a position of take it or leave it. You either accepted the pit closures, or you could do what you want. She threw the gauntlet down. We had to take it up.

The new school term began, and my youngest daughter started school. As the days shortened, transporter trucks took the drilling rigs away.

A few days before Christmas 1984, the CEGB said that the Druridge site was indeed suitable for two nuclear power stations with the option of a third, and they purchased the land from the farmer.

The next year, in July 1985, when the Sizewell Inquiry was completed but the inspector's report not yet published, the CEGB purchased the houses at Druridge hamlet, all but two of the owners of the dozen or so properties selling and leaving.

And so it seemed our bay was doomed.

"The strike was about communities and employment. During the 80s unemployment was going up and up. If you were made redundant from the pit, there was no alternative for you."

George Ferrigon

1984 - miners employed in Northumberland 5,219

Fighting back with funding

1986

Doomed or not, opposition continued. In order to increase the momentum, the Druridge Bay Campaign needed an office, and staff. The county and district councils donated enough to run an office and two part-time staff. In April 1986, the office opened, and I and my co-worker Wendy Scott began to work. Without the financial support from the local authorities, the next eleven years of work could not have continued.

Employees would work when volunteers got weary, or moved, or took a few years out to have a family. The earlier Druridge Bay Association had lasted two years on voluntary effort, before the members became worn out. From 1986, DBC staff would put in twenty hours of work each week. Our annual turnover started at about £10,000 in 1986, later rising to £17,000 by 1992, then falling back to £13,000 by 1995.

It was riches, compared to working from corners in our houses, in our spare time. We had an office, two part-time workers, and a band of volunteers, with which to counter the power of the Central Electricity Generating Board.

The public is forced to think about radiation - Chernobyl

It was one of those events where you always remember what you were doing when you heard the news. It was Saturday 3 May 1986. I was on a cycling weekend in Northumberland with my daughters, then aged nine and six. We had been soaked in a heavy shower at Embleton. That night in the youth hostel, we saw on the news that radioactive rain had fallen across the country.

Andrew Home and his baby Jake take a radiation reading.

In those days, public opinion on the nuclear power issue was split fairly clearly along political lines. If you tended to be conservative in thinking, respectful of authority, you tended to like it. If you were more radical and rebellious in thinking, leaning more towards the left in politics, you tended to dislike it. The Chernobyl accident changed all that. At last, the real dangers of nuclear power became apparent to everyone.

The accident happened just after we had opened our office, and just after we had obtained our first radiation monitor. We had decided to obtain background radiation readings in Northumberland and Tyneside, so that we had evidence against any future changes which may be caused by CEGB emissions at a nuclear power station at Druridge Bay. We hoped this would be a deterrent to the CEGB, but in the worst case it would be useful information.

Local people knew we had this equipment, as we had been on TV taking readings in MPs' gardens. It was as though our radiation monitoring programme had been set up ready for the Chernobyl accident. Our monitor registered 50% above the background readings we had taken in Felton, Northumberland, during the two weeks prior to the accident.

At that time, the local authorities had no radiation monitoring programme of their own. We were one of the very few sources of freely available information about radiation increases in the country. We made dozens of visits to families who wanted radiation readings in their gardens, even though we pointed out that without a prior reading, the measurement lacked significance.

The accident brought us new members, and some of them began to investigate the health effects of radiation for themselves. Libby Paxton, a member from Morpeth with young children, and Toni Stephenson, a teacher from Warkworth, began to go to conferences. They met children's cancer consultants in Newcastle hospitals.

National networking

The Sizewell Inquiry, which had started in February 1983, finished in March 1985. There was a mountain of evidence to be analysed. The inspector finally reported in January 1987. From start to finish, the Sizewell Inquiry had caused a four-year delay.

If the government of 1965 had decided to let the CEGB build PWRs when it wanted to, instead of going for the British designed AGR, this inquiry could have been similar to the 8-day Torness inquiry. That earlier decision may have changed the course of the landscape history of this country. We might have had thirty-two new nuclear power stations. It's not so incredible as it sounds. France made the decision to go for PWRs in 1970, and now has about 40.

Everybody expected that the CEGB would get its approval, and it did. The inspector Frank Layfield recommended that the Sizewell reactor should be built in the national interest, which "overrides the local interest in favour of conservation". Although critical of the CEGB on safety issues, he concluded that such matters could be left in their hands. He also criticised their economic case,

The Miners

After the strike

1985 - miners employed in Northumberland 5,219

"After the strike, the government would say 'We've got to shut your pit'. We would say 'Oh no! It's viable', and try to prove it.

"They always produced the counter case. We always lost. Finally Heseltine would just shut it, and that was it. There was no way you could save your neck then. Even if you got a reprieve, they would come back after two years and say 'Sorry, you're not making money. You'll have to close.'

"After the strike ended, Blyth, Ashington, Lynemouth, all the smaller pits closed. Employment went down drastically. Some miners took redundancy. Others got transferred to other pits, in Durham, anywhere."

George Ferrigon

1992 - miners employed in Northumberland 1,400

concluding that Sizewell had a one in four chance of losing the nation money. Nevertheless, national need for electricity dominated. A local area had to be sacrificed for the national good.

The inspector's report was not allowed to take account of anything that had happened since the end of the inquiry, so it ignored the Chernobyl accident, and ignored the slump in coal and oil prices which meant that a coal-fired power station could be cheaper. In principle, the PWR programme would go ahead.

Our destiny appeared to be decided.

Off to Parliament

1987

Friends of the Earth organised a lobby of the House of Commons for the Sizewell Debate, in February 1987. We joined in with gusto.

We were part of a network of anti-PWR groups at Sizewell, Hinkley, Dungeness, Winfrith and Trawsfynydd. Jonathon Porritt was director of Friends of the Earth at the time.

At the House of Commons lobby on the Sizewell debate, February 1987.

We wrote to 21 North East MPs, mainly Labour, one Liberal and two Conservatives, on the theme that "A Vote for Sizewell is a Vote for Druridge". We sorted the replies, those who supported our theme, those who didn't, and those who didn't reply. We made big placards with all their names on, stating how they would vote. Those who hadn't replied were into the "THESE MPS DON'T KNOW?" category. A coach load of supporters took our banners and our round placards with our Druridge No! emblems to London.

It was our first venture to the far off power-centre in the capital. Perhaps we would never have made this first step without the stimulus from Friends of the Earth. At the lobby, we met people from the other PWR campaigns and Jonathon Porritt. As well as performing for the TV and newspapers outside the House of Commons, we went in to the Grand Committee Room where Friends of the Earth had organised speakers. Our members met their MPs and we built up new and influential contacts.

My youngest daughter, Laura, was seven years old. She had the day off school so that she could come with me. She can be seen in the centre of the photo.

We felt the glamour of being in the ancient building where all those important-looking decision-makers passed to and fro. A long way from our windswept beach in Northumberland.

Nuclear power or privatisation?

In the early 1980s, the Central Electricity Generating Board had boundless confidence. Our long experience was beginning to show us that, over time, even the most daunting odds can change. The Sizewell Inquiry had delayed the CEGB plans, and Chernobyl had shaken public opinion. Now the Conservative government wanted to privatise the electricity board, which owned the land at Druridge.

Privatisation of the electricity industry meant that potential purchasers would be scrutinising the nuclear economics closely.

From this point onwards, the Druridge Bay Campaign began to develop closer contacts with the Parliamentary process, which I describe in more detail in chapter four. Our campaign was maturing, gaining confidence.

The Privatisation of Electricity White Paper was published in February 1988. We decided not to get into the pro- or anti-privatisation debate, but to work for three positions. The first was that nuclear power should not be protected from hard market forces. The second was the right to a full public inquiry, which could take account of all wide-ranging issues. Thirdly, we wanted legislation on energy efficiency, which would reduce the need for new power stations.

Tony Blair, shadow energy spokesperson, comes to Druridge in 1989. With Jack Thompson MP and Bridget Gubbins.

Once again we joined a Friends of the Earth lobby. Alan Beith booked a committee room in the House of Commons to which we invited our own North East MPs. Later we followed the standing committee's clause by clause examination of the Bill, pushing for our three points through our MP contacts on the committee.

Tony Blair comes to Druridge

Tony Blair was then shadow energy spokesperson, and on the standing committee. In March 1989, Jack Thompson brought him out to Druridge Bay. Standing on the sand dunes with Jack and me, he spoke to the reporters and the TV crew.

"It would be a great shame to spoil this bay as an amenity for the local people and as an area of beauty. It is quite clear that the opposition will continue until the plans are laid to rest. Because of the pressure, I think it increasingly less likely that the board will want to site a power station here. That should be an incentive for people to keep up their efforts."*

He was a relatively powerless opposition MP. None of us dreamed then that he would one day be prime minister.

As the Privatisation of Electricity Bill went through the House of Lords, we joined another Friends of the Earth lobby. This time, Lord Glenamara, formerly Labour MP Ted Short from Newcastle Central, advised us. At the lobby, he

Our Campaign - Your Campaign

The Feeling of Hopelessness

You've been campaigning as hard as you can, and you feel you can't possibly win. They've got their planning permission for the new road. The public inquiry went against you and you're exhausted and broke. The protesters have been removed from the site, and the bulldozers are in. Everything is hopeless.

Yes, you may lose. That's very hard to accept.

The drilling rigs were at Druridge for the second time, in 1984. The CEGB were doing six months of detailed investigations that would enable them to design the power stations. Then the farmer sold his land to them. Everything was against us.

But totally unexpected things happened. There was the Chernobyl accident which changed public opinion. Then electricity privatisation revealed the real costs of nuclear power. The worst didn't come to pass.

Remember

If you lose, you did your best, so pat yourselves on the back. You will certainly have learned skills in the process.

The unexpected may happen, even after all seems lost. So dig in. Victory may yet be yours.

introduced us to Lord Williams of Elvel, the opposition energy spokesman, and to other sympathetic peers. Lord Williams spoke out for Druridge in the debate in the House of Lords. This sort of thing made very attractive media stories, and got us television coverage.

Whenever I could, I took one or more of my children to local events, to London, sometimes taking them out of school. We used our Family Railcard to keep costs down, and stayed in youth hostels. My daughters have been with me to the Houses of Parliament several times. My younger son, Daniel, was sixteen when he came to the electricity privatisation lobby.

Not economic after all

One of the main problems in privatising nuclear power was the unknown cost of decommissioning old nuclear power stations and disposing of the radioactive waste. One report by city brokers claimed that it could be as much as £12 billion, more than the value of the nuclear generating plants themselves. The Government's pledge of a £2.5 billion subsidy towards these costs was quite inadequate.

We had come a long way from the confident CEGB who had been claiming since at least 1979, and throughout the Sizewell Inquiry, that nuclear power was cheaper than coal. On 24 July 1989, energy minister Cecil Parkinson announced that the Magnox reactors, the older UK first generation of nuclear power stations, were not to be sold off after all. They were not saleable.

* *Quoted in the Northumberland Gazette, 3 March 1989.*

The revealed true costs of nuclear power was really shaking the Conservative government's ideas. This information changed public opinion even further away from the former clear-cut politically left/right positions on nuclear power.

In August, Tony Blair revealed that privatising the AGRs presented an even worse financial risk than the Magnox reactors. There were revelations that the costs of Sizewell B had risen by 10%.

The delay over Sizewell, the Chernobyl accident, and now privatisation. Gradually the shadow over Druridge was lifting.

Global warming - a crutch for nuclear power?

During 1988 and 1989, the nuclear power people began to promote their industry as clean and green, an answer to environmental problems. In the late 1980s, electricity was still supplied principally by coal and nuclear power. Coal power was dirty, they said. As well as emitting acid rain pollutants, it was a major emitter of carbon dioxide, the principal gas contributing to global warming. We Druridge campaigners produced our own carefully researched arguments as to why there should not be more nuclear power stations as an answer to global warming. We concentrated on the dangers of nuclear power, the tens, or even hundreds, of thousands of years' heritage of radioactive waste, and the unknown problems of decommissioning old power stations.

The earliest taste of victory

On 9 November 1989, the day the Berlin Wall came down, Energy Minister John Wakeham announced in the House of Commons that the nuclear industry would not, indeed could not, be privatised along with the rest of the electricity industry, and that there would be no new nuclear power stations until after a government review in 1994.

Even up until the last minute, we had not really been able to believe that this could happen, so used had we become to living with the threat. We were exhilarated, and yet cautious. It was a reprieve, yet not a conclusion.

In March 1990, the Druridge Bay Campaign went into a new phase. Members voted to keep up a constant watch on the bay until the 1994 review of nuclear power, when new nuclear power stations would be considered. We agreed to free ourselves to speak out against the nuclear industry, broadening out our simple opposition to nuclear power at Druridge only stance, and to campaign against other threats to the bay.

The old Central Electricity Generating Board had had its day of domination and Druridge Bay was safe - for the time being.

The lightening shadow

Spring 1990

How much more the sunlight seemed to glow at the bay, then. You could crest the dunes, and there the great open ocean was laid out before you, blue and grey and white, glistening, framed by the sands, the spiky grey-green beach grasses. You could breathe more freely. You could smile.

The Inn on the Park doorman remonstrating with Queen Jane Gifford about leafletting shareholders.

Stopping the Sand Extractors

Chapter 2

At the AGM

The Inn on the Park is a very smart hotel near Green Park and Hyde Park Corner in London. One chilly May day in 1993, the Rolls Royces and Bentleys were pulling up as usual at the grand front entrance. The wealthy patrons were ushered respectfully inside by the doorman in his black and gold braided uniform.

A mini-bus arrived a few yards along the road. Out of it tumbled a red-bearded king, with a wine-gum jewelled crown and flowing robes, a crowned queen adjusting her snow-white wimple, and a rag-tag assortment of slaves and serfs in sackcloth clothes. The serfs unrolled a huge banner, 30 feet long, which stated READY MIXED CONCRETE - STOP DESTROYING DRURIDGE BAY, and positioned themselves along the pavement in front of the hotel.

The king and queen had handfuls of leaflets, and they started to offer them to the surprised hotel guests as they climbed out of their limousines. The doorman moved into action. He addressed King Canute and his queen. It is definitely not allowed to stand outside this hotel here. It is private property. The guests must not be handed leaflets. The Queen remonstrated with the doorman. The broad-shouldered King, holding himself erect, moved around handing out more leaflets while the Queen carried on the dispute.

Shareholders began to arrive at the Ready Mixed Concrete Group's annual general meeting. The King and Queen didn't know which of the guests were shareholders, but they and the serfs gave out leaflets anyway. Passers-by stared. TV arrived. The King was interviewed, and he explained that he had come to tell the shareholders of RMC what their company was doing, and to speak to the chairman.

King Canute had a single share. It had cost £5. Three others of his court were named on the share as joint holders, and all four could according to the rules therefore attend the company's AGM.

The TV reporters began to interview the arriving shareholders. Mr Rolfe from Sussex was asked what he thought of RMC taking sand from a Northumbrian beach, and upsetting all the local people there. He had never been on TV before. He said he was surprised; that RMC is a very respectable company, and he was sure that when the chairman understood what was going on he would do something about it.

The King, Queen and two of the court went into the plush-carpeted entrance, and up the marble stairs, joining the suited ladies and gentlemen at the shareholders' meeting. RMC's public relations man smoothed the way. The directors were getting agitated behind the scenes, but he convinced them they had better make the best of things. Into the chandeliered room went the Northumbrian visitors, and sat among the shareholders. On the platform was a row of seats with wooden nameplates engraved for each of the directors. Quiet fell when the dozen powerful men took their seats.

The chairman, Mr P J Owen, reported on the annual progress of the company. He asked the various directors to give summaries of finances, of dividends, and the agenda was about to move on. King Canute's own personal public relations officer (me) nudged him. Up he got onto his feet. Why, he asked, was a company of the size and respectability of the RMC group ruining a Northumbrian beach?

The chairman had been well briefed before we came. The extraction is perfectly legal he said. The amount of sand they are taking is very small compared to the size of the bay, and other factors are causing erosion. In any case, the extraction *helps* the local environment by clearing sand from the bed of the stream, and hence stopping flooding.

King Canute disagreed. The sand levels are falling, the dunes are being eroded, and the damage can never be made good. Once the sand has gone, nothing can bring it back. Was it worth all the bad publicity for a few thousand pounds of profit a year?

The chairman repeated that the company did not accept responsibility for the erosion, as its operations were very small scale.

When the formal part of the meeting was over, the directors and shareholders moved into the room where the buffet was being served. The King, Queen and court had travelled down overnight, a crowded uncomfortable minibus journey from the north of England. The serfs holding the banner outside were cold and tired. The King wrapped up some of the sandwiches and delicacies in paper napkins and sent the food down to his hungry serfs. He and the Queen mingled and talked with the shareholders. I invited the shareholders to look at a collection of newspaper cuttings from north east local newspapers, describing the company's activities, showing the erosion of the beach. Some looked with interest, and smiled sympathetically. One well-dressed woman said: "You ought to be ashamed of yourselves, coming here like this. You're disgraceful."

Our Campaign - Your Campaign

Buying a Share in a Company

Your group needs to agree that you have no objections in principle to buying even one share in the company you oppose. Could you bear to benefit, even by a few pence a year from their activities?

If for any reason your group cannot or will not buy a share, but you need one for access to the company's AGM, a willing member may do it.

There are books you can read about using shares to make companies more accountable. Look at our bibliography.

Nick Scott, our King Canute, telephoned stockbrokers Wise Speke. He paid £5 for one share, and we passed the hat round at a meeting to cover the £25 brokers' fee.

Four people were named on the one share, and could attend the AGM. The principal shareholder receives the company's annual report, and details about the AGM. The report probably cost more than the value of your share, so you've already contributed to losing them some money.

At the AGM, you will be plied with pleasant drinks and snacks, of which you will want to take advantage so as to further reduce their profits.

Remember

Buying a share and attending the AGM of a company is a relatively cheap and easy way to make big publicity for your cause.

As a shareholder you're entitled to information about the company and its activities.

You are not seeking to increase the company's profits for your own own benefit like most shareholders. You may be trying to reduce its profits, for the benefit of the general public, or the environment.

AGM actions are becoming more commonplace, and thus less media-attractive. But your local media should be interested, especially if you can prepare an interesting action to support going to the meeting.

That evening, as the directors knew, the company's name would be broadcast for all to see on north east television, and it would be in the papers the next day.

Some of the directors must have been asking themselves and their subsidiary company Northern Aggregates why they were taking the sand. Was it an essential part of their operations? And others may well have counter-argued that they had no need to stop their legal and profitable activities just because of a few sensation-seeking environmentalists.

RMC's digger loading up beach sand to be carried away by the lorry.

Shovelling away the beach

The beach was being shovelled up, and removed. Villagers at Cresswell, Ellington and Widdrington watched it disappear by the lorryload. Park wardens checking on wild bird movements saw the trucks loading up and driving away. Visitors strolling along the sand were shocked to see the digger at work. It was unforgiveable vandalism.

How could a situation have arisen where a company openly, and legally, was digging away a Site of Special Scientific Interest?

We must look back many decades. Historical diggings were made in the duneland adjoining Cresswell village, as we can see by "sand pits" marked on old maps. Beach sand was being extracted at Druridge until the second world war using hand shovels, and horses and carts.

In 1960 and 1965 there were two planning inquiries in Morpeth, about two separate sand extraction sites at Druridge. Northumberland County Council and what was then Morpeth Rural District Council lost both appeals. Few conditions were imposed on the operators, and there were no restrictions on the number or size of lorries which may take sand, on the hours of working or on the amount of sand which may be taken. No conditions were imposed to check the state of the bay, or to review the operation. As a result extraction under current law could legally continue until 2042.

Northern Aggregates, which is a subsidiary of the RMC Group, has been working at both these sites. Since 1982, they dug on the Blakemoor Burn site which they had purchased. In addition they had an agreement with the landowner to extract sand at another site at Hemscott Hill, although this work had ceased in 1987.

Druridge Bay Campaigners had all read reports by experts showing that erosion at Druridge was worsened by sand extraction, though there were two other factors, mining subsidence, and the lowering of the land level relative to the sea, which is happening all along the east coast of the country. Also, we learned that the sand in a bay moves in a closed system. It may cycle round the bay or move up and down the beach, according to the season, the wind direction and the tide. But new sand does not come into the system. If therefore it is removed at one point, the bay as a whole suffers.

At some places in the north of the bay, 12 metres of dunes had been lost since 1986. In the south of the bay, near the extraction site, you could see huge exposures of glacial pebbles and clays which underlay the sand deposits. Peat forests were also exposed, from trees which had once been growing at that location when it was land. These deposits were being rapidly eroded by the sea.

Since Northern Aggregates obtained the land and rights to extract sand at the Blakemoor Burn site, the extraction had been increased. Thus in 1960, 14,000 tonnes of sand were removed annually, but by the 1990s, 40,000 tonnes were disappearing. Red and yellow Thompson's lorries were regularly moving away from the burn site, through Cresswell village, to concrete-making sites on Tyneside.

Fighting a multinational company

Autumn 1990

Campaigners had been fighting the state-owned nuclear industry about building nuclear power stations at Druridge for over a decade. We'd learned the style, the tricks and the sorts of arguments to use. We'd learned about lobbying Parliament, about using the democratic process and the media. Now we were preparing to tackle a multinational company, a business which exists to earn money for its shareholders. We had a lot to learn.

A new type of member was attracted to the sand campaign. Angry, green-waxed-jacket wearers would come to meetings fresh from the dunes, with sandy boots and binoculars. Sand extraction was very much an immediate, visible activity. These people, who were involved in day-by-day care of the bay, could see the digger taking away the sand, and see the dunes eroding. They were from the National Trust, Northumberland Wildlife Trust, Druridge Bay Country Park and Castle Morpeth Borough Council.

We drew together all the information from every available source. After listening, reading and thinking, we deduced that there were four principal ways in which the sand extraction could be stopped.

The first, and the most unlikely, was that the company could stop voluntarily.

The second was for Northumberland County Council, as mineral planning authority, to revoke the planning permissions. If they did this, they would have to pay several hundreds of thousands of pounds compensation to the company, for loss of business. In the era of government cutbacks, pending village school closures and teachers' redundancies, the county council could not afford to do it. Councillors believed they had no moral duty either, as planning permissions had been given by central government.

The third option was for Castle Morpeth Borough Council to impose a Coast Protection Order and refuse a licence to the company to continue extraction. The problem to be faced there was whether or not the council would have to pay compensation for the value of lost business, and the need for the council to prove that sand extraction was a real cause of the erosion at the bay.

The fourth option was for the Secretary of State for the Environment to revoke the planning permission, and pay the compensation.

A four point strategy

In November 1990, the Sand Group agreed a simple four-point strategy, which became the basis of three years of actions.

1. to raise the issue locally, using the media
2. to place pressure on Ready Mixed Concrete
3. to encourage Castle Morpeth Borough Council to use the Coastal Protection Act
4. to support Northumberland County Council in lobbying the Secretary of State for the Environment to stop the sand extraction.

A characteristic of our campaign was the particular way we related to our local councils, perhaps unusual among environmental campaigns.

One of the earliest protests against sand extraction in November 1990, with TV crew.

There was an unwritten understanding between us. We were the grassroots local people, while they acted officially. Northumberland County Council paid an annual donation of about £7000, Castle Morpeth about £700, and neighbouring Wansbeck about £1000 to the Druridge Bay Campaign. The county Minerals Planning Officer, Andrew Brack, was allowed to brief us and attend Sand Group meetings, as did Castle Morpeth's Countryside Officer Colin Marlee, who managed the dunes adjoining the sand extraction site,

The councils paid their annual donations and left us to get on with things. A feeling of mutual trust had grown up over the years since 1979. We did the outrageous and entertaining things. We dressed up and took our banners and placards to meetings where the councillors and their officers behaved formally. We specialised in Druridge issues, always on the lookout for an opportunity to make a public point, at the same time making sure our written reports, letters and public statements were accurate. We kept RMC under the spotlight.

Round the seasons at Druridge Bay

Alan Beith MP and Bridget Gubbins at the unveiling of the first sign, adjoining the sand extraction site, in May 1992.

During the next three years, we followed our strategy, and constantly referred to the four ways in which RMC might be coaxed or forced to stop. Many of our activities took place at the bay, in bad weather and good, round the seasons.

On a cold wet miserable sea-fretty muddy day in November, a dozen of us went to the bay, armed with our placards and new leaflets. The digger driver and the lorry drivers who took the sand away weren't the main enemy. They were tools of the big companies, and possibly didn't like what they were doing. We had decided to face them on the site, and encourage them to support us, to ask if their trade union would back us.

TV and newspaper reporters turned up. The digger driver and lorry driver tried to go on with their work. Toni Stephenson, our vice-chair at that time, tried to hand leaflets to the very embarrassed lorry driver, who had never imagined that part of his work would be appearing on local TV. He was filmed answering her questions about how much sand he was taking away every lorry load. Another lorry was filmed manoeuvring through the protesters and the placards, as it left the site.

The digger driver was harsher. He told us to get away from private property, refused to take a leaflet, and tried to shut his digger door on Toni. All this was filmed, against the stunning background of crashing waves. It made grand TV. It cost us nothing. It would be very difficult for Ready Mixed Concrete to counter such bad publicity.

During the autumn months, the sea stripped the already depleted sand from the beach at the southern end of the bay. There were ugly exposures of mud and peat. I took a photo of two local officials on the mess, with the digger working in the background. At Christmas time, we sent all RMC's 10 company directors a card with this photo on. We'd already written to them all, with newspaper cuttings. One of the directors, a Mr J B Cooper, replied. "No evidence has been produced by Northumberland County Council or their consultants to suggest that the properly authorised (and relatively minor) activities of Northern Aggregates are having anything more than a superficial impact on the sand deposits in the bay."

In the spring, our reserves wardens got their hammers, saws, and paintpots out, and made a big wooden sign, saying SAVE DRURIDGE BAY - STOP SAND EXTRACTION. We got permission from Castle Morpeth council to erect it on their land next to the extraction site. In May, Alan Beith unveiled the sign. TV reported it, and there were picture stories in the papers.

A summer picnic was a good opportunity to expose RMC's sand digging. In July, we organised a Save Our Beach picnic. Children from local playgroups came to the beach with their parents, near the extraction site. An aunty-like councillor,

Members' children have fun scaring away the digger driver at Halloween. Behind the masks are Jenny, Paul and Eric Greveson, and George, Sophie and Freddy Paxton.

Isabel Smail, came as our VIP. We brought a special cake we had made with a digger on, while the vehicle itself dug out the sand nearby. We wore our new home-made badges showing a sobbing toddler, and the slogan Save Our Beach, SOB.

At Halloween, a group of us with young children let them make masks and dress in up scary costumes. Off we went to Druridge Bay to scare away the digger driver, the young children making hideously ugly faces and screechy noises.

In March, we livened things up a bit by sending RMC's chairman an invitation to collect a Green Duffer Award on the first of April, at the beach. One of our members, Catherine Spoor, made a long scroll with a green rosette and ribbons, saying:

To the Chairman of Ready Mixed Concrete
Green Duffer Award
for
Creating a Sand Free Picnic Spot
on the Beach

We went to the beach, with a bottle of imitation champagne. The chairman neither answered our invitation, nor turned up for his award. We, however, sat and ate our sand-free sandwiches, and drank the fizzy pear wine.

Sitting in front of the digger

The weather in our cold, exposed northern bay often made campaigning difficult. Despite this, two members of our Sand Group began to plan in April their own action, to sit down in front of the digger. Terry and Carole Drummond live at Ellington, a mile from the beach.

It was on Terry's 69th birthday, in May, when he and Carole took their folding chairs, a big beach umbrella, a flask of coffee and a book each, and sat on the beach in the path of the digger driver. Carole had informed *The Journal* and TV. Here is the TV dialogue.

> *BBC reporter: It's not the ideal day for a beach party. It's cold and overcast. But that didn't stop Terry and Carole Drummond from sitting there with a book, in a silent protest. Anybody trying to take sand would have to run over the Drummonds. It left the man from Northern Aggregates not knowing which way to turn.*

(The camera focuses on Terry and Carole on their beach chairs on the beach)

Terry (angrily): I'm trying to draw attention to the fact that they're *ruining the beach*. It's criminal.

BBC to Terry: It's not the ideal way to spend your birthday is it?

Terry: It's a *good* way to spend my birthday, to draw people's attention.

BBC reporter: Eventually the police came, after complaints from Northern Aggregates about the beach party. But Mr Drummond wasn't going to let the foreman from the company spoil his big day.

(A policeman, the digger driver and Northern Aggregates' foreman clamber across the piles of sand, and approach the Drummonds.)

Foreman (dubiously as he's on TV): I've been on to my head office...

Terry: Fine...

Foreman: ...and they say you are on freehold land...

Terry: Am I? Fine! What are you wanting to do?

Foreman: I'm asking you to leave.

Terry: I'm *not* leaving!

Foreman: You're not?..

Terry: No! I'm exercising my right to sit on the beach, as an Englishman.

Foreman (doubtfully): Can I have your name and address please?

Terry: Why do *you* need my name and address?

Foreman: Because the company asked...

Terry: I'm not *giving* you my name and address. I'm not giving it to you. I don't know *who* you are. I've never seen you before. You could be a ... a ... *coastguard!*

BBC Reporter: The police couldn't interfere unless there's a breach of the peace. So off they went (the policeman, the foreman, and the digger driver) not being able to work out if the Drummonds were on private land.

Terry: I'm getting very angry!

BBC reporter: The company is now telephoning their legal man to see whether they have the right to remove the Drummonds so they can carry on with their work.

BBC reporter, turning to Terry: You can't come here every day though?

Terry: Of *course* you can. You can if you're so *determined!*

(Turning to Carole, tenderly...) The thing is they're not taking sand away all the time that we're sitting here. So I suppose that's something isn't it?

Terry and Carole on their beach sit-down, May 1993.

Carole kept a diary of the events. On the afternoon of the second day:

2.30 Lorry arrived and driver came down to us and threatened to drive the JCB up the ramp and if we didn't move we could get hurt. We didn't move. Tide is coming in fast. Just another 20 mins and he won't be able to drive on the beach.

2.45 Digger half filled lorry from rear of site.

3.15 A Mr Leese (young whiz-kid) from RMC arrived and told us we were trespassing, preventing their legal right to remove sand etc etc and a heated argument took place. He advised us to seek professional advice, and left.

On the third morning:

9.00 The Richardsons (local residents) informed us lorries had been loaded throughout the night.

9.20 We arrived at the site. Same lorry driver who threatened us yesterday was waiting for us with another lorry driver and the digger driver. None of the hoped-for support from other local residents was present. Driver said he would "smack Terry in the mouth" if we made any attempt to stop them filling the lorries with sand. We had no choice but to stand and watch. Lots of people walking on the beach. NOT ONE PERSON CAME NEAR TO GIVE US SUPPORT!

Lorries arriving every 20 minutes and leaving with full loads.

11.15 Sand piles flattened. All gone. Lorries and digger packed up and left at 11.30 am. We left at 11.55 am.

WILL NOT RETURN. NO SUPPORT

No-one cares about the beach. Why bother?

Terry and Carole felt that RMC could have been stopped months earlier than they did if others had joined them. Only one couple from nearby Cresswell had supported them, on and off, and others had dropped by from time to time.

Although nothing seemed to change as a direct result of their action, there was immense symbolic importance in their sit-down. The TV and newspaper photographs recorded for history the pensioner and his wife who stopped the digger, and the bewildered response of the powerful company.

Spring, summer, autumn, winter. Whenever a group of us could organise something, we were at our bay, in mud and rain, sun and wind, damp and penetrating chill, in all weathers and all conditions. We weren't there all the time. There were only a couple of dozen active campaigners. But RMC never knew when we would turn up, and the digger driver never knew when he would next be embarrassed.

Lobbying and winning support

Our campaign was all about saving our bay, but not all our actions had to take place there. We worked out and about in the public arena, winning support and influencing people. We wanted to build up such a level of reproach against RMC that they would be unable to hold up their heads for the shame of what they were doing. We worked on many fronts during the years 1990 to 1993.

One of the earliest actions was our approach to local builders, asking them not to use sand from Druridge. Only two builders responded to our letters. That might seem depressing, but there is always some gain. We had told the papers about the letters, and one reporter from *The Journal* tracked down an enthusiastic spokesperson from a large local builder, who agreed that his company would not use Druridge sand. Either he was brave or tactless. The company squashed him, and nothing further happened. The company refused to reply to our follow up letters.

Other outlets for sand to be sold were through the DIY stores, with whom we corresponded. We learned that B & Q were selling Ready Mixed Concrete packs of building sand. We wrote to their Environmental Co-ordinator Dr Alan Knight, drawing attention to their four policies on non-replaceable peat, and the similarities with non-replaceable sand. Dr Knight investigated their sources, and later wrote to us guaranteeing that none of the sand came from Druridge. Did he communicate with RMC? We don't know who knows who, in the world of business. Certainly the exposure in the media ensured that RMC knew about these letters.

We wrote to local councils. Would they please request any contractors who undertook work for them to agree not to use sand from Druridge. Wansbeck District Council which had an active Green Committee overcame the legal difficulties, and banned Druridge sand. Later Castle Morpeth Borough Council decided they could not square the circle of legal difficulties. Many times over the months, the debating and eventual decisions appeared the newspapers.

At the first local council election following the start of our sand campaign, we invited all the prospective candidates for a walk along the beach, to show them the damage, and most of them came. We asked them to work within Castle

Candidates for Castle Morpeth Borough Council election 1991, being taken on a tour of the damaged beach near the sand extraction site.

Morpeth to stop sand extraction, if elected, and they nearly all said they would, as we expected. We sent photographs to the local papers of them on the beach. It was more weight again to our cause.

Before the 1992 general election, we wrote to all the main parties' environment spokespeople asking them to review historic planning permissions for minerals extraction. Then we wrote to all the candidates in 24 local constituencies asking for their support if elected. They almost all said they would, and once again, it was reported in black and white in the newspapers.

These are very simple ways to gain support from elected representatives, though it would make life very difficult for these people if every single interest group required a response in this way.

One way to alert local people to the problem, and to learn how much sand was leaving the bay, was to try to count the number of lorry movements. Catherine Spoor was at that time an unemployed theatre costume designer who worked voluntarily in our office several days every week. She designed and produced our "Sand Spotters" form. This encouraged people who lived in Cresswell and Widdrington village to record the lorry movements. We wanted to work out for ourselves exactly how much sand was leaving, and in which direction it was going. We had always had to rely on RMC's own statements that they were removing between 30,000 and 40,000 tonnes every year.

Bobbie Parsons, a local member, delivered the forms to every house in Cresswell. The most regular reports came in from the village shop. The owner caught most of the truck movements passing south through Cresswell. His shop was strategically placed at the junction of routes. After ten months of observations, a council officer took the records and calculated that over 103,000 tonnes had probably been moved in that time. This information formed part of our bargaining package with RMC.

That great campaigners' standby, a petition, had to be used to influence people. Nick Scott, who was a warden for Northumberland Wildlife Trust, organised a petition against sand extraction during the Gateshead Garden Festival in 1990. The Trust had a pond at the festival, and there Nick and his co-wardens gathered 12,000 signatures. The Mayor of Castle Morpeth agreed to receive the petition at Druridge. *The Morpeth Herald* took a splendid picture of him accepting it with the digger scooping up sand in the background.

Sometimes we had to lobby for support within our own close contacts. RMC offered a contract to Northumberland Wildlife Trust's subsidiary Northumberland Ecological Services for environmental works at one of their Northumberland gravel sites. We challenged the Trust not to work for them, and we had meetings and some passing back and forth of letters. Eventually they agreed not to, while RMC continued to extract sand at Druridge.

We used the whole gamut of classical campaigning activities to build up our support. We spoke at local meetings frequently. We wrote to housing associations asking them not to use Druridge sand, and letters to the Cleveland Wildlife Trust objecting to them allowing Northern Aggregates to be one of their corporate sponsors. This led to another minor upset with Northumberland Wildlife Trust. We met the Countryside Commission to discuss why Druridge was not a designated Area of Outstanding Natural Beauty. Between us, we prepared leaflets, and distributed them round the villages and towns of our region, and through the libraries. Members sought sponsorship in the Druridge Bay Campaign's annual Beach Run. Others met council officers.

We wrote to local garden centres, we distributed the petition, we kept in close contact with Castle Morpeth and its attempts to use coastal protection legislation. Some of our ideas fell by the wayside, such as producing a video for distribution; the presentation of a Greensand award to DIY shop managers; the attempt to bring Sir John Hall, later of Newcastle United fame, into the campaign, as he owns a house in Cresswell; a lorry trailing exercise.

Victories never come quickly and easily, but every small step informed the wider world about sand extraction, and gained us support.

Copied (T) THOMPSONS WAGONS MAY '94

DATE	TIME AM/PM	PLACE	DIRECTION OF VEHICLE (see back of page eg C→L)	DESCRIBE LORRY eg name of company, colour of vehicle	OTHER COMMENTS (loaded or unloaded etc)
13/5/94	14-08	CRESSWELL ICES	LYNEMOUTH - DRURIDGE	THACKERAY TRAILER	EMPTY
13/5/94	14-30	"	DRURIDGE - LYNEMOUTH	"	LOADED SAND
13/5/94	15-01	"	"	"	"
13/5/99	15-20	"	LYNEMOUTH - DRURIDGE	"	EMPTY
13/5/94	15-36	"	DRURIDGE - LYNEMOUTH	"	LOADED SAND
13/5/94	15-55	"	LYNEMOUTH - DRURIDGE	"	EMPTY
13/5/94	16-18	"	DRURIDGE - LYNEMOUTH	"	LOADED SAND
13/5/94	16-55	"	LYNEMOUTH - DRURIDGE	RED/YELLOW [illegible] (T)	EMPTY
13/5/94	17-10	"	DRURIDGE - LYNEMOUTH	" (T)	????
14/5/94	07-32	"	"	THACKERAY TRAILER	LOADED
14/5/94	08-01	"	LYNEMOUTH - DRURIDGE	"	EMPTY
14/5/94	09-26	"		"	LOADED SAND
14/5/94	09-45	"	DRURIDGE LYNEMOUTH	"	LOADED SAND
14/5/94	09-46	"	"	"	EMPTY
14/5/94	10-01	"	LYNEMOUTH - DRURIDGE	"	LOADED SAND
14/5/94	10-20	"	DRURIDGE - LYNEMOUTH	"	EMPTY
14/5/94	10-28	"	LYNEMOUTH - DRURIDGE	"	LOADED SAND
14/5/94	10-43	"	DRURIDGE - LYNEMOUTH	"	LOADED SAND
14/5/94	11-00	"	"	"	EMPTY
14/5/94	11-01	"	LYNEMOUTH - DRURIDGE	"	EMPTY
14/5/94	11-21	"	"	"	LOADED SAND
14/5/94	11-24	"	DRURIDGE - LYNEMOUTH	"	LOADED SAND

Maurice Brown fills in his sand spotter form. He is one of the local residents who tracked movements of the sand lorries past his house at Druridge Bay.

The Journal takes on sand extraction

For years, we had had a good working relationship with our local media on the nuclear power stations threat. The sand campaign had probably even more media attraction, as it was so visual.

Philip Young was one of our members, and a local freelance journalist and writer. He later became deputy editor of *The Journal*. In 1990, he was nominated as one of ten top prize-winners in the Northern Short Story Competition. His story, "When Fascination Comes Around", was about a man taking a walk beside a river, contemplating both a decision in his personal life and the extraction of beach sand from Druridge. The story appeared in the local papers with Philip seated on the dunes and the digger behind.

He wrote an article for *The Observer's* Sunday magazine in October 1992. It was about Nick Scott and his personal protest beside a big hole in the sand on the beach. For once we had got national coverage for our issue.

Local coverage was fairly continuous, but the head of steam was kept going by a remarkable proposal in April 1993 from Tony Henderson, environment editor of *The Journal*, the North East's regional daily paper. He asked if we would like the newspaper to take on sand extraction as an issue. Of course we were very excited about the opportunities this offered.

The Journal

SAVE OUR BAY CAMPAIGN

END SAND EXTRACTION AT DRURIDGE BAY — *NOW!*

We the undersigned call upon Northern Aggregates–part of the Ready Mixed Concrete Group – immediately to stop taking sand from Druridge Bay

Name	Address	Signature

Please return to: Druridge Bay Campaign, Tower Buildings, Oldgate, Morpeth, Northumberland, NE61 1PY

The petition printed by The Journal.

Tony Henderson, his photographer, Countryside Officer Colin Marlee and I went out to Druridge. The photographer took dozens of pictures on the bright day, with blue sky and clouds, and the digger removing the sand. *The Journal* drew up a SAVE OUR BAY logo, with a picture of the yellow digger. A double page colour splash launched *The Journal's* campaign. Almost everyone in the North East would learn about the issue.

In early May, Tony had a petition printed in *The Journal*. It said: "We the undersigned call upon Northern Aggregates - part of the Ready Mixed Concrete Group - immediately to stop taking sand from Druridge Bay." He had sheets printed and sent to us. Readers were invited to write to the newspaper for copies, and we distributed them through our networks. Later, more had to be printed. Tony would record over the months the rising number, and by the end of the year there were 20,000 signatures.

The articles stimulated letters to the newspaper both from our own members and the public. Every time a letter appeared, the SAVE OUR BAY logo did too. It appeared in the reporting of our annual Beach Run when we awarded a yellow digger as a booby prize to RMC; when MPs signed the petition; at events organised at Druridge over the summer; when visitors expressed concern at what they were seeing on the beach; when rare birds appeared at the bay; every time any of the councils made a comment or discussed the issue; as the petition numbers crept up; when VIPs and organizations like the Council for the Protection of Rural England and the World Wide Fund for Nature were asked by Tony to comment.

At least 39 times before the end of the year, articles appeared in *The Journal*. Letters were published in the paper, and editorials objected to what RMC was doing.

Naturally, we played to our audience. The more opportunity we had, the more ideas we came up with.

In Parliament

We could never expect sympathy in the House of Commons, except from the opposition benches. All our campaigning years were spent under the Conservatives, for whom only a minority of people in the North East voted. We developed the mentality of not expecting help from government, but protesting nevertheless, as if against a brick wall. Our political representatives helped us.

On 10 December 1990, Alan Beith challenged Tim Yeo, Parliamentary Under-Secretary of State for the Environment, in an adjournment debate. His argument, with which most people in our area would agree, was that as it was government inspectors who gave us our problem in the first place, it was the government which should pay any compensation involved in undoing the planning permissions.

Tim Yeo did not agree. He said that it was not the government's job to revoke the permissions. "The county council ... is in the best position to strike the right balance of supply of sand and gravel against the environmental costs. It also has the power to revoke or modify the existing planning permission." He said that there was no provision for the Secretary of State to pay compensation.

The adjournment debate took place between 12.36pm and 1.06am on the night of 10 December. Civil servants in the Department of the Environment had been required to prepare a full briefing for Tim Yeo. There were three full pages in *Hansard* reporting the debate, which RMC are sure to have seen. And it was televised on BBC's North of Westminster the following Sunday. Many more people were finding out about the dirty deeds of RMC.

It was the usual stalemate. The mineral planning authority, which was the county council, could not afford to revoke planning consent. No-one would or could pay for sand extraction to stop at Druridge Bay.

During September 1991, the Environment Select Committee was taking evidence on coastal zone protection. They were looking at risks to coastal settlements and ecosystems. We found this out at very short notice, and also that John Cummings of Easington, one of our MP supporters, was on the committee. We hadn't time for detailed research. I quickly prepared a short case, summarising the issues, and presented it neatly with coloured and black and white photographs. I contacted John Cummings, and he agreed to point out our submission to the committee.

When the committee published its report, our evidence was listed in the Unpublished Memoranda section. That was the full extent of its direct influence. But as usual it made useful local publicity for us. John Cummings allowed us to inform the media that he was supporting us, and sent photos of himself at the House of Commons, so I could attach them with the story for our Northumberland newspapers.

In December, Alan Beith and Jack Thompson both spoke in the House of Commons debate on the report of the Environment Select Committee. Alan said: "One thing that ought to be considered is the situation at Druridge Bay, where sand continues to be dug from the beach on the basis of a planning decision granted on an appeal decades ago."

Jack said: "The problems being experienced now, arising from some 25 years of removing sand from Druridge, are evident all along this part of the coast. The extraction of some 1.5 million tonnes of sand is causing damage which may never be overcome."

Again, at the end of December 1991, Alan Beith addressed an oral question in the House of Commons to Under Secretary of State Tony Baldry. "Since it was central Government, not the local communities, who allowed sand extraction to happen, the Minister must surely recognise that central Government must play some part in bringing this disgraceful practice to an end."

Tony Baldry replied: “It is for the mineral planning authority to decide whether or not to revoke the planning consent for extractions and whether such action is warranted.”

Thus we raised our voice in Parliament on sand extraction. RMC knew what we were doing. But sand extraction would not be stopped by our political masters.

King Canute

In 1991, King Canute came to our aid. The real King Canute was Danish, and according to my *Encyclopaedia Britannica*, conquered all of England except London in 1015. His fierce Viking nature apparently became tamed when he became a Christian, and the encyclopaedia says “his humility is finely illustrated by the old Norman poem which describes how he commanded the rising tide of the Thames at Westminster to go back”. From schoolgirl comics, my own idea of him is of a king uselessly attempting to command the forces of nature.

Our sand group had the idea of linking him with RMC, digging the coastal defences away, and at the same time commanding the tide not to come in and flood the land. We came up with the symbol

Royal

Monarch

Canute.

In March 1991, a costumed group of Vikings somehow got themselves out to Druridge. There was a king with a crown and flowing cloak over striped pyjamas. There were serfs carrying his throne, and assorted Viking-type characters with placards. We had a wheelbarrow and spade. We marched down the country lane, chanting

“Dig the sand at Druridge Bay

Canute will keep the sea away.”

We plodged across the track to the beach where the digger was working, and put the king on his throne next to the water. Half of us dug sand out with the shovel and wheelbarrow, while the others waved their placards pleading with the king to stop.

TV followed us all the way, and newspaper photographers.

King Canute sat at the edge of the waves, waving his sword at the tide, and commanding it to stay back. His Anglo-Saxon trainers and striped pyjamas got wetter and wetter, and his throne was sucked giddily into the sand. Still he waved on his lop-sided seat, and told the sea to stay back.

It was totally silly, and all playing up to the TV. From then on, King Canute became the protector of Druridge Bay. On this occasion, the king was played by Niall Urquhart. Later, Nick Scott took the job, and later still Ken McDonald. They were all bearded, big men.

We used him regularly, but sparingly. We had to try to sense how often to play games for the media, among other techniques, and he was our best act, to be brought out at special times.

In October 1991, King Canute and court marched through the streets of Yarm, a market town in Cleveland, to deliver a proclamation at Northern Aggregates' head office. Yarm wasn't used to the antics of protesters, and the people stared as the court processed down the high street, being filmed by local TV. Northern Aggregates officials came to the front door, to hear the majestic King request them to stop ruining Druridge Bay.

King Canute's first appearance at Druridge Bay, March 1991. He (Niall Urquhart) is trying to keep the sea at bay. With Bridget Gubbins, Ian Douglas, Mike Greveson and volunteer coastal wardens.

Direct encounters with Ready Mixed Concrete

During 1992, the RMC Group were applying to have an extension of existing sand and gravel extraction at Powburn in Northumberland, about 30 miles inland of Druridge. There was a planning inquiry. We decided to embarrass RMC and made a short submission to the inquiry explaining that RMC could not possibly claim to care for the environment of Northumberland while they were destroying Druridge Bay. Seven or eight of us assembled with our placards, and stood outside Powburn village hall, giving out leaflets. County council officials smothered grins as they passed us. Expensively suited RMC executives were very irritated.

That was the first time we met Tim Stokes, RMC's public relations man. He tried to get friendly, and buy us cups of tea. We talked to him, but paid for our own cups of tea in the nearby transport café. He gradually became a kind of middleman between his employers and ourselves.

As well as going for planning permission to extend their Powburn site, RMC were applying to extract sand and gravel at Haltwhistle, on the River Tyne's banks, thirty miles west of Newcastle. We took our placards and stood outside the church hall in the village street. Later, Terry Drummond had a vicious verbal battle with Chris Leese, Northern Aggregates' Estates Manager. Chris Leese obliquely refers to this in a letter to us which appears in chapter eight.

During the autumn, Fiona Hall, our vice-chair at the time, was in discussions with Tim Stokes. The company was making tentative approaches to us. Here are some extracts from the correspondence.

Dear Bridget *9 September 1992*

It was a great pleasure to meet you and some of your colleagues from the Druridge Bay Campaign at the Powburn Appeal yesterday...

I hope that an improved level of dialogue can be achieved in the future...

Tim Stokes

Public Relations Executive

Following this, a meeting was arranged between us, Northern Aggregates and RMC.

Dear Ms Hall *30 November 1992*

We enclose our proposed agenda for your consideration. We confirm that four representatives of the Company will be attending. We understand that four members of the Druridge Bay Campaign will be in attendance. We hope that our suggested agenda will provide the basis for a useful discussion.

Chris A Leese

Estates and Development Manager

The agenda was a straightforward laying out of the positions of both sides, until Item 4, which read: "Consideration of any positive measures that could be taken to alleviate concern, setting to one side any question of a cessation of operations." Fiona wouldn't let that pass.

Dear Mr Leese *6 December 1992*

The draft agenda you propose is satisfactory except for Item 4, where the Campaign insists on deleting "setting to one side any questions of a cessation of operations". The belated introduction of this restriction is contrary to the spirit of open discussion in which the RMC Group first proposed this meeting.

Fiona Hall

Vice Chair

Dear Ms Hall *10 December 1992*

Item 4 was intended to promote a discussion on positive measures we may be able to consider taking other than a cessation of our activities. We still wish to have this discussion but will remove Item 4, and now hope the enclosed amended agenda will prove satisfactory.

Chris A Leese

Estates and Development Manager

The meeting was chaired by Alan Beith, in the Community Council for Northumberland's building, where the Druridge Bay Campaign had its office. When the RMC people rang our bell, they noted Victim Support's bell, and made wry comments about needing its services. The big important, rich men in suits, travelling first class from their London west end office, to our little meeting room in the building for voluntary groups. They certainly had the power, the wealth. We had something different - genuine concern, and the interest of the media who reported our David antics against the Goliath multinational.

At the meeting we all aired our views, though neither side budged from its position. The minutes of each side went back and forth for correction and final approval three or four times over the next four months.

It's hard to know what it achieved, other than perhaps each side knowing the other's humanity.

King Canute goes to the capital

Autumn 1993

We decided to present the petition to RMC in London when it reached 20,000. This was clearly going to be before the end of 1993. Alan Beith arranged a meeting for us with Tony Baldry, Under-Secretary of State for the Environment, at the DoE building in Marsham Street.

Many of our VIP supporters had signed our petition. They were actresses Julie Christie, Juliet Stevenson and Emma Thompson, actor Richard Briers and actress and writer Beryl Bainbridge, environmentalist Jonathon Porritt, playwright Edward Bond, the Bishop of Newcastle, Baroness Stedman, architect Sir Richard Rogers, conductor Sir Charles Mackerass, former CND general secretary Bruce Kent. Tony Henderson got quotes from Emma Thompson, Beryl Bainbridge and Juliet Stevenson.

Because of the widespread advance publicity, our plans were well known. RMC and the leader of the county council, Ian Swithenbank, decided to upstage our action, and organise a surprise for us. On 21 November, the day before we left, we discovered that they were going to announce an eventual end to sand extraction at County Hall.

A minibus of King Canute and serfs had another uncomfortable drive to London. We all met Alan Beith at Marsham Street. The doorkeepers wouldn't allow the merry court inside. Some of our group had stayed at a roads protest squat the night before, and gathered extra supporters. Therefore, we had musicians, strolling players and jugglers to support the King, the Queen who this time was my seventeen-year-old daughter, Jeannie, and his court. TV came.

His Majesty and his court were not welcomed into the Department of Energy, and had to wait outside. Alan Beith, Jack Thompson, Bob Clifton, an engineer who had studied the effects of sand extraction, Fiona Hall and I went in to meet the very important Tony Baldry. He was welcoming and pompous, short, tubby and bristling with self-importance. We were ushered into a meeting room, where he half listened to our case, expressing glib delight that RMC had announced earlier the same day that it would be stopping sand extraction at the bay. He said he and his staff were singing the Alleluia Chorus in the lift.

Tony Baldry waved us goodbye and sailed off to other more important business. We went to join the King and courtiers. The TV crew organised the musical, juggling protesters into a parade, led by King Nick Scott Canute. In his interview he said, with a serious and noble demeanour: "I am glad that RMC have seen sense. They have listened to the King, and they have obeyed me!"

RMC will make a "phased withdrawal"

The TV crews had been active at both ends of the country. While we were in London, RMC and the County Council held their press conference at County Hall in Morpeth. They released a joint statement which said that RMC would make a "phased withdrawal". The points of substance were:

- that Northern Aggregates would make a "phased withdrawal" over an agreed period of time, subject to consent being obtained from the county council for further suitably located sites, and subject to other mineral-bearing land in which they had an interest being included in the county minerals plan;

- when these conditions were met, RMC would surrender its planning consent at Druridge, and do restoration work on the dunes.

We had seen a faxed copy of their press statement which had arrived in Alan Beith's office. We were glad, but it was not exactly a statement that they intended to stop.

Meanwhile, we had not finished our antics in London. Using our A - Z, we paraded through the west end streets to RMC's Georgian house in Chesham Street, where the media had been alerted to look out for us at 4 o'clock. Together with our road-protester supporters, we knocked on the door. Director Bryan Frost opened it. He was filmed receiving the 20,000 signature petition. He invited a group of six of us in for an exchange of views, including naturally MPs Alan Beith and Jack Thompson. But I protested. Surely he would invite the rest of the group in for a cup of tea. Tim Stokes had said that we would be welcome. Mr Frost was being filmed. He could hardly refuse. After some behind-the-hand whispers, one of his staff escorted the gang into the front room, where they were served tea. They made themselves comfortable on the cosy furniture, and the children played roly-poly on the deep-piled carpet. Herbal smoky smells filtered downstairs, while the select six exchanged polite but frosty remarks in the basement meeting room.

It all made marvellous television. Our video recordings of those days have us rolling around with delight. I wonder if RMC could share the jokes at their expense. Was their self-importance pricked?

A long three-year wait

After this announcement, which was portrayed in the local media as a win for the Druridge Bay Campaign, we had to wait while RMC applied for planning permission for new sites in Northumberland. It created an activity vacuum. Although RMC constantly told us that they were moving as quickly as they could, and that planning permissions of this nature take a long time, we were impatient. Sand was being removed at the same rate as ever before. Whether or not RMC were moving as quickly as they could on alternative sites, the bay was being badly damaged. During the last five months of 1993, the dunes had been broken through at Druridge in new places, at least three times.

Strong north easterly winds and high tides in September 1993 break through the dunes at one of RMC's former sand extraction sites near Blakemoor Burn. The dune in the foreground was once continuous with those further away. Straw bales have been placed across the gap in an ineffective attempt to repair the damage.

We let up the pressure somewhat, and were busy working on the nuclear issue. Coverage in the media didn't stop, though it was less concentrated. It was just enough to let the company know we were still alert. RMC got its permission to extract sand and gravel at Haltwhistle. Attempts were made to repair the dunes at Druridge, by the British Trust for Conservation Volunteers, using old Christmas trees around which windblown sand could collect.

At RMC's next AGM in May 1994, we organised another double action. We made a new sign and erected it in the place of the old one, with the slogan HOW LONG RMC? The Mayor of Castle Morpeth, Cllr Tom Simpson, unveiled it. On the same day, I was dispatched to RMC's AGM, with a Castle Morpeth Cllr Peter Angus, whom I had persuaded to come with me. When we got there, he wasn't allowed to speak at the meeting, as he wasn't one of the joint share-owners. Therefore I had to stand up and ask the Chairman why progress was so slow, and why they were still removing sand after giving the impression that they would be stopping.

After the meeting, I was given a wigging by Mr J B Cooper, one of the directors, who said we were making it very difficult for them. Really our actions were counterproductive now that they were trying so hard to find alternative sites. Nevertheless, the shareholders were still interested. I met Mr Rolfe, and told him how much we had enjoyed his TV appearance last year.

Prize poem, *Way of the Buffalo*

In 1994, we organised a poetry competition, and *The Journal* underwrote the prize money. Here is one of the winning poems, written by Ann Coburn.

WAY OF THE BUFFALO

These photographs, these framed reductions
Fail to catch the scale of it,
The vast, the endless spread of it,
They cannot show the long stampede of dunes,
The tawny, bristled hides shouldering down to the sea.
The thunder of waves is silenced here,
And how can frozen colours show their muscled flow,
Their rolling eye-whites and their foam-flecked flanks?
A photograph can never tell the rank, brash, salty smell
Of life.
Our bay.
It was - a marvel.
And we, whooping wild and windswept
With salt-lick skin and scabby knees,
We thought it was for ever.

Back then, we never dreamed our bay would go
The slow, sad way of the buffalo.

Then they came, the suit men
The white-faced, busy-eyed men.
They stood with their backs to the sea and calculated
Profit.
Time was nothing to them.
They strapped time to their wrists and made it bleat
Like a lamb.
It took a thousand years to make the sand
Which filled their shiny shoes,
But they scraped away the centuries in a few short years.
Our sand is in their roads, now.
It shapes their brandy glasses.

Yet still, we never dreamed our bay would go
The slow, sad way of the buffalo.

RMC get their first alternative site

By November 1994, the first of RMC's hoped-for alternative sites was named, at Wooperton, in Northumberland. In January 1995, storms breached the dunes more seriously than ever before, and sensational pictures of floods appeared on TV and in the papers.

By May 1995, RMC stated that it would reduce extraction at Druridge if it got the planning permission it wanted at Wooperton. The county council had always said that new sites would be examined entirely on their merits, and not as part of an exchange for Druridge. Nevertheless, RMC would have discussed whether or not it was worth proceeding with Wooperton, and informally had hinted that we should encourage our council to grant the permission to hasten getting them out of Druridge. We never did this.

In November 1995, RMC got planning permission for Wooperton, two years after they said they would stop. They still intended to get another planning permission, and wanted a third site to be included in the area of search in the forthcoming Minerals Local Plan, before they would stop at Druridge. Meanwhile, the beach was disappearing, and the dunes still eroding.

Ready Mixed Concrete want to dig out another beauty spot

By April 1996, a new twist to the tale started. RMC put in their second planning application which if achieved would put an end to extraction at Druridge. Gradually, it dawned on us that the site was almost at the boundary of the Northumberland National Park, in the sensitive and lovely Ingram Valley. Unsurprisingly, people there rose up in protest.

At first, it looked as though the confrontation-loving media would try to play one group against the other. We felt hampered. We didn't want another lovely area of Northumberland to be ruined, yet sand was still being dug at Druridge Bay.

After the summer, we carefully thought through our strategy. We agreed that we should approach the group campaigning to save the Ingram Valley and join forces. The group was called STRIVE, Save The Real Ingram Valley Environment.

We entered into careful negotiations. Ingram Valley residents were farming people, with ties to business and the Conservative Party. They were distrustful of the Labour dominated county council. Perhaps they saw the Druridge Bay Campaign as vivid and forthright, even exhibitionist. We did however agree a Joint Statement, which we made public.

1. Druridge Bay Campaign does not want Druridge to be saved at the expense of another much-loved beauty spot.

2. STRIVE has never argued that sand should continue to be extracted from Druridge, in order to keep the threat away from the Ingram Valley.

3. The two campaigns jointly oppose RMC for its attack on these two Northumberland beauty spots.

4. Each campaign continues to be structurally independent. Druridge Bay Campaign's remit is to protect Druridge Bay. STRIVE's current remit is to fight any quarrying proposals in the Ingram Valley.

5. RMC has a planning permission at Wooperton which will give them enough sand equivalent to that taken from Druridge to last them until 2022. They should stop extracting sand at Druridge immediately.

6. RMC should not be greedy. They have 26 years to find a non-controversial alternative source of sand.

Planned joint actions collapsed rather. Our idea that they provide a Saxon princess for our King Canute, and that we proceed from our locations on the west and east of the county to a meeting in the centre for a wedding, with horses, costumes and media attention, fell flat. STRIVE preferred to do things their own way.

I don't know how much our combining with STRIVE affected the internal thinking at RMC. It may have had some influence, as the divide-and-conquer strategy had failed. I was much happier once we had made the decision to work jointly with STRIVE.

Three years and still extracting

Autumn 1996

It would soon be three years since RMC had said they would stop. We decided to plan our own, hard-hitting actions. All this had to be co-ordinated with our nuclear campaign, and we had to try not to bombard the media with too many complicated stories at the same time.

Christopher Hampson was the North East's representive on the new Environment Agency, which has a Flood Defence committee. He was also RMC's chairman. There were very good exploitation possibilities there.

We decided to bring King Canute out again. He had been lying low since November 1993.

I spent one Sunday with tins of orange and black paint, and made a GREEDY RMC sign. We planned a double action, first in Morpeth, then moving on to Druridge Bay. On 11 November 1996 we paraded down the street with Ken McDonald as our king, Debbie Davies as the Queen, and various little princes and princesses, some in pushchairs. We had drums, and we chanted

GREE - DY R - M - C

HANDS - OFF DRU - RIDGE - BAY

Then we piled into vehicles, drove to Druridge, and repeated the performance parading down the country lane with the new sign. Terry, in serf costume, nailed the sign on top of the old one. TV covered us, and the papers reported it.

The end was getting close, though we didn't realise it. Three weeks later, Charles Bowden, an independent film producer, had a group of us out at Druridge for a three-episode documentary he was preparing for Tyne Tees. We showed him the eroded beach, and provided him with interviews. Clearly something odd was happening. Charles Bowden kept disappearing out of the wind into the sand dunes to listen to messages on his mobile phone. Then he said that RMC were about to make some kind of announcement, but he wasn't sure what. Would I agree to be interviewed expressing delight that they had agreed to stop extraction. I wouldn't. I couldn't react without knowing what the announcement actually was.

And then they stopped

We all stopped what we were doing and drove back to County Hall in Morpeth, where there was to be a press conference. We rushed to the committee room, complete with our SAVE DRURIDGE BAY flag. We were only just in time. TV, Tony Henderson, local reporters were all there. The council officers smothered grins and avoided our eyes, while we smiled at everyone around. Bryan Frost made RMC's presentation. He said that RMC had decided to stop sand extraction at Druridge from that moment, and that they were giving up their planning permission. They would dispose of the land they owned at Druridge for pence, to the County Council or to a suitable charitable trust. They were dropping their application for Ingram too. They would seek another less controversial site in Northumberland. Environmental values had changed over the years, and they realised that they could not go on with what they were doing.

Well! This was a surprise. We cheered. Tony Henderson, and Adrian Pitches for Look North, asked questions about the new location. Terry Drummond remained bitter. Who, he wanted to know, was going to repair the damage to the beach? After the formal business, I actually shook hands with Bryan Frost, managing to feel positively friendly towards him. Tim Stokes was there, smiling and diplomatic in the background.

Thus it was that the great destroyers were halted. They stopped voluntarily, it is true. But they did it because of the disgrace that was being attached to their name. A giant company with a turnover of £4.5 billion, with quarries and subsidiaries around the globe, submitted to the psychological pressure of a handful of powerless people. The company gave up its legal rights, and abandoned a small but profitable operation. Sometimes, the little people of the world can celebrate.

King Canute (Ken McDonald) brandishes the third sign opposing sand extraction.

Demonstrating outside Morpeth Post Office before dispatching a giant postcard to energy minister Tim Eggar, February 1996.

"Sell the Land" Pressing, Pursuing, Persuading

Chapter 3

Round the Central Station with the piper

Newcastle's Central Station is a cold and draughty place at half past eight on a November morning. And on this particular morning, the commuters were pouring out of the local trains, over the footbridges, across the main concourse and out of the columned exit. London and Edinburgh inter-city trains were pulling in, pulling out, and the announcements were called out over the speakers. Just a usual sort of day, office workers carrying briefcases, moving briskly, speaking little. Everything as would be expected, except that there was a sound of bagpipes coming from somewhere. A raucous sound of bagpipes being tuned.

Hiding in the shadows, a skinny whiskery man with fingerless gloves was pumping his bellows, listening to his drones, adjusting them. From time to time, he breathed warm air onto his frozen fingers, shook his hands. From here and there, from out of the underground, people dressed unlike city workers, joined the piper. Two of them wearing anoraks carried a big wooden placard. One had golden and green in her hair, another was wearing an Oxfam shop-best black and white herring-bone coat. A round-bonnetted woman, wearing a pale blue padded coat, carried a huge Lever-Arch file.

The maroon-uniformed information people kept an eye on things. The pipes began to sound a little more like some kind of music. Then the piper, wearing a feathered hat, stood up and shook himself, and began to play *...over the hills and far away...* The rest of the group arranged themselves behind him, and held up the wooden placard, and a flag. The person in the blue coat obviously had some important documents in the file she held in front of her.

TV people with a woolly microphone and a camera arrived. They identified the group, who had begun to follow the piper around the concourse. The dark suited people moving in two directions turned their heads, attracted by the piper's sounds. They might have glimpsed the words and stars on the placard as they passed. 40,394 signatures. Juliet Stevenson. Emma Thompson. 6 Lords. 2 Baronesses. Edward Bond. Jonathan Porritt. 6 Civic Leaders. Sinead Cusack. Richard Briers. 16 MPs. Alan Bennett. 10 Professors. Michael Williams.

The group went round the concourse three or four times. SAVE DRURIDGE BAY said the flag. *Oh yes, Druridge Campaigners*, a few people probably thought. *Them again. I agree with that.* Perhaps one or two may even have thought *That's the petition I signed.*

The group then marched up the sloping gangway to the footbridge, towards the Kings Cross train. They shuffled in between the moving commuters *...and all the tunes that he could play...* and across the bridge to the platform on the other side, following the piper's feathered topknot. The TV camera man trotted along beside, spurted ahead and whizzed around to face the group.

They went along the platform to a carriage where Blue Coat clambered on. She opened the file, and showed it to the TV cameras. It was a rather untidy pile of papers, with hundreds and hundreds of signatures on. She waved to the group, and they waved back, as the doors closed, and the train left the station. *...over the hills and far away...*

* * *

At Kings Cross, Blue Coat left the train and went into the underground, still carrying the big black file. She came out at Westminster, into air that was still damply chilled. Over the traffic lights by the House of Commons, past Westminster Abbey to Victoria Street, to the new glass-house office building which houses the Department of Trade and Industry.

Waiting there were two men, one wearing a black knee-length wool coat, one a fawn trench coat. And a TV cameraman and microphone man. A press photographer. Blue coat and the two men posed obligingly, flicked through the pages of signatures, gave interviews. It took half an hour or so. Cynical seen-it-all Londoners barely turned their heads as they rustled past. And then the man in the black coat went in to the DTI and said something. A few minutes later, a woman came out and took the file. She put it in a trolley and wheeled it into the building. Those outside the frosty glass watched it disappear.

...over the hills and a great way off... All those signatures. Hours and hours of knocking on doors. Of stopping cars at the car park behind the sand dunes. Of posting sheets for signing in countless mailouts. Of approaching people at Newcastle's Monument. Of frozen fingers, ball-point pens on strings getting tangled, of sweaty sun-burnt backs leaning over cars in the east-wind-wicked sunshine of a northern bay. All wheeled away, and gone.

Then, Blue Coat and the two men smiled at each other, and shook themselves, and went their ways. That was that done.

* * *

Some of those commuters saw on their television screens that night a replay of the morning in the station. *I thought that's who it was.* But thousands more who watched would have thought *I signed that. That's my name going to London.* One in ten adults on Tyneside and in Northumberland could have thought that.

Then they would see the Tyne Tees reporter track down the important government minister in the glassy building.

> *Jerry Foley: You're keeping Druridge Bay in public hands. Why don't you give a commitment that no power station will be built there?*
>
> Tim Eggar: I'm obviously looking as quickly as I can at the issue of the future ownership of the site. I'm very well aware of the considerable pressure coming locally, and the strongly held feelings locally, and I'll take those into account.
>
> *Jerry Foley: You said exactly that in a letter to Alan Beith, that you would take it into account. If you genuinely listened to what people say…*
>
> Tim Eggar: I have genuinely listened to what people say. I will be looking as soon as I can at the issue of exactly what is going to happen to that land. I have responded to their immediate concerns that it would not go into the private sector. I've given Druridge Bay residents and people concerned locally that assurance, uniquely. Nobody else in the country has got a similar assurance. And I will be looking as soon as I can at the issue of exactly what is going to happen to that land.
>
> *Jerry Foley: When will the final decision be taken?*
>
> Tim Eggar: I hope during the course of this year.
>
> *Jerry Foley: In a matter of months, if we're lucky?*
>
> Tim Eggar: If you're lucky, yes.

We want the Druridge land

The main aim of the Druridge Bay Campaign was to get the land owned by the nuclear industry out of their hands. We achieved many other useful things in the process, including the stopping of sand extraction, which had been important work between 1990 and 1993, with another intensive period in 1996. We worked on the land sale in parallel. The new Energy Group and the Steering Committee made sure the sale of the land was a high profile issue with government and Nuclear Electric.

Writing letters

Immediately following the announcement on 9 November 1989 that the nuclear industry would not be privatised, and that no more nuclear power stations would be built pending the 1994 Review, both the energy minister and the state-owned Nuclear Electric which inherited the land, were bombarded with letters, and Alan Beith had asked two parliamentary questions before the end of December 1989. Their answers left us in no doubt that the nuclear industry still wanted Druridge, and thus we were determined not to give in. Here are some extracts from the correspondence.

From the Corporate Director of National Power to Jack Thompson MP.

Dear Mr Thompson *6 December 1989*

The Government made clear (in the 9 November announcement) that the new company will retain the ability to construct and operate new nuclear capacity, and explained that it continued to value the diversity benefits for electricity generation that nuclear power could bring.

Mr John Collier, the Chairman of the new company, Nuclear Electric plc, has stated that it is his ambition to build more nuclear stations ... I believe it would be prudent not to abandon any suitable sites in the present circumstances.

Sam Goddard

Corporate Director of Planning and Construction

From the Under Secretary of State for Energy, giving a gleam of hope.

Dear Alan (Beith) *31 January 1990*

Nuclear Electric, although being retained in the public sector, will be required to operate on a commercial basis. It therefore will be in the company's own interest to reach a decision on the use of their site at Druridge Bay as any unused land asset will be a commercial liability.

Tony Baldry

To Cllr Flaherty, chairman of Northumberland County Council's Planning and Economic Development Committee, from Sam Goddard who had now been transferred to the new company.

Dear Cllr Flaherty *5 February 1990*

As I explained to you in my letter of 6 July 1989, nuclear sites are difficult to find, and Druridge, because it offers an acceptable balance of technical and environmental factors, is considered by Nuclear Electric to be a valuable asset which it will be retaining for possible future nuclear power station development.

Sam Goddard

Nuclear Electric

From the new chairman of Nuclear Electric.

Dear Mr Thompson *21 March 1990*

I can confirm that we do not have any detailed plans for this site which we continue to hold as a potential site for possible future development.

John Collier

From Nuclear Electric's company secretary.

Dear Mr Thompson *15 April 1991*

I should explain that we continue to regard Druridge Bay as a suitable site for further nuclear developments. The technical criteria required for nuclear sites are very onerous and locations such as Druridge which offer an acceptable balance of technical and environmental factors are difficult to find.

Rex Melville

From Nuclear Electric's Government Relations Manager, somebody lower down the chain of command, who sent a similar word processed letter to us at the Druridge Bay Campaign.

> *Dear Ms Gubbins* *17 April 1991*
>
> *Thank you for your letter of 25 March concerning Nuclear Electric's plans for the land it owns at Druridge Bay. You might be aware that we have received a similar letter from Mr Jack Thompson MP.*
>
> *I should explain that we continue to regard Druridge Bay as a suitable site for further nuclear developments. The technical criteria required for nuclear sites are very onerous and locations such as Druridge which offer an acceptable balance of technical and environmental factors are difficult to find.*
>
> *P M Haslam*

From Rex Melville to Jack Thompson again.

> *Dear Mr Thompson* *4 March 1992*
>
> *I can confirm that the Druridge site has not been subject to opencast activity ... Nuclear Electric continue to regard Druridge Bay as a suitable candidate site for nuclear development.*
>
> *Rex Melville*

From the Druridge Bay Campaign to the newly appointed managing director of Nuclear Electric.

> *Dear Mr Hawley* *11 June 1992*
>
> *Owing to the stated wish of John Collier to build a series of new PWRs, we would be very much obliged if you would agree to meet us to discuss our concerns. Alan Beith MP would like to attend such a meeting, and Cllr Kevin Flaherty, Chairman of Environment and Economic Development Committee at Northumberland County Council may be able to attend, depending on commitments. We would like to suggest 7, 8 or 9 of July.*
>
> *Bridget Gubbins*

From the very pressurised managing director of Nuclear Electric

Dear Ms Gubbins *17 June 1992*

As I am sure you will understand, my schedule for the first few weeks after joining Nuclear Electric is very busy, and I would therefore be unable to join you on any of the dates you suggest.

As you know, there is a moratorium on all new nuclear power station construction until the government holds its review of nuclear power in 1994. Even then, Druridge is unlikely to be the first site to which we will turn.

Dr R Hawley FEng

Frank Dobson and Simon Hughes come to Druridge

Jack Thompson arranged for us to meet Frank Dobson, the current shadow energy spokesman, when he was on a visit to the north, in October 1991. He listened carefully to us, and said that a future Labour government would ensure that Druridge Bay is not a site for a nuclear power station.

Alan Beith had helped us to meet Simon Hughes the Liberal Democrat energy spokesperson in December 1991. He agreed to support us however he could.

Changing minds - energy ideas into action

If a campaign is against a proposal, it needs to have an alternative strategy in place. We didn't want nuclear power. Therefore we needed to think how else electricity should be provided. Our local coal reserves, upon which so many communities depended for their livelihoods, were an asset which we should use in as wise and non-polluting way as possible. We wanted to move towards renewable energy.* We had done a lot of talking over the years about alternatives to nuclear power. Now we wanted to see real projects up and running. We wanted to change our energy ideas into action.

The time was right for anti-nuclear groups to take on a more positive approach. The trends were happening round the country. In London, Friends of the Earth started a renewable energy campaign. In Scotland, the Scottish Campaign to Resist the Atomic Menace, which had co-ordinated opposition to Torness, renamed their *SCRAM Journal* as *Safe Energy*.

By autumn 1990, the Druridge Bay Campaign had an Energy Group. It was a specialist sub-group, of five or six of us. Fiona Hall, Toni Stephenson and I brought our growing campaigning skills to the group. We three women were all non-technical people. There was Adrian Smith, a Newcastle City Council planner who was allowed to spend a certain amount of his work time supporting

* *Details of the arguments against nuclear power at Druridge Bay and for alternatives can be found in Generating Pressure. See bibliography.*

the Druridge Bay Campaign, as the council's way of endorsing our work. He was at the focus of the council's energy work, having promoted a city combined heat and power station. He'd been one of our energy advisors for some time.

Dr Nigel Mortimer was our most long standing expert energy advisor. He had been a research associate at Sunderland Polytechnic Renewable Energy Centre, and he now runs the Resources Research Unit at Sheffield Hallam University. Other people came in and out of the group at various times, but we five were at the core.

Our idea was to use local resources as much as possible. The CEGB had originally stated that a new power station would be needed in the North East to supply an expected increase in demand in the area. Originally they had thought a nuclear power station would be up and running by 1990. The region had managed very well in the meantime, partly, whether we liked it or not, with electricity from Torness. A large gas-powered station was being built on Teesside.

Our work was threefold -

local renewable energy,

clean coal and combined heat and power,

energy efficiency.

We want local renewable energy

Seven years ago, when this work started, there was only one wind farm in the UK, in Cornwall. Blyth Harbour windfarm, in Northumberland was being planned. In theory, all environmental groups supported renewables. There had been no anti-wind reaction, or talk of lavatory brushes against the skyline. Wind, solar, biofuels, wave and tidal energy were seen as benign and desirable.

Our Energy Group and our close contacts knew as much about renewable energy as anyone else in the region. Nigel brought together a group of people from Sheffield Hallam University, from Sunderland University, and from the Hexham company Border Wind which was building the Blyth Harbour windfarm. We called ourselves North East Wind Associates, and began to talk to farmers and landowners about their wind resources. By the end of 1992, the group had become a private limited company of consultants, North Energy Associates, with a Morpeth office.

Nigel Mortimer, Adrian and Nicola Smith and Garry Jenkins, a colleague of Nigel's from Sunderland University, and I were directors. North Energy Associates found and assessed windfarm sites, produced a renewable energy strategy for Durham County Council, has designed a new 15 - 20 kilowatt wind turbine, and has extended its area of work into biofuels. The company has been totally separate from the Druridge Bay Campaign since 1991, and has carried on in a practical way some of Energy Group's objectives.

Supporting clean coal and combined heat and power

The Druridge Bay Campaign had always had a close link with the National Union of Mineworkers. Dennis Murphy was the secretary of Northumberland NUM Mechanics. He later became leader of Wansbeck Disctrict Council, and following Jack Thompson's retirement, he became Wansbeck constituency's MP in 1997. In the late 80s, he and his colleagues set up an organisation called the Regional Energy Foundation. Its aims were to promote coal, to keep the deep mines open and miners employed, and to promote clean coal technology.

Our Energy Group supported these aims. We had a social concern in that jobs for miners were a mainstay of the regional economy, but we wanted to see cleaner, more efficient power stations. The Druridge Bay Campaign sent a statement of support in February 1991.

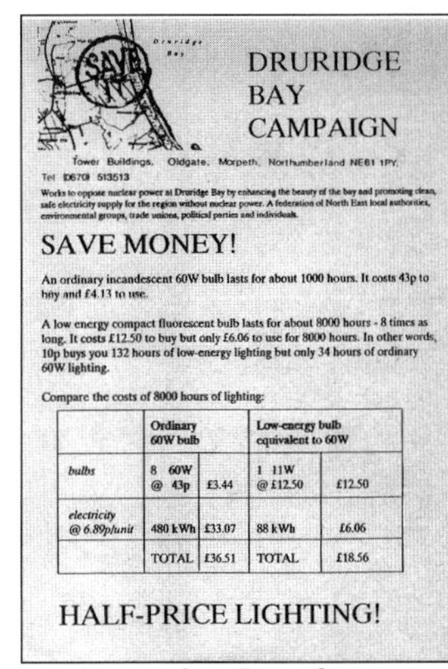

DRURIDGE BAY CAMPAIGN

Tower Buildings, Oldgate, Morpeth, Northumberland NE61 1PY. Tel (0670) 513513

Works to oppose nuclear power at Druridge Bay by enhancing the beauty of the bay and promoting clean, safe electricity supply for the region without nuclear power. A federation of North East local authorities, environmental groups, trade unions, political parties and individuals.

SAVE MONEY!

An ordinary incandescent 60W bulb lasts for about 1000 hours. It costs 43p to buy and £4.13 to use.

A low energy compact fluorescent bulb lasts for about 8000 hours - 8 times as long. It costs £12.50 to buy but only £6.06 to use for 8000 hours. In other words, 10p buys you 132 hours of low-energy lighting but only 34 hours of ordinary 60W lighting.

Compare the costs of 8000 hours of lighting:

	Ordinary 60W bulb		Low-energy bulb equivalent to 60W	
bulbs	8 60W @ 43p	£3.44	1 11W @ £12.50	£12.50
electricity @ 6.89p/unit	480 kWh	£33.07	88 kWh	£6.06
	TOTAL	£36.51	TOTAL	£18.56

HALF-PRICE LIGHTING!

Druridge Bay Campign leaflet about energy efficiency.

Improving energy efficiency

Fiona Hall produced a leaflet in March 1991, which we distributed through regional libraries, about energy saving lightbulbs. She calculated that UK lighting consumes the output of four power stations of the size proposed for Druridge Bay. And if each of Northern Electric's 1.3 million domestic customers replaced their three most heavily used 60 Watt lightbulbs by energy savers, demand would be reduced by up to one sixth of the output of the power station proposed for Druridge. The slogan on the leaflet was

SAVE MONEY

SAVE ENERGY

SAVE DRURIDGE BAY.

By the end of November 1993, we had produced another leaflet called *Electricity and Heating your Home*. This criticised the newly privatised Northern Electric for its heavy promotion of electric heating. We pointed out that electricity is a much more polluting and expensive way to heat homes than direct heating by gas. Because electric fires are much cheaper to install than a gas central heating system, we called for grants to be made available for low-income households.

Northern Electric were running their own Envirocare 2000 project, encouraging wise use of energy at the same time as pushing for a larger share of the heating market. In our wisdom, we advised them through the leaflet that the company should continue its programme of encouraging energy efficiency, but should stop promoting polluting electricity heating systems.

Our energy policy is an exam topic

We were just a small group with big ambitions. We got our message out wherever we could. In 1993, we produced our energy policy statement.

Although we would have liked to produce a well-researched work showing in detail an ideal electricity supply system for the region, we simply didn't have the resources. Instead our statement was a kind of wish-list for action. In 1995 it was used as part of a Geography A Level exam. At the moment, the ideas within it are being used as a starting point by Northumberland's Agenda 21 Energy Group. Its principles later formed the basis of a successful European bid for funding.

Campaigning is partly about changing minds. It is about achieving alternatives, about preparing fertile furrows ready for new ideas. Back in 1979, electricity supply was a battle between nuclear and coal for dominance. Power stations were polluting and inefficient, renewables were virtually non-existent, and no-one had heard of the concept of energy efficiency. It is not easy to assess what influence our small group actually had, but we were part of the national change of consciousness.

The Miners

Heseltine and the pit closures

1992 - miners employed in Northumberland 1,400

"Heseltine said 'Right we are going to shut 30 pits.' 30,000 men will be out of work. We thought, how can they do that? Why are they doing it? The pit is a community. You shut the pit, you shut down the community. There's nothing else. There wasn't at the time. There still isn't. We said 'What are we going to do?' The pit is the only employer in the area. It wasn't like in the 60s when people could get other jobs. You knew, whether you were 20 or 50, you were finished. Most miners are just miners. Not trained to be anything else. They're unskilled. Very skilled in the pit, but unskilled out of it. The shock of it. They would say 'I'm only 25. I've got two children and a mortgage.'

"There was nowhere you could be transferred to. I think that's when compulsory redundancy first came home to roost.

Achievements via privatisation

Why should a local group tackle a national injustice?

While working on local energy issues, we were constantly bearing in mind the need to be ready for the Nuclear Review scheduled for 1994. This would settle whether or not there would be government backing for new nuclear power stations.

I would ring round the other groups periodically to find out what they were doing. Friends of the Earth's energy campaign, Stop Hinkley Expansion, SCRAM in Edinburgh, the Shut Down Sizewell groups. Eventually, a network was set up by the secretariat for the Nuclear Free Local Authorities, in Manchester.

The Druridge Bay Campaign took a small but stubborn part in the work, insisting on playing a part alongside the major groups like Friends of the Earth, Greenpeace, and the Consortium of Local Authorities from South Wales and the South West, known as COLA, against a new PWR at Hinkley in Somerset.

By summer 1993 our Energy Group had decided that we wanted to expose the inadequate third party insurance of nuclear power.

Friends of the Earth were focussing on the forthcoming proposal by NIREX, the Government's radioactive waste disposal organisation, to build an underground nuclear waste laboratory under the Irish Sea, near Sellafield. Greenpeace were opposing the opening of the new THORP reprocessing plant at Sellafield. COLA was commissioning detailed analysis of the financial liabilities of the nuclear industry. The Druridge Bay Campaign had very small resources relative to these bodies, but we wanted to be heard too.

Back in 1983 I had become aware for the first time that if there should be nuclear accident, the nuclear industry was not required to compensate the general public, at that time beyond a paltry £20 million, with the Government supporting this with another £192 million. As an ordinary lay-person, I was horrified that this should be allowed, and whenever I could, I asked questions, wrote letters, discussed the topic.

We applied to Wansbeck District Council for £500, and to the Nuclear Free Local Authorities for another £500. When we got this money, we were able to commission a short research project which would be overseen by Nigel Mortimer in his spare time. By Christmas 1993, Helen Brownlie, a planner who worked with Adrian Smith in Newcastle City Council, had been given her outline brief.

What's wrong with the way the nuclear industry insures itself?

Although it is very seldom mentioned, the whole history of the civil nuclear industry is tied up with the way it has been protected from having to insure itself.

Walter Patterson, in his book *Nuclear Power*, described how the nuclear industry got round its insurance difficulties. In the early 50s, American reports declared that the likelihood of a major accident happening was one in a thousand million. On the other hand the consequences would be horrifying, with costs of thousands of millions of dollars, and deaths and long term injury to hundreds of thousands of people.

Commenting on these reports in 1976, Walter Patterson wrote that the remote likelihood of a major accident happening, combined with the astronomical consequences, set the insurance business an "unparalled poser". The US government wanted a civil nuclear programme so Congress got round the difficulties by passing the Price Anderson Act in 1957. This is how Walter Patterson described it.

> "Private utilities will not build and operate nuclear power stations if they may be bankrupted by claims arising from a major nuclear accident. Therefore, let a private utility be instructed to purchase from private insurers as much coverage as they will sell, against nuclear third-party liability. Thereafter the government will kick in an additional $500 million from Federal funds. Beyond this total there shall be no further financial liability."

Thus, "a maximum of $500 million from government plus $60 million from private insurers would be available." That was all.

The principle was followed by other nuclear nations, including the UK. In 1960, Parliament passed the Nuclear Installations (Licensing and Insurance) Act. Limits were set even lower than in the US, at £43 million from the Government and £5 million from private insurers. This amount has been raised since 1960, and is currently £280 million.

"Heseltine made his announcement, not knowing hardly what a pit was. After the furore, he pulled the reins back a bit. But he never changed his mind. The closures went ahead. In 1993 and after, it was done by stealth. It felt like that anyway. He would close ten. Then have another review, then close another ten.

"At first when the pits closed, there was a little bit of euphoria. People got their redundancy money. Holidays. When they came back down to earth they would say 'What am I going to do with the rest of my life?'

"Ellington was re-opened, with 300 men where there used to be thousands. We had to be grateful. We're so desperate in this area. 300 jobs is 300 jobs. If people come with factories now, they're not big employers. The factories take up a lot of space, but only have jobs for 10 or 12 people."

George Ferrigon

1997 - miners employed in Northumberland 435

Part of this cover must be paid for by the nuclear industry itself in the form of insurance. In the UK, this is £140 million. The remaining £140 million is not insurance at all. It is simply a sum of money guaranteed by the Government, to be provided out of its contingency funds. Beyond that, there is no legal obligation to compensate the public. Any further payment is at the discretion of Parliament. There is no money put aside for the purpose.

Walter Patterson wrote: "Since other energy supply industries must provide their own third-party coverage out of working funds, there is little doubt that the nuclear industry gains a distinct competitive advantage from the provisions."

There is absolutely no doubt that these limits were set to enable the nuclear industry to grow. They were not set for the protection of the population. The limits were, and still are, so low that the general public bears the risk, usually without being fully aware it is doing so.

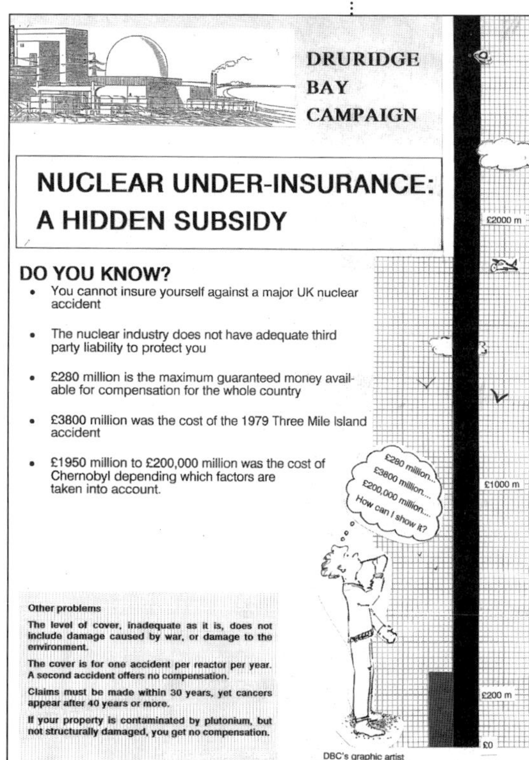
DRURIDGE BAY CAMPAIGN

NUCLEAR UNDER-INSURANCE: A HIDDEN SUBSIDY

DO YOU KNOW?

- You cannot insure yourself against a major UK nuclear accident
- The nuclear industry does not have adequate third party liability to protect you
- £280 million is the maximum guaranteed money available for compensation for the whole country
- £3800 million was the cost of the 1979 Three Mile Island accident
- £1950 million to £200,000 million was the cost of Chernobyl depending which factors are taken into account.

Other problems

The level of cover, inadequate as it is, does not include damage caused by war, or damage to the environment.

The cover is for one accident per reactor per year. A second accident offers no compensation.

Claims must be made within 30 years, yet cancers appear after 40 years or more.

If your property is contaminated by plutonium, but not structurally damaged, you get no compensation.

Nuclear Under-Insurance public information leaflet.

The nuclear industry has been very quiet about the topic. And it is not an attractive one. It doesn't make light reading when one comes home from work, or in the odd five minutes at home during the day. Chernobyl has already shown that the victims of a nuclear accident in a poor country can never be properly compensated. The reality will only come home to us if there is a major nuclear accident which affects us, a rich country. You and I, the general public, are shouldering the insurance risk, and we ourselves will pay the consequences after an accident. Is it good enough to let things remain unchanged, and rely on hope that an accident will never happen?

Our local, barely funded Druridge Bay Campaign decided to air the issue and make it publicly comprehensible.

Nuclear Under-Insurance: a Hidden Subsidy

In September 1994 Helen Brownlie and Nigel Mortimer produced probably the UK's first report from a non-official body on the mysterious and unknown subject of nuclear under-insurance. We sent a copy of *Nuclear Under-Insurance; a Hidden Subsidy* to Energy Minister Tim Eggar for the Government's review, and to every sympathetic MP we knew. We circulated it to a list of city people looking at the economics of nuclear power. And we produced a public-friendly leaflet which we arranged to go through the library systems in Northumberland, Newcastle and the Tyneside metropolitan boroughs.

Of course we were a small voice in the wilderness. Of course our leaflet was done on a tiny budget, and of course our research was done in volunteers' spare time. But if we hadn't done it, no-one would have.

Much of the awareness there is on this subject within the UK is to a large extent due to the Druridge Bay Campaign.

Quoting statements from the Government that, if privatised, nuclear power should not be subsidised and that market mechanisms should rule, Helen and Nigel attacked the huge hidden insurance subsidies by the public to the nuclear industry.

They described studies which showed that an accident could cost up to £4,500,000 million. Chernobyl had cost up to £200,000 million. The amount of money available to compensate UK citizens after a major nuclear accident in one of our power stations was £280 million. The likelihood of it happening was also evaluated from other studies. Unsurprisingly, Nuclear Electric in its submission to the 1994 Review said: "The high safety standards in the UK mean that the probability of a major nuclear accident is insignificant." The Health and Safety Executive said that the chance of an uncontrolled release is between 1:100,000 and 1:1,000,000.

By contrast, one US study, based on what had historically happened, estimated that there will be on average a core meltdown once in eight years among the world's 400 reactors.

Nigel Mortimer calculated that, based on the various risk and cost estimates, if the nuclear industry took out proper insurance, its electricity would cost between one third to one hundred times more.

Our report argued that in a free, open, competitive market, the nuclear industry should not have such a subsidy. The Government then and frequently since replied that the UK is governed by international conventions. We know that the conventions allow each government to set its own level of protection as high as it wishes. The limit of £280 million is a minimum amount. There is no maximum. We argued that other electricity generators had to pay their full insurance costs, so the nuclear industry should too.

Outside the House of Commons in December 1994, demonstrating for full nuclear insurance. The £5 notes represent the amount of compensation that would be received by the average UK family after a nuclear accident in this country.

We certainly did not expect that the Government would pay any attention to our arguments. We were doing it because the job needed to be done.

We did get a fair amount of publicity. By December 1994, we had made presentations to Wansbeck District Council, to Northumberland County Council's Environment Forum, and to a House of Commons meeting which we had organised. Through our contacts in the media, we had triggered in December an item in Radio 4's *Costing the Earth*, featuring interviews with Nigel Mortimer, Geoff Warren from the Lloyds Atomic Insurance committee and me. At the launch of our report, we had run our own press conference at County Hall in Northumberland which resulted in coverage from BBC TV's Look North and Radio Newcastle. And on our behalf, Llew Smith MP had tabled five Parliamentary written questions to the Secretary of State in December 1994.

When the Government nuclear review was published in the following May, 1995, as *The Prospects for Nuclear Power in the UK*, it mentioned our submission only in passing, criticising one of our lesser recommendations and substantially ignoring the rest. It didn't surprise us. Like all doughty campaigners, we just kept battling on.

Under-Insurance: a Nuclear Liability

submission from
Druridge Bay Campaign
about taxpayer subsidy to a
privatised industry

to the Trade and Industry Committee

Autumn 1995

Report to the DTI select committee, with David Simonds' cartoon reproduced on the cover.

Submission to DTI Select Committee

In May 1995, we found out from the *Guardian* newspaper that the Trade & Industry Select Committee planned to conduct an examination into nuclear privatisation. We learned that the committee would look at the scale of nuclear liabilities and how they would be covered.

Over the course of the following year we got closer and closer to the decision-makers of the future, those who are now important members of the new Labour government. We asked our MPs how we could present evidence. Jack Thompson told us to ring the Trade & Industry committee clerk, and to inform Michael Clapham, a Labour MP on the committee. The clerk sent us the committee's timetable, and told us we would be put on the list of those submitting written evidence.

Over the summer, I produced another report on the back of the first. Helen Brownlie and Nigel Mortimer's report had produced the hard evidence, and sent it to the DTI Select Committee. Mine was written with the intention of being very accessible, so that MPs would read it. It even further simplified Helen and Nigel's arguments, listed all the attention being given by the media to the issue, and tackled some points of detail which our critics had raised following the first report.

Informing Liberal Democrats

At the Liberal Democrat federal annual conference in September 1994, the Berwick upon Tweed Liberal Democrats, prompted by Fiona Hall, amended a conference clause on nuclear power. They included nuclear under-insurance with the other suspect costings of radioactive waste disposal and decommissioning of old power stations. Fiona's speech featured in national radio coverage.

During 1995 and 1996, Fiona served on the Lib Dem energy working group. As a result, the phrase "The nuclear industry should carry a greater share of third party insurance" appears in the party's document, *Conserving Tomorrow*.

Our Campaign - Your Campaign

Presenting Evidence to a Select Committee

You may find out that a House of Commons select committee is going to take evidence on a topic of relevance to you. This happened for us when the Department of the Environment Select Committee examined risks to coastal settlements and ecosystems, and when the Trade and Industry Select Committee examined nuclear privatisation.

The best way to find out if this is happening is to be in close touch with a friendly MP, who will inform you. You'll probably read about it in the newspapers or the newsletters of related organizations, or on the Internet. It's unlikely that it will escape your notice.

As soon as you find out that the committee will be taking evidence, you should ring the committee clerk. Get the name and number from the House of Commons Public Information Office, 0171 219 4272, or the switchboard 0171 219 3000. Ask the clerk to put you on the list for supplying evidence. Discuss your ideas with him or her, and ask how likely it is that you may be called in to give oral evidence.

Find out which MPs are most likely to be interested in your case, either from the committee clerk or your MP. We always looked first for a sympathetic local MP. If no-one local is on the committee, ask your own MP to advise you who is most likely to share your concern. Make contact and once the MP on the committee has agreed to take an interest, ask if he or she will make a statement of support, and send you a photo for you to send to the local paper.

You must prepare your evidence. Don't worry if you can't afford to commission an expert to provide detailed evidence. Do it yourselves. Make your points simply and clearly. Use illustrations, and present the work attractively.

Our presentation on coastal erosion at Druridge took me one day to write, find pictures, bind and post. As we only found out at the last minute, that was all the time I had before the deadline. However I was able to make press statements about it when I dispatched it, when John Cummings MP agreed to speak up on our behalf about it, and when the committee's report was published. Also, MPs Alan Beith and Jack Thompson spoke up in the Parliamentary debate which followed.

Our submission on nuclear under-insurance was more substantial. We had obtained funding of £1000 towards the cost. When it was submitted, we organised a press conference, attracting local TV and newspapers. Following that, a Radio 4 reporter used it as the focus for an item on *Costing the Earth*. Our second report on nuclear privatisation took five days of my work time, and again we maximised media coverage. Thus as well as informing the select committees, we were able to broadcast our message to our public and to our opponents.

Remember

A short, well-produced, illustrated submission may be as effective as a longer, more detailed one. The media are only interested in the key points, and MPs are bombarded with information. You need to produce something they will actually read.

Present your arguments clearly. Always see how many words you can cut out of the text, without losing the essential meaning. You'll be surprised!

Use tables, cartoons, photographs or other illustrations where this is possible.

Make sure the submission is accurately typed. Have one or more members read it to check for clarity and errors. They'll almost always find something wrong, which you will then correct before despatching a perfect copy.

In the national media

The media began to focus on the forthcoming nuclear privatisation. In May 1995, a *Guardian* report by Mark Milner stated that the UK's nuclear industry has an easy time with nuclear insurance compared to Germany or the US. In June, we had a letter published in the *Guardian*. In September, Labour's trade and industry spokesman Brian Wilson said: "In the event of privatisation going ahead, an incoming Labour government will comprehensively review the share of (nuclear) liability to be borne by the taxpayer and private sector respectively. We owe the taxpayer no less an obligation."

In September, another *Guardian* article had a cartoon by David Simonds which showed a nuclear privatisation lorry loaded down by tanks of liability, one of which was insurance. We contacted him, and he agreed that his cartoon could be used on the cover of our report to the DTI committee. We had another letter in the *Guardian* in September. In October, a *Guardian* item covered nuclear insurance, and a letter was printed from Peter Godwin of Teesside Green Party. Peter had also been conducting correspondence with MPs about nuclear insurance in connection with Hartlepool. He was another lonely voice in the northern wilderness.

We sent our second report, *Under-Insurance: a Nuclear Liability*, cheerfully displaying David Simonds' cartoon on the front, to all the relevant and friendly MPs we knew, and to all the city financiers. We never once had a response from any of the city people. Whether they simply binned our reports, or read them and judged that no government would be likely to change the nuclear industry's financial obligations, we shall probably never know.

The CBI have heard us

In September 1995, the CBI's energy policy researcher asked to see Nigel and Helen's report. In their evidence to the DTI Select Committee, the CBI included the following statement, showing the influence of our arguments.

> "The Government could consider raising the limit on the required insurance cover or act as the underwriter for commercial insurance. Any remaining Government guarantees should be transparent."

The DTI Select Committee report

Never before had the unloveable topic of nuclear under-insurance been so thoroughly publicised.

On 14 February 1996, *Guardian* journalist Simon Beavis reported on a leaked draft of the report. As I was having my breakfast on Valentine's Day, I read the headline "INSURANCE THREAT TO NUCLEAR FIRMS". The article read as follows.

> "The privatised nuclear power industry may face a soaring insurance bill to protect itself against the risk of a major disaster if the recommendations of a key report by MPs is accepted by the Government."

The draft report was confidential, and the MPs on the committee were to meet that day to agree the final wording. The article went on as follows.

> "The recommendations on nuclear accident insurance ... will be critically important for the privatised firms' revenues.
>
> "Unusually the British nuclear industry operates under a generous insurance regime. The industry has a limited liability for a single incident capped at £140 million. The Government picks up the next £140 million and then must provide further funds if Parliament agrees.
>
> "MPs on the influential cross-party committee want the industry brought in line with other industrial companies which have to cover themselves for much higher sums.
>
> "But in a further sting, they want the nuclear company being lined up for privatisation to pay an extra premium to the Government for any state guarantee beyond the higher amount insured."

This was too amazing to be true. In fact the wording in the final report was completely revised. Despite phoning the *Guardian* journalists several times, and asking MPs on the committee, we never saw the draft version.

The final recommendation only asked the Government to see if normal commercial cover could be obtained for sums exceeding £140 million, jointly with other signatories to the various international conventions. In other words, nothing would be done.

Informing opposition MPs, who will one day be in government

The previous December, Graham Stacy, a Morpeth man who had become interested in nuclear under-insurance, Nigel Mortimer and I had gone to London to meet John Battle, then shadow energy spokesman. In the end, he couldn't come to our meeting, but we had met his researcher, Peter Metcalfe.

Nuclear privatisation was to happen before Parliament went down in summer 1996. The Labour Party chose it for an opposition debate in March. We didn't find out about it until the Friday before the Tuesday for which it was planned. Hastily, I consulted Graham. We prepared a one-sheet briefing for all the friendly Labour and Liberal Democrat MPs. We sent it to Margaret Beckett as opposition spokesperson for trade and industry, to John Battle and to all the Labour MPs who had been on the DTI committee, to Jack Thompson and to Matthew Taylor, Liberal Democrat environment spokeperson. Peter Metcalfe was very helpful in advising us, and in passing on briefings.*

* *According to a* Guardian *article by Ian Willmore, 23 July 1997, Peter Metcalfe "moved smoothly over to British Nuclear Fuels Ltd when the Labour Party took office."*

The Miners

1960 - miners employed in Northumberland 34,200

"Of course I'm sure this Labour government is going to open up the pits again. (Laughing) The coal is there if the country ever wants it, if it's needed. There's 200 million tons of it at Druridge Bay, up towards Amble.

"Once, if you had to retire after an accident, you might take a light job like being a hospital porter for a few years. But now - they are premium jobs. Young lads are doing that now because that's all there is.

"Blair, we're looking to Blair. He's a North MP. But you cannot replace 20,000 jobs at a crack. Like the shipyards closing, losing another 20,000 or 30,000 jobs. Consett now, it's just starting to get on its feet after the closure of the steel industry, after 20 years.

"The sad thing is that we might not be able to keep the community together. If the young people say there is nothing for us here, and move, the place will die. It'll be sad."

George Ferrigon

1997 - miners employed in Northumberland 435

I phoned Alan Beith's secretary to ask her to send me *Hansard* after the debate, which she did. It arrived on Friday, on my day off. I felt tired, and I wasn't in the mood for wading through Hansard. I went home for the weekend without reading it.

On Monday, feeling in a better mood, I read the pages. I was astonished. A week after the event, I discovered that Margaret Beckett had made nuclear insurance the second major topic of her speech, in opposition to Tim Eggar. Here was our case, in black and white. His arguments refuting what she said were weak. Later in the debate, Matthew Taylor and Ken Purchase raised the issue again.

Immediately, Graham and I analysed the weaknesses in Tim Eggar's arguments. We wrote to Margaret Beckett and the other MPs with our analysis. We had a reply from Margaret Beckett, thanking us, and asking us to keep in close touch with John Battle.

In May, the Government published their belated response to the DTI Select Committee's report, within which we found inaccuracies. We transmitted these to Tim Eggar, via Alan Beith, and once again we found that his replies, presumably prepared by some civil servant given the tedious job of examining our detailed arguments, did not stand up to criticism.

In July 1996, John Battle spoke at a meeting in Newcastle upon Tyne. Some Druridge Bay Campaign members were present, and I asked a question about the land at Druridge Bay. Despite the variety of topics of all sorts under discussion, John Battle's eyes lit up when I said Druridge Bay Campaign, and he said: "Oh yes, Druridge Bay Campaign - nuclear insurance!"

As I write this in June 1997, we have a Labour government. The nuclear insurance work has been taken over by a group detached from the Druridge Bay Campaign, under the name of PIANA - Proper Insurance Against Nuclear Accident. Nigel, Graham, Fiona and I are part of PIANA, along with friendly specialist legal advisors and researchers into nuclear economics. We still haven't got any funding, and are in the process of trying to get some at present.

Now is the time to see how the Labour politicians can help remove this unfair anomaly, and put the burden of full third-party liability against a major nuclear accident where it belongs. That place is on the back of the nuclear industry, not on the backs of the people of this country.

Our vitality has given birth to other groups

The Druridge Bay Campaign's Energy Group was a hotbed of ideas and activity. As well as North Energy Associates, which took over its renewable energy work, and PIANA, which took over nuclear under-insurance, we stimulated the founding of the Wansbeck Energy Company.

During 1995 and 1996 I had attended Wansbeck District Council's Energy Panel meetings on behalf of the Druridge Bay Campaign. This panel was one of a series designed to stimulate economic development following colliery closures. While there, and partly owing to my work in North Energy Associates, I found out about a European fund to devise regional energy management strategies. It was a way of getting cash and other resources for a regional energy policy, which our Energy Group had never been able to afford.

Using the DBC's energy policy statement as a basis, and getting the go-ahead from Wansbeck District Council, I devised the application with the help of Adrian Smith. I planned the scheme, worked out the costings, helped obtain European partners, and made revisions according to the directions of the directorate in Brussels.

The plan included an assessment of energy use within Wansbeck and Castle Morpeth districts, and a strategy to use fossil-fuel and renewable energy efficiently. It would replicate this work within the region as a whole. Nuclear power was not to be considered. The grant was worth 325,000 ecus (approximately £243,750) over three years. Forty per cent of this would come in cash, and 60% would be provided locally by work in kind and cash contributions.

By mid 1996, Wansbeck Energy Company was formed, and appointed consulting engineers to do the energy assessment. By February 1997, a ten-point strategy was agreed. It includes urban combined heat and power and district heating, clean coal technology, renewable enegy - wind, woodfuel, solar, landfill gas. Just what the Druridge Bay Campaign has been calling for since the mid-1980s. An alternative to the big ideas of the CEGB.

Writing, demonstrating - Sell the Land

We never forgot the land at Druridge. It was still in the hands of the nuclear industry.

In 1989 the nuclear power stations were not privatised with the rest of the electricity generating industry. They were kept within a state-owned company Nuclear Electric, as was the land at Druridge. In 1996, the Conservative government planned to privatisate nuclear power. The land at Druridge would either go to a private company owning the newer nuclear stations, British Energy; or it would stay in the state-held rump containing the old stations, Magnox Electric. In either case, we wanted the land to be sold.

Ellington Colliery Band lead a march at Druridge Bay, in July 1994

In parallel with energy and nuclear insurance work, and at the same time as keeping a watch on sand extraction developments, we ran what we called our Sell the Land campaign.

In July 1994, we had a march at Druridge, following Ellington Colliery band, and with a big launch of balloons. Catherine Spoor made a five by two metre banner with huge letters saying NUCLEAR ELECTRIC SELL US OUR LAND

BACK, and a hundred or so members followed it, with the band, down the country lane behind the sand dunes. Jack Thompson MP was there, and we were on TV.

1995

On 4 April 1995, *The Journal* interviewed Robert Hawley, chief executive of Nuclear Electric. The newspaper headline read "WE WILL BUILD AT DRURIDGE", and reported him saying "We want to retain that land to put a future nuclear power station on in a long long time into the future." He said that by the time the bay was looked at, he expected protests would have largely died down as people realised nuclear power was needed.

He had a letter published on the letters page two days later. It included the following.

> "I took great trouble to explain to your reporter that any decision about building a power station at Druridge Bay will be taken by future generations for future generations and in the light of the energy requirements well into the next century. It is simply not on the agenda at the moment and it would be foolish, not to mention selfish, of us to take a decision now that could have profound effects long after we have gone."

Nothing would satisfy us, after that, other than an outright declaration that the land would be sold.

At our summer festival, Alan Beith MP and Northumberland county councillor Kevin Flaherty were the first to sign our Sell the Land petition, closely followed by the mayor of Castle Morpeth. In November, we took the petition to Grey's Monument in Newcastle, amid the busy shoppers with our banner which took three people to hold it up.

Before our AGM we had a mini-march through Morpeth, behind a highland piper. Our obliging local police stopped the traffic so that our street-wide banner could be carried along.

The next drama was an announcement in December by Robert Hawley that the new soon-to-exist British Energy would build no new nuclear power stations.

This then was the ignominious end of the CEGB's nuclear power stations building programme. British Energy had dropped plans for building Sizewell C, for which actually they had been refused planning permission. They would not build Hinkley C, for which they had had planning permission, though it had expired. "Sell the land at Druridge Bay" we clamoured, louder and louder.

We sent our VIP supporters a copy of our petition inside their Christmas cards. By February we had signatures from all the celebrities named on the placard that went round the Central Station, and many others.

The letters started winging their way to London and back. Here are some extracts.

Dear Dr Hawley *12 December 1995*

In view of the huge publicity that your statements to abandon plans to build new nuclear power stations has engendered, please could you let us know what Nuclear Electric intends to do with the land at Druridge Bay, during the privatisation process. Will you sell the land?

Bridget Gubbins

From Dr Hawley back to us.

Dear Ms Gubbins *21 December 1995*

It is the Government which will decide whether Druridge Bay remains in the public sector or is placed with British Energy

Dr R Hawley

As soon as the Christmas period was over, we acted in response.

1996

Dear Alan (Beith) *6 January 1996*

Please could you ask the minister what the Government plans to do with the land? Is it to be sold back to the community? Is it to be included in the privatised package, with the new power stations? Is it to remain in state ownership? And when will we know their decision?

Fiona Hall

DBC Chair

To the DTI's Nuclear Privatisation Team

Dear Sir or Madam *6 January 1996*

Robert Hawley has told us that it is the Government who will decide whether the Druridge Bay land will remain in the public sector or is placed with British Energy. Please could you let us know what the Government intends to do? Whatever happens, until the land is sold there will be a strong feeling of restlessness in our area, and a continuing campaign.

Bridget Gubbins

From the DTI to DBC

Dear Ms Gubbins *11 January 1996*

The Government is considering how to allocate the land currently held by Nuclear Electric, and the final decision is expected within the next few weeks. I will write to you again at that stage, but please let me know if you have any questions in the meantime.

Mary Tait

Naturally, a friendly letter like that invited a response.

Dear Ms Tait *16 January 1996*

Please will you tell the relevant minister that we are running a petition asking Nuclear Electric to sell the land, which we will now present to the Government. So far, we have signatures from the following VIPs who will offer us further support if we ask them. (The names are then listed.)

Bridget Gubbins

I telephoned the DTI too, and found out that the decision on Druridge was to be made imminently. So I quickly phoned Alan Beith, and he responded immediately by writing to Tim Eggar MP, Minister for Energy.

Dear Tim *22 January 1996*

If as I believe there is no realistic prospect of a nuclear power station being built at Druridge, then the threat should be removed by the release of the land. I am therefore making this urgent plea that the land should not be conveyed to British Energy, and that discussions should then begin about its release.

Rt Hon Alan Beith MP

Next, Druridge Campaigners prepared an A3 sized postcard to Tim Eggar. A few telephone calls later, a group of members paraded outside Morpeth post office with our street-wide banner, and posed for the newspapers. His postcard was a coloured picture of the bay, and this message in giant script.

Dear Tim Eggar *23 January 1996*

Please sell the land at Druridge Bay owned by Nuclear Electric back to the community.

From Druridge Bay Campaign

Morpeth, Northumberland

Tim Eggar replied to Alan Beith.

2 February 1996

Dear Alan

The Druridge Bay site is to be assigned to Magnox Electric, and will therefore remain in the public sector. We will of course take full account of the concerns expressed by the Druridge Bay Campaign and the strength of feeling in the North East.

Tim Eggar

He wrote a similar letter to us, signed with his turquoise blue ink, and thanking us for our postcard.

Getting closer

Tony Henderson, our great supporter at *The Journal*, backed our postcard action by agreeing, in discussion with us, to print a special cut-out letter for readers to sign. On 3 February, the headline read, "YOU HAVE THE POWER TO RESCUE DRURIDGE", with a coloured photo of the bay, and an addressed letter, saying

Dear Tim Eggar

Please sell the land owned by Nuclear Electric at Druridge Bay back to the community.

Signed

Signed

Signed

We will never know how many were sent, but without doubt this all had some entertainment value with the DTI's Nuclear Privatisation Team. I think they put the postcard on their mantlepiece.

Next we decided to present our petition in London. Naturally we wanted to make the most of the event. We had a 6,000 signature star-studded petition at this point, and we dusted down the earlier one which had been piling up in our cupboard since 1983, making a total of over 40,000 signatures.

The send-off and delivery is the story at the beginning of this chapter.

On 14 February, Alan Beith asked the President of the Board of Trade, in oral questions in the House of Commons, if the Druridge land was to be released for sale. Richard Page replied that the land would be staying with Magnox Electric, and that "those working on the site will be consulted, and I hope that a satisfactory solution will be achieved".

There had been no admission so far that the land would actually be sold. Tony Henderson managed to ask Tim Eggar this, and on 15 February he was able to report in *The Journal* the minister saying: "That may very well be the final outcome. I don't rule that out as an option." Tim Eggar also said that he had already responded to the Druridge Bay Campaign by retaining the land in the public sector, and added: "If the attitude of this campaign is going to be immediately we are given one thing they ask for something more, they undermine their own case."

Obviously he didn't like our stubbornness, but that couldn't deter us. Not content with knowing the land may be sold, we also wanted it to be sold in such a way that nuclear power stations could never be built on it in the future. What would stop a future government buying the land back, should there be an energy crisis, or a rebound in the fortunes of nuclear power? People had campaigned for eighteen years, for a whole generation, and we wanted to take no chances.

Next to be done was to gather all the bodies together who managed land at Druridge. We needed a statement upon which they could all agree, asking that the land be sold in a way that meant it could never be used for any kind of industrial development. Into this process, we invited to our office the National Trust, Northumberland Wildlife Trust, Castle Morpeth Borough Council, the County Council's Countryside Service, English Nature and the Countryside Commission. We began to discuss what we would ideally like to be done with the land.

Fiona our chairperson had had the idea that she had sat next to Mark Baker, the new chairman of Magnox Electric, at a Liberal Democrat conference meeting. On 4 April I wrote to him again, only days after Nuclear Electric had been split up between British Energy and Magnox Electric, asking him to assure us that consultations on selling the land at Druridge would start soon, and that Magnox Electric had no plans now or in the future to build a nuclear power station at Druridge Bay. His reply was brief and personally signed.

> *Dear Ms Gubbins* *11 April 1996*
>
> *As you may know, Magnox Electric plc has been in existence for barely a week and we have not yet had time to give any consideration at all to dealing with Druridge. I will write to you again when we have had time to consider the matter properly.*
>
> *Mark Baker*

We received a letter from Ray Hall, Magnox's chief executive.

Dear Ms Hall *1 July 1996*

We are currently reviewing our future intentions in relation to the company's land holding at Druridge Bay as part of a general review of the property portfolio we have inherited. We are very aware of the importance of local needs and interests. I do not expect this review to be completed before the year end.

R W Hall

We raised the Druridge land issue with shadow energy minister John Battle MP at a meeting at Northumbria University, where he was addressing local Labour members, as mentioned earlier.

At the end of July, the newer nuclear power stations had been privatised, and Tim Eggar retired. Perhaps we had added a little light relief to a tedious and complex job.

Immediately, we asked Alan Beith to contact the new energy minister, to ensure he was as well-informed as Tim Eggar. This turned out to be Lord Fraser of Carmyllie.

From the Rt Hon the Lord Fraser of Carmyllie QC to Alan Beith.

Dear Alan *16 August 1996*

The Government has given an undertaking to take the views of local people into account when the long term future of the land is decided. Magnox Electric are currently looking into the long term options for Druridge Bay, taking into account commitments given by the Government and the legal rights and interests of the current tenants. I would be happy to talk about this with you later in October when Parliament returns.

Peter

Fraser of Carmyllie

The Sell the Land meetings continued in our office. We were discussing the placing of a legal protective covenant on the land, with a neighbouring landowner such as the National Trust. We wanted a joint statement from all these bodies, and from Northumbria Tourist Board as well. The statement would be ready to for Alan to take to his meeting with Lord Fraser on 27 November.

Ownership of land for power stations at Druridge Bay

1984

CEGB drilled and purchased 300 acres from farmer.

1989

Electricity privatisation.

1990

Nuclear Electric, non-privatised nuclear power company, inherits land at Druridge.

1996

Nuclear privatisation.

1996

Magnox Electric, non-privatised rump of Nuclear Electric, inherits Druridge land.

1997

Magnox Electric sells land back to farmer.

Diagram 3.1

These were the most important points of our joint statement.

> As Magnox is a publicly-owned company, we invite it to sell its holding at Druridge in such a way that the land
>
> maintains its rural character
>
> and
>
> increases its overall landscape and ecological value
>
> and
>
> can never be used for building nuclear power stations or other unsuitable development in the future.

It was signed by Alan Beith, Northumberland County Council, Northumberland Wildlife Trust, Castle Morpeth Borough Council, Northumbria Tourist Board and the Druridge Bay Campaign. The National Trust and the Countryside Commission sent messages supporting any action which would increase the conservation and landscape value of the bay.

We were so anxious that Magnox didn't make any decisions affecting the fate of the land at Druridge before the meeting between Alan and Lord Fraser that we wrote to inform Magnox about what we were doing, and of the joint statement we were preparing. We received a polite reply from Magnox's company secretary, Rex Melville.

> *Dear Ms Gubbins* *4 November 1996*
>
> *I confirm that we shall certainly bear these events in mind in reviewing our future intentions for Magnox's land holding at Druridge Bay. I have also asked David Hall, our Property Adviser, to arrange to meet you when he is next in the Morpeth area.*
>
> *Rex Melville*

We didn't know until later that Mark Baker, the chairman of Magnox, was highly indignant that we should presume to advise him what the company should do with its own property. We got strong hints from his colleagues not to direct future correspondence directly to him. But I cannot see why he should be so irate. He is after all paid from public funds to run a public company. Probably he felt his dignity had been affronted.

The land will be sold

The prettily mounted Joint Statement went to Alan in time for his 27 November meeting, with Lord Carmyllie. As Energy Minister, we assumed that he would be in close contact with the state-owned nuclear power company. Undoubtedly this was so, because before the meeting took place, Magnox decided to make their own move.

We issued our own press release about the meeting on 25 November, embargoed until 1.00am Wednesday 27 November. On 26 November, Fiona rang me to say that Alan had told her that Lord Fraser's staff at the DTI were asking him questions, and that it was likely they might make an announcement to upstage our meeting.

On 27 November, the phones in the DBC office started ringing. Reporters told me that Magnox had made a statement. They read it out to me over the phone, and faxed it. Lord Fraser said: "I welcome the decision announced today by Magnox Electric that they do not wish to retain the land at Druridge Bay for future power station development, and that it should therefore be released for sale.

"The company will be drawing up detailed marketing plans to sell the estate for continued agricultural and residential use. Magnox will take full acount of the rights of the estate's tenants in this process. I believe this will reassure local people about the long term future of this land."

As I write this now, six months later, in June 1997, I can feel my skin tingling as I hear those words. After eighteen years since the first announcement; after thirteen years of the nuclear industry owning the land. It was so very, very important a statement.

Adrian Pitches of BBC's Look North wanted to know if a group of campaigners could go out to Druridge for the lunchtime programme. Quickly, Liz my co-worker and I rang round to see who could come. A dozen of us turned up with our huge banner NUCLEAR ELECTRIC SELL US OUR LAND BACK. We made a display next to the Cairn, on the land behind the sand dunes. The BBC's link unit transmitted us live for the lunchtime programme, as well as doing interviews for the evening shows.

What will you do now? Adrian asked us. Have a party, we said!

A miner

I met him at the Miners' Picnic, in Ashington in June 1997. He was in his mid-40s, there with his wife. I'd known him for years as a Druridge Bay Campaign member. "What are you doing with yourself these days?" I asked. "I'm a house husband," he said. "My wife bosses me about. She's always got something for me to do. Haven't you pet?"

Lord Glenamara being interviewed outside the Houses of Parliament for the Druridge Bay Campaign, April1989.

A Pressure Group and its Influence on Government

Chapter 4

Before I started writing this chapter, I assembled some academic books about pressure groups. During the fourteen years in which I personally had been campaigning, I had never questioned whether or not we actually were a pressure group, though various students had used us a model in their studies.

As I read, I felt a great sense of our localness, and how provincial we may seem to the professors. I also realised that the citizens of this country are woven into complex sets of groups lobbying government for their interests, which are as varied as multinational consortiums, trade associations, local parents' associations and environmental groups.

What is a pressure group?

HMSO's book *Pressure Groups* says: "Pressure groups are organisations which aim to influence Parliament and Government in the way decisions are made and carried out, to the benefit of their members and the cause they support."

Dr Rob Baggott in his book *Pressure Groups Today* produces a list of nine definitions of a pressure group from other books. Here are some of them.

Rob Baggott: "A pressure group is an organisation which seeks to influence the details of a comparatively small range of public policies and which is not a faction of a recognised political party."

Wyn Grant: "A pressure group is an organisation which seeks as one of its functions to influence the formulation and implementation of public policy, public policy representing a set of authoritative decisions taken by the executive, the legislature, and the judiciary, and by local government and the European Union."

Alan Ball & Frances Millard: "In general, pressure groups are social aggregates with some level of cohesion and shared aims which attempt to influence the political decision-making process."

Pressure group types and tactics

HMSO's book *Pressure Groups* says that in the voluntary section alone, it is estimated that one-third of the population is involved in regular work for voluntary organisations, many of which are pressure groups. The academic works I have looked at by Rob Baggott, Wyn Grant, Geoffrey Alderman, Alan Ball & Frances Millard, and A G Jordan & J J Richardson all have sections categorising the groups, and defining the many different ways in which the thousands of organisations act as pressure groups. It is obviously an extremely difficult subject to sort out, and they all have chapters analysing each other's attempts to do so. Groups which may act as pressure groups at times, if not all the time, are as varied as the Automobile Association, the Child Poverty Action Group, the Church of England, the Institute for Public Policy Research and the Cats Protection League.

The HMSO book distinguishes between groups which represent the interests of people in a particular section of society, such as coal miners or doctors, which it calls *sectional* or *interest* groups, and those which campaign for a particular issue or cause, such as protection of animals, which it calls *promotional* or just *pressure* groups.

Geoffrey Alderman in his book *Pressure Groups and Government in Great Britain* differentiates between *sectional* groups and *cause* groups. *Sectional* groups operate in the interests of a section of the community, whereas *cause* groups campaign at the level of ideas and beliefs. *Cause* groups do not produce goods which people want, or provide services which people need. Their strength depends largely on the amount of popular support they can muster.

Wyn Grant divides pressure groups into *primary* and *secondary* categories. Primary groups exist principally to act for political change, such as Greenpeace. Secondary groups exist mainly to provide services for their members, such as the Automobile Association, and campaign on transport issues without necessarily representing the views of those who purchase their services.

He then classifies groups not so much on what they do, or who they represent, as on their different strategies, and on the response of government to those strategies. He divides groups into *insider* groups and *outsider* groups. "*Insider* groups are regarded as legitimate by government, and are consulted on a regular basis. *Outsider* groups either do not wish to become enmeshed in a consultative relationship with officials or are unable to gain recognition."

Another way of looking at *outsider* groups, he says, is as "protest groups which have objectives that are outside the mainstream of political opinion. They then have to adopt campaigning methods designed to demonstrate that they have a solid base of popular support."

Insider groups, which many *outsider* groups eventually try to become, need to be near the focus of the UK's centralised political system, in other words in London. Their effectiveness "increasingly depends on the ability to develop well-researched critiques of existing policy".

Wyn Grant shows that insider groups have to learn how to talk the language of civil servants, that of "veiled understatement". He says that in this way, the state sets the rules of the game for pressure groups activity. It creates incentives for groups to act in a particular way, thus becoming tamed and domesticated, with only the ideological rejectionists remaining outside the system.

He explains that groups, or the many groups comprising a movement such as the animal rights movement, "exhibit every form of political action from the presentation to government of informed position papers to terrorist actions". Governments choose who they are prepared to listen to, ie the *insider* groups, but groups themselves may choose not to "bargain with government, engage in dialogue with scientists, or influence public opinion." They believe in direct action, he writes, to damage the economic interests of those who use animals, and they see conventional pressure group methods as ineffective.

Wyn Grant divides groups into six categories, ranging from those most tied to government, to those most rejecting it. *Prisoner* groups depend on government funding. *Low-profile* insider groups work largely behind the scenes. *High-profile* groups use the media and cultivate public opinion to back their influence on government. *Potential insider* groups are close to gaining insider status. *Outsider* groups lack the political sophistication to become insider groups. *Ideological outsider* groups reject the political system.

Other academics produce a third category between insider and outsider, that of *thresholder,* which oscillates between the two strategies.

These books assume that the role of pressure groups is to influence decision makers, principally the national government or Parliament, and thus they concentrate chiefly on national level groups rather than local or regional groups like the Druridge Bay Campaign. Our work, once it passed the level of ensuring virtually total local authority support, was addressed increasingly at the Government and Parliament.

Working through Parliament - is there any point?

Reading through these books about pressure groups leaves me with the strong impression that the academic writers feel that decision-making by government in this country is really influenced not so much by the process of elections and what happens in Parliament afterwards as by who knows whom in the corridors of power. A G Jordan and J J Richardson, in their book *Government and Pressure Groups in Britain,* say that "much of the most important pressure group influence is wielded by groups which do not need to conduct high-profile public campaigns. Policies are developed in private arrangements between civil servants and their pressure group peers." They say "it will be a theme of this book that there are often, indeed usually, shared interests between groups and government departments."

The authors say that groups who have established their credentials with government may find that, rather than clamouring to be heard, they are hounded for advice. And with groups such as the CBI, the TUC and individual companies and unions, the Government may actually want to influence them, rather than the other way round.

They say that *promotional* groups usually lack the blunt power of insider groups. "Promotional goals such as redistribution of income or abolition of hunting cannot normally be attained in the private politics of consultation." Yet sometimes a government department may seek to co-opt and hence silence protest, or it may invite pressure, in the achievement of departmental goals.

Jordan and Richardson introduce one of their chapters by quoting those who make the case that as the influence of Parliament is decreasing, groups such as the CBI don't expend much energy in Westminster. The relevant cabinet minister presents packages in the House of Commons agreed between his or her civil servants and representatives of powerful outside groups. Whips prevent backbenchers challenging their government. This "appears at odds with the sheer volume of group activity exerted at the parliamentary level".

At the House of Commons lobby on privatisation in November 1988.

Why do pressure groups emerge?

If policy decisions are made between civil servants and influential organisations acting in unseen ways, and presented by the minister to the House of Commons, why would any inexperienced group begin to protest? When the nationalised Central Electricity Generating Board wanted to build a series of new PWR nuclear power stations in the late 1970s, and Energy Minister David Howell announced this to the country, what would be the point of a national organisation like Friends of the Earth, never mind any group such as ours, even beginning to oppose nuclear power stations in a local area? Yet the opposition emerged regardless.

Perhaps people become active in pressure groups because they feel they cannot stand by and do nothing, or that they think decision-makers may change their minds when public opinion expresses itself. Perhaps they believe that in a democracy they should have a voice, at a personal level as well as via their elected representatives.

Druridge campaigners, probably like many other groups, didn't stop to read books about pressure groups. Perhaps it was as well that we didn't understand what we were getting involved with, and just got on simply with what it seemed necessary to do. This was to co-ordinate opposition, and be a visible expression of it. Gradually, with experience, we came to learn that the Parliamentary process was available to us, if not the *insider* contacts with ministries.

A pressure group interacting with Parliament

Rob Baggott lists and summarises the ways in which Members of Parliament can be influenced, or can help pressure groups. I'll use the list and summary here, and discuss briefly how the Druridge Bay Campaign used these ways. Readers can assess their effectiveness, and, if members of a group, can think about what methods might be useful for them.

The adjournment debate

MPs can initiate what is known as an adjournment debate, a short debate at the end of a parliamentary day. Such debates will not provoke the government into action, but nevertheless can focus attention on an issue.

Working closely with us, Alan Beith decided to have an adjournment debate challenging Tim Yeo in December 1990, which I described in Chapter 2. As government inspectors had given permission against the wishes of the local authorities in 1960 and 1966 to allow sand extraction to take place, it should be the government not the local authority which pays any compensation owing to the operator if they are forced to stop. The midnight debate was televised, and our video recording has raised many a laugh as Tim Yeo on the government side and Alan Beith on the opposition side were the only MPs in the House. It didn't look like a very popular issue. All the tired MPs had gone home. But local TV reported it, Tim Yeo had been required to ask his civil servants to research his answer, and once again it had added to the general awareness-raising exercise at home and in the centres of power.

Parliamentary committees

Select committees scrutinise the work of government departments. They always have a majority of MPs from the Government's party, but may be chaired by opposition MPs, and will contain MPs from all major parties. They examine closely particular issues. Examples are the DTI Select Committee's examination of the proposed closures of the coal industry in 1993, and of nuclear privatisation in 1995/6.

If an issue is being reviewed by a select committee, pressure groups have the chance to participate. It doesn't mean once again that they will obtain the changes they would like, but they will get an airing for their point of view. They can send written evidence, and offer to give verbal evidence. Rob Baggott points out that more than two fifths of the evidence to select committees is submitted by outside organisations.

The Druridge Bay Campaign has submitted evidence to certain of these committees. I have mentioned the submission to the Environment Select Committee on coastal erosion at Druridge.

The weighty submissions to the Trade and Industry Select Committee, on the under-insurance of the nuclear industry, were more significant. As I have described this in Chapter 3, it is enough to say here that a local group like the Druridge Bay Campaign gathered the courage and competence to put together a good case, which was noticed. We followed up our reports with further harrying of the minister as we learned that the government could not produce plausible arguments against our case.

All-party committees have members who wish to work on a particular topic, from any political group. They can and often do work very closely with pressure groups, tabling parliamentary questions or early day motions. Sometimes pressure groups help with research or take on administrative duties for the all-party committee. The RSPCA for example services the Animal Welfare All-Party Committee.

The Druridge Bay Campaign had a loose connection with the Parliamentary Renewable and Sustainable Energy Group, which was chaired by Stockton North MP Frank Cook and vice-chaired by our own Wansbeck MP Jack Thompson. We had a position on renewable energy within our energy policy statement, read this committee's briefings, and knew it was there as a resource.

Standing committees examine bills put forward by government clause by clause, and recommend amendments. They are in both Houses. In the House of Lords the standing committee stage takes place on the floor of the House, whereas in the House of Commons it takes place in a committee room. As with select committees, the government will always have a majority of MPs. Pressure groups can brief MPs or lords, but are seldom called upon to give evidence. They may however suggest amendments.

The Druridge Bay Campaign did encourage our MPs to suggest three amendments to the Privatisation of Electricity Bill described in Chapter 1. We put the points to them, and left it to their judgement or goodwill if they used them. Alan Beith served on the House of Commons' standing committee on the bill, so we were in close contact with its proceedings. Tony Blair was on the committee, as shadow energy spokesperson. At the House of Lords standing committee stage, Lord Glenamara advised us to give the lords the exact wording of the amendments we would like to be submitted.* In 1989, energy efficiency as a concept was very new. One of our amendments encouraged energy efficiency to be emphasised in the new law. Friends of the Earth had promoted a similar amendment which was passed by the Lords, whereas ours was not. Nevertheless we added to the weight of the argument.

Thus if legislation is going through Parliament on an issue affecting a group, the standing committee process is accessible, with the support of an MP or a member of the House of Lords.

** The detailed lobbying undertaken by the Druridge Bay Campaign is described in Generating Pressure, by Bridget Gubbins. See Bibliography.*

Lobbies of parliament

Rob Baggott describes lobbying at the House of Commons as a tactic which often fails. "In order to be effective, mass lobbies have to be extremely well-organised to ensure that those involved actually do see their MP and get their view across. To maximise the impact of a mass lobby, it is also important to attract as much publicity as possible in the media, and this depends very much on other events happening on that day, which cannot easily be predicted beforehand."

Geoffrey Alderman describes much "lobbying" as not actually lobbying at all. Rather than participants meeting their MPs and seeking to persuade them of a particular viewpoint, it means quite simply holding a mass demonstration *outside* the Houses of Parliament and obtaining maximum media coverage thereby. "In the modern mass lobby, numbers count almost as much as arguments. When tens of thousands of people converge on Westminster, only a few hundred gain admittance to the Central Lobby of Parliament. There, only constituents with advance appointments can be reasonably sure of seeing their MPs; and if they do, the interview is likely to take place in a cramped corner of the lobby or in some alcove ... Many constituents, even those with specific written appointments to see their MPs, are never allowed into Parliament at all, for the press of people simply cannot be accommodated within the precincts."

I've described the three lobbies we joined in, in Chapter 1. The first was in 1987 at the Sizewell debate, and the second two in 1989 during the privatisation of electricity procedure. Friends of the Earth, based in London, did a professional job of the organising, and we simply fitted in with the arrangements. We always made a good visual display with banners and posters, and with the help of Alan Beith, organised our own meetings for local MPs in committee rooms, where we presented our cases in detail.

Alan Beith hosts presentations critical of nuclear privatisation. With Fred Barker, Helen Brownlie, Nigel Mortimer, Jamie Woolley and Jane Roberts.

In December 1994 the Druridge Bay Campaign initiated our own meeting in the Grand Committee Room during the nuclear privatisation procedure. We provided a platform for four speakers to address MPs on their objections to the nuclear industry's economic case, based on their submissions to the DTI Select Committee. Alan Beith helped us arrange the meeting, and acted as chair. Alan had invited city financiers, we had invited other energy campaigning groups, and we had both invited MPs. Including our own group, there were about fifty people in the Grand Committee room. The various nuclear industries sent representatives, and campaigners from across the country and a few MPs turned up. Not a single city financier either replied to Alan Beith's letter or came to the meeting.

Druridge Bay Campaign's presentation was on the under-insurance of the nuclear industry. It was harder to excite the media about nuclear insurance than the direct threat of nuclear power stations at Druridge Bay. After the formal meeting, twenty or so of us with children paraded outside the House of Commons carrying big placards of enlarged £5 notes, the amount of compensation for the average family after a major nuclear accident. We got newspaper coverage but not TV, though the campaigners from Sizewell who came to the event did. There was an important budget debate the same day, which probably accounted for the low turnout of our own supporting MPs.

In spring 1996, at our suggestion, Jack Thompson booked a committee room and invited northern Labour MPs to hear our case on nuclear insurance. Three of us travelled down to London, and not one MP turned up. Jack was mortified, and we were naturally disappointed. That is the chance we took. It is a tactic which can fail.

How did the Druridge Bay Campaign's lobbying activities rate, according to the paragraph I quoted earlier by Rob Baggott? Were our lobbies "extremely well organised"? When we followed the careful advice and good organisation of Friends of the Earth, they certainly were. Those of us who had pre-arranged to see our MPs did so. We all got there in time, by coach, train or other means, and we ensured at the DBC end that everyone, including all the media, knew all the details. Through our MPs, we arranged our own committee room presentations to other MPs. When we organised lobbies ourselves, they were less successful in attracting MPs and TV, even though they were still well organised.

Did we maximise the impact of the events by attracting the maximum publicity? We always gave the media every opportunity to follow us, and usually we got regional TV as well as newspaper cover. Where we didn't, it was because our nuclear insurance issue was not so popular, or because we were unlucky as other more interesting Parliamentary business took precedence. As Rob Baggott said, such events cannot easily be predicted.

Petitions

If a group wants to petition the House of Commons or House of Lords to demonstrate public opposition to a particular policy, or to make a plea, they must follow the formal and ritual wording procedure in the petition. It can then be presented by an MP or peer in the relevant House.

Petitions are awareness-raising exercises. They will scarcely ever get what they ask for, but they inform the government of the degree of concern about an issue, and they focus the minds of the people who are asked to sign them.

There have been various petitions organised over the years by the Druridge Bay Campaign. More than once, we started a petition in a burst of enthusiasm, without carefully thinking about exactly how and to whom it should be presented. The petition against sand extraction could not be presented in the House of Commons because, as Alan Beith pointed out to us, "the words on the signature pages must conform to Parliamentary requirements, and a subsequently added sticker would not be acceptable". We presented it with equal effect however to RMC as described in Chapter 2.

The same thing had happened with the petition against nuclear power at Druridge Bay. There were 40,000 signatures which had been gathered over many years. It couldn't be presented to the Government, via the House of Commons. Instead, we presented it at the Department of Trade and Industry, as I described in Chapter 3.

Early day motions

Early day motions express support for a policy, and are sponsored by one or more MPs, who ask other MPs to add their signatures. The names are printed in the daily House of Commons order paper, and the list gets longer as more names are added over time. The government is likely to pay attention to any early day motion which has many signatures from its own backbenches.

A group can suggest an early day motion to a supportive MP. The Druridge Bay Campaign tried to get a motion backing the full insurance of the nuclear industry put forward, though not successfully. We have however written to encourage our own MPs to support those put forward by other groups, particularly in regard to the Home Energy Conservation Bill.

Parliamentary questions

If a group wishes to obtain information, or raise an issue, it can ask an MP to frame a parliamentary question. Supportive MPs will use this technique readily. Up to 20,000 questions are submitted each year, the vast majority of which receive written replies. Some questions are answered orally in the House.

Rob Baggott points out that although questions rarely bring about a change of policy, they concentrate the minds of civil servants and ministers, who may want to know whether or not they are part of a broader lobbying campaign.

MPs Alan Beith and Llew Smith have both asked parliamentary questions for us about nuclear insurance, and Alan asked an oral question about sand extraction in December 1990.

Private members' bills

Private members' bills provide opposition or government MPs with the chance to promote new laws on issues which specifically interest them. Sometimes pressure groups have ready-drafted legislation waiting to be sponsored by MPs. Bills most likely to succeed tend to be those which draw cross party support. MPs submit their names in an annual lottery every autumn. The first names drawn are the most likely to get parliamentary time, with perhaps six annually doing so.

The government can prevent the bill becoming law if it wishes by using its parliamentary majority. Sometimes however if many government MPs show signs of supporting the bill, a compromise may be negotiated. This happened in the case of the Home Energy Conservation Bill of 1995 which became law with negotiated amendments.

The Druridge Bay Campaign had an influence in the Home Energy Conservation Bill. We had produced a statement on energy policy for the North East, in March 1993. It included a section on energy conservation, because we were sure that a thorough programme of saving energy would reduce the need for new power stations. The Green Party had drafted what was then called the Energy Conservation Bill in 1993, following 327 MPs' signatures on an Early Day Motion. All active energy groups in the country were looking out for a likely MP to promote it. We wrote to all our 22 north east MP supporters, asking them if they would consider promoting the bill, if they were lucky in the autumn lottery. Seven replied saying they would consider doing so.

By very good luck, in November 1993, our own MP Alan Beith came second in the lottery, and agreed to put forward this bill which actively required local authorities to promote energy conservation in all housing in their districts. We wrote to all our MP supporters, 22 from the North East and 15 others, and most agreed to back the bill.

It failed because the Government put 216 amendments to it, and enforced a three line whip in November 1994. However, the following year, another Liberal Democrat, Diana Maddock MP promoted the bill. With a new, co-operative energy minister, and a government modification protecting itself from financial responsibility for the work of the local authorities, the bill became law.

The free vote

The free vote is a time when MPs are freed from party discipline. Although such cases are rare, they have been allowed in recent years, on abortion, embryo research and restoration of the death penalty. These free votes make openings for relevant pressure groups to influence MPs. There was never one of relevance to the Druridge Bay Campaign.

Changing government policy - our route

In Chapter 3, I have described our work on nuclear under-insurance. Diagram 4.1 shows a simplified version of the complex routes we took to influence government policy. The parallel routes work from left to right, over the course of six years.

The central, fourth, row shows the main stepping stones and publications, and our route through the government process.

The second row shows the endless articles, press releases and letters which we issued in parallel.

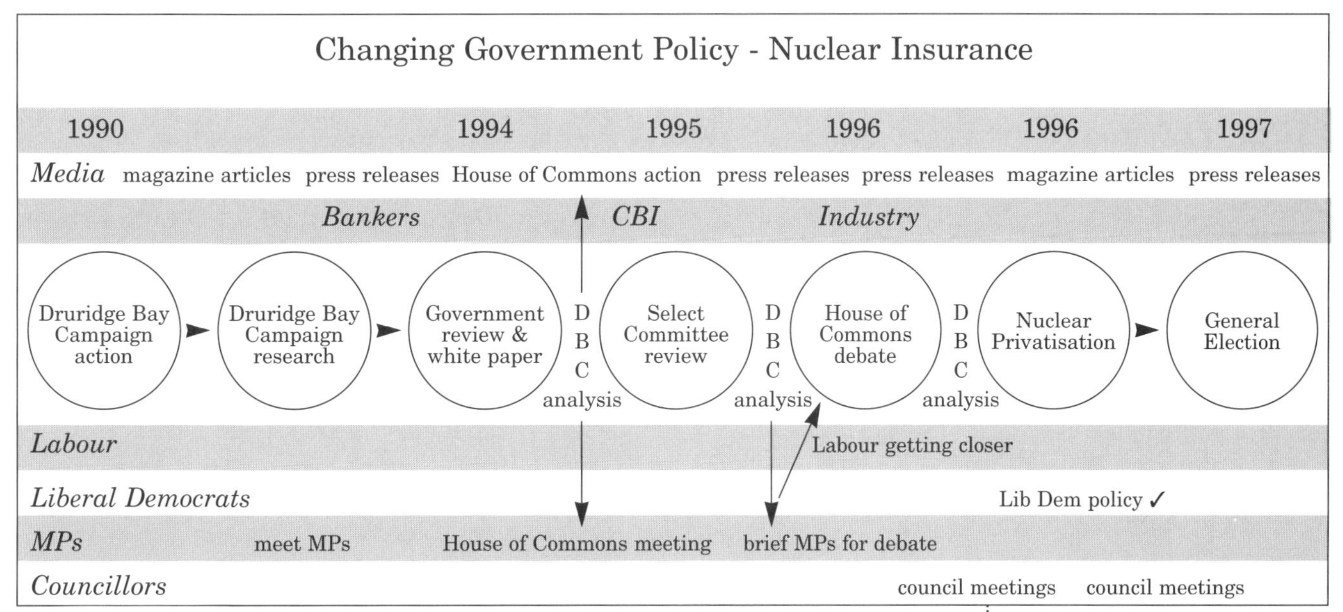

Diagram 4.1

The third row shows our contacts with industrialists.

The fifth and sixth rows show our work to influence policies of opposition parties, via letters, briefings, and Fiona Hall's work on the Liberal Democrat energy policy working group.

The final two rows indicate our presentation at council committees in the North East, and our meetings with MPs and their researchers.

Now that there has been a general election, and a change of government, the work will go on under the new group, Proper Insurance Against Nuclear Accidents, or PIANA.

Did we make a difference?

Having described some of the ways in which *outsider* groups like ours can interact with Parliament, it is worth thinking on whether or not our events had any useful effect.

Rob Baggott examines why, if policy making is dominated by the executive arm of government, pressure groups invest so much time and effort in parliamentary lobbying, and identifies three reasons. First, groups perhaps naively think Parliament has more influence over policy than it actually does. Second, it could be a kind of last resort where pressure elsewhere has failed. Third, groups actively believe parliamentary lobbying will bring benefits.

My reaction to those points is to say that, in the case of the Druridge Bay Campaign, we did not think naively that Parliament had more influence over policy that it actually does. We used the system to raise the issues, and sometimes to influence the course of the debate. Secondly, in our case, it was not a last resort where pressure elsewhere had failed, but rather a first step on an uphill process. We started from a local base, with little influence. As to whether or not parliamentary interaction brings benefits, although at first we perhaps were not aware of its consequences, we learned that it did bring us benefits in terms of high profile at home in the North East, new contacts and ideas. Not least we gained the support of local MPs who became our friends, and who at that time of entrenched Conservative power we could scarcely have imagined eventually becoming powerful members of a new government.

Those are my opinions. I asked Alan Beith and Jack Thompson, the two MPs with whom we worked most closely, to comment on the role of an *outsider* group like ourselves, and our effectiveness with the Government and Parliament.

Alan Beith's opinion

As well as being Deputy Leader of the Liberal Democrat party, Alan Beith is the MP for the Berwick upon Tweed constituency, which ranges from the Scottish border in the north to the southern end of Druridge Bay in the south. The bay is thus his particular concern. He has supported the campaign against nuclear power there since at least 1983, when he laid the foundation stone of the Cairn. This is what he said.

> "The Druridge Bay Campaign used the parliamentary process in the most effective possible way, to highlight issues and to gain access to ministers. I was pleased to co-operate closely with the campaign members. I can imagine that, as a constituency MP, I would have had a very hard time if I had not been a willing participant in the process!
>
> "As a group, they were very dogged and persistent, but also rational and persuasive. Colourful and robust campaigning was backed up with a 'charm offensive' of polite and responsible pressure.
>
> "In my position as an MP, I can meet ministers, and insist they listen to our case. Sometimes the Druridge Bay Campaign asked for my help, and at other times I suggested it. Over time, we managed to impress several of them. The meeting I set up with campaigners and environment minister Tony Baldry in 1993 prompted RMC to make the original announcement that they would eventually stop extracting sand. The advance knowledge that the meeting was taking place concentrated the minds of the company, and Tony Baldry had to get himself briefed.
>
> "Then the constant approaches to Tim Eggar and earlier energy ministers over the years left them in no doubt about local feelings on the nuclear issue. It was crucial to keep up the pressure, until the economics of

nuclear privatisation collapsed around the industry, so as to prevent any early move to build the power station. The area was never free of the danger of the nuclear industry moving in, until the axe finally fell.

"After the nuclear privatisation process was completed in 1996, the Druridge Bay Campaign immediately wanted the land held by Magnox Electric to be sold. They asked me to arrange to talk to Lord Fraser of Carmyllie, the new energy minister, about this. The sudden announcement that Magnox would sell the land came early on the morning of the same day that I had arranged to meet him.

"In both these cases, the knowledge of the meetings and the attendant publicity concentrated the minds of the ministers, and of Magnox Electric and RMC. When the Druridge Bay Campaign brought a protest to London, it meant that civil servants at all levels had to get their files out. The effectiveness of the Druridge Bay Campaign was such that every ministerial meeting was also an occasion when the minister had to be ready to give a TV interview. A line of defence had to be worked out so that the minister was not left naked in the room. A high level of regional media interest led to a high level of ministerial involvement. This added to the pressure for the minister to make an announcement in our favour. If he can get rid of an irritant, he might as well do so.

"The various lobbies and presentations to MPs were of less value than specific meetings with ministers. They were good for the morale of the Druridge Bay Campaign members, and they helped to publicise the issues at home. North East MPs like Jack Thompson and Frank Cook took a personal interest and gave moral support. This helped to encourage support beyond the immediate Druridge area. But it was like talking to the converted. The ministerial contacts were the most influential."

Jack Thompson's opinion

Jack Thompson has been Labour MP for Wansbeck since 1983. Wansbeck constituency is immediately to the south of Alan Beith's, and two or three miles south of Druridge Bay. Like Alan Beith, Jack has supported the DBC consistently from when he was leader of Northumberland County Council in 1981, and continued when he became an MP in 1983. This is what he said.

"So-called *outsider* groups are becoming much more powerful and sophisticated. I have seen a very fundamental change in how they operate, since I was elected in 1983. In those days, until perhaps the end of the 80s, there were often big demos in London, like CND or the poll tax, with maybe a quarter of a million people. That seems to have gone out of fashion.

"They were not all that effective, as lobbies. I've been to some where they don't really get their message across. I once looked out of the window, and on the other side of the river, outside St Thomas' hospital, there was a huge demo about the health service. I couldn't hear a thing. If I hadn't looked out of the window, I wouldn't have known it was happening. You're cloistered in the House of Commons.

North-East MPs, Joyce Quinn, Gerry Steinberg, David Clark, Alan Beith and Marjorie Mowlam, at House of Commons lobby by the DBC during the privatisation of electricity debate, 1989.

"The benefit of such lobbies is more for the people doing them than for any impact it has on MPs. It's a publicity exercise.

"You'll remember when you came to see me once about a lobby you were organising in London. I said there's no point in coming to see me. I can meet you at home. In terms of spending money it's not sensible. It's better to see those MPs you need to influence, like the two Tories in our region, Neville Trotter and Alan Amos. Less obvious ways can be more effective.

"I am sure that groups like Greenpeace, the Green Party, and you in the Druridge Bay Campaign, who can show there is strong public support for what they believe in, have had an impact on Labour Party environmental policies.

"Again, by linking with other groups across the country, at other nuclear power station sites, the Druridge Bay Campaign doubled the strength of the arguments. The Labour Party knows about the country's feeling about nuclear power stations from various messages, letters, actions, presentations at public inquiries, approaches to MPs. All these have more impact, and are cheaper and easier to organise than huge demonstrations in London.

"Every day, my secretary puts my mail in three piles. The first is from constituents, and every letter gets a reply. The second is about matters related to other parliamentary work, such as any committees I may be on, and I read it and reply to most of it. The third is by far the biggest, from lobbyists seeking support. Most of that goes straight in the bin.

"When other north east Labour MPs get letters from the Druridge Bay Campaign, they would generally answer them, and be supportive. They know I would raise the matter at the next meeting of the northern Labour group. We support each other's matters of regional concern."

From the point of view of these MPs, ministerial contacts are more influential, and working closely with MPs in their own constituencies is more effective than House of Commons lobbies. They both appreciated the close contact between them and us, the way we made our views felt, and the local support they knew we commanded.

Our Campaign - Your Campaign

Making Friends with your MP

You will benefit hugely from the support of your MP. She or he is probably the single most important friend you need. If you don't know who your MP is, your local library will tell you.

Perhaps you are opposing his or her party's policies. You should still be in close contact. MPs will always listen to their constituents, and reply to their letters, despite a difference in politics. In the unlikely event that they are not helpful, a quick letter to the newspaper mentioning this will work wonders.

However an MP who agrees with you will naturally be more helpful, and it is important to keep searching. It's likely that at least one of your group is the constituent of an MP who can take an interest in helping you.

If your friendly MP is in the party in government, you're lucky. If not, and ours weren't for a full eighteen years, times will change. Perhaps one of your local MPs will end up in the cabinet, or as prime minister. One of ours did - Tony Blair!

How do you meet your MP? They have surgeries where their constituents can meet them. Sometimes information about surgery times, dates and places are published in local papers. If not, ring the House of Commons on 0171 219 3000, and ask for your MP by name. Sometimes they answer the phone in person. If not, and their secretary or researcher knows you're a constituent, they'll be helpful. They'll give you the MP's local office, and tell you how to arrange a meeting.

The secretaries and researchers can provide you with lots of help and information, and its well worth getting to know them. For example, your MP can get any HMSO publication, including committee reports, without payment, and pass it on to you.

Remember

Your MP needs your good opinion, as much as you need his or her help.

Whenever possible, return their favours by mentioning them in your press releases, and invite them to your events.

They are the servants of their constituents, but they are vulnerable human beings too. They need to feel appreciated for their efforts.

Cultivate a mutually beneficial relationship.

In June 1996, I was invited by a British Studies lecturer in Oldenburg University to describe our work to students. They were amazed at the seemingly close contact we had with the parliamentary process. It is quite true that, for all groups in this country, MPs are accessible, and the House of Commons is there for us to make our views known.

Pressure groups and democracy

Whether or not pressure groups play a beneficial role in a democracy is a subject of academic interest. Does it undermine or add to the democratic process?

Rob Baggott identifies various schools of thought. Some, he writes, see pressure groups as key political institutions in modern democraties. They point out that since groups are numerous and diverse, they are able to represent a wide range of interests and preferences. While some are more powerful than others, the sheer volume of groups, their cross-cutting interests and the freedom of people to form and join groups, makes it unlikely that a single pressure group will be able to dominate policy making.

The New Right perspective he says maintains that pressure groups are broadly not to the gain of democracy. Groups are self-interested, may distort the views of the public, and some are too powerful. They prevent democratically elected governments from taking a clear view of the public interest, and undermine government authority. They are also able to block vital economic and political changes.

One gets the picture again that powerful insider groups have huge influence. Some of this may be for the good, some not, depending on one's point of view.

Jordan and Richardson see *interest* groups on balance, as "a strength in democracy. A complex society, with dispersed political power, may be difficult to govern but who would want simplicity?"

Geoffrey Alderman in his book *Pressure Groups and Government in Great Britain* describes a reason why people form pressure groups. "People who wish to change Parliament's mind, to influence government thinking or simply to bring about the public airing of a grievance or point of view, do not join a political party. Neither do they wait until a general election forces their MPs to pay attention to what they have to say. They form or join pressure groups. In consequence a great deal of the time of government and Parliament is occupied with the consideration of the views these groups put forward. Not only are there more pressure groups active in British government now than there have ever been; these groups appear to wield more power than previously and (some would argue) more power than is perhaps healthy in a democracy like ours."

He also says: "If there are anomalies in the present first-past-the-post electoral system, then the activities of pressure groups can help redress the balance. If the organs of central or of local government seem remote from the mass of the population, then participation within pressure groups can help restore a sense of participation in government. And if the complexities of modern society distance policy-makers from issues, then the existence of pressure groups of all sorts can only serve to strengthen the governed against those who govern. This cannot but be for the public good."

I can't enter the academic debate on the rights and wrongs of the role of pressure groups as a whole, in democracy. I can only describe what we did as well as I can, and leave the arguments to others. However the right to freely express our opinions in action was very important to me. It would have been quite inadequate to talk to our local councillors and MPs, and leave them to do what they felt was right, with the opportunity to put a cross on a ballot slip every four or five years, in the hope of exchanging one person for perhaps another, with no certainty they will be more helpful. The opportunity to act freely for change, sometimes in co-operation with politicians, but very often

Our Campaign - Your Campaign

Making Friends with His Lordship or Her Ladyship

Legislation passes through the House of Lords as well as the House of Commons. You can get welcome support, and useful publicity thereby, from a friendly peer.

But how do you meet a Lord or a Lady?

Your friendly MP may introduce you to one, if you ask. Another approach is to contact the House of Lords Public Information Office, on 0171 219 3107, and ask them to send you a list of all members of the House of Lords. You'll probably recognise some by the names of local stately homes or castles. Write to them. You've nothing to lose.

We once wrote to the Duchess of Northumberland. She sent a short and sweet refusal, and signed the letter "Elizabeth Northumberland". Hmm!

You can also write to your local bishop, who has a seat in the House of Lords. You'll almost certainly get a friendly reply. And he (I don't think I can write "she" yet) may well recommend you a friendly local lord, or even introduce you if your cause is worthy enough.

One of our members met Lord Glenamara at our Sizewell lobby of the House of Commons, while he was with his MP in the House of Commons bar. Shortly afterwards, Lord Glenamara came to one of our beach runs. Later I met him and Lady Glenamara over tea and scones at a National Trust teashop, and he gave me a detailed briefing on how to approach the House of Lords during the Privatisation of Electricity Bill.

Remember

Peers don't need your good opinion in the way that MPs do.

They're not accountable to an electorate, and don't have the same obligation to be helpful.

You've a good chance of finding a friendly one however. There are lots of them.

quite independently, was essential. I am sure I speak for Druridge Bay Campaign members when I say we valued the right to express creatively our concern with others of like mind.

The local group and local corridors of power

The academic analyses I have looked at concentrate more on important nation-wide pressure groups than small or regional groups like ours. The writers sometimes admit that this area is little studied but of growing interest.

Wyn Grant describes five types of relationship between local authorities and local groups:

- Left wing Labour authorities in urban areas, often with good relations with trades unions, tenants' and community groups but less so with business groups.

- Soft-left councils which are less likely to support radical cause groups and more willing to work with business.
- Urban areas with centre-right Labour or Liberal Democrat influenced authorities, working with a wide range of groups.
- Suburban or rural authorities dominated by Conservatives or Liberal Democrats. Farming and environmental lobbies will be accepted, but not those with extreme left wing views.
- New Right Conservative authorities which will work with groups such as business interests, amenity societies and residents associations, but would be hostile to those of the voluntary sector viewed as left wing or "political".

He says that in general, "there is not the same tradition of long-term routine consultation as at the national level. Local pressure groups generally have fewer staff than their national counterparts, whilst local authority officers are less dependent on them as a source of information and consent than civil servants" but "the range and sophistication of such activity would seem to be growing".

Rob Baggott asserts that pressure-group activity at the local level has increased in recent decades. Local authorities have often encouraged this. In some cases, privatisation has drawn private contractors and voluntary groups into closer consultation with local decision-makers. On the other hand central government has sometimes discouraged local authorities from going beyond the statutory minimum. And the setting up of quasi-governmental agencies by the Conservative government has by-passed local decision-making, and reduced the impact of local groups.

The problem of analysing local groups is definitely going to be as difficult for the academics as that of analysing national groups, as they are so many and varied.

The Druridge Bay Campaign interacted with local authorities of the first four of the five types described above by Wyn Grant. Our members were from all of those areas, and we gradually built up support in their councils. The councils on Tyneside and south east Northumberland are urban left-wing and centre-left Labour. In north and west Northumberland we have Liberal Democrat/ Conservative councils. There was no council of the overwhelmingly Conservative type in the region in which we mainly operated, from the Scottish border in the north to County Durham in the south.

We used different styles, and emphasised different aspects of our work with the various local authorities. Over the years, they all supported us, the main ones being Northumberland County Council and Castle Morpeth Borough Council as the two councils with direct responsibility for Druridge Bay; closely followed by Wansbeck and Blyth Valley district councils.

What bound us together in this work was the local opposition to national government policy, and in the case of sand extraction to a multinational company's activities. Our work took place almost entirely within the rule of the Conservative government from 1979 to 1997. It was an alliance between our local authorities and ourselves, against national government. They funded us, and we exchanged information. It was mutually supportive.

So what is the Druridge Bay Campaign?

According to the academic definitions, I think we probably can agree that we are a pressure group, in that we seek to influence a small range of public policies, on nuclear power, and we are a *social aggregate with some level of cohesion and shared aims.*

We can be described as a *cause* group, as at least in our later epoch we represented the particular principle of opposition to nuclear power, and one of our strengths is the large amount of popular support we gradually mustered. We can also be described as a *promotional* group which campaigns for a particular interest or cause. We were equally a *primary* group as we existed to act for political change, and an *outsider* group in that we certainly in our earlier days operated outside the mainstream of political opinion, and had no opening to the corridors of power.

We could also be called a *thresholder* group or *potential insider* group, in that we sometimes dabbled with *insider* strategies as we gained experience.

The Druridge Bay Campaign worked within the eighteen years of Conservative government. It learned how best to interact with that government, and how to use the channel of Parliament to express its point of view. It was not a powerful *insider* group, as defined by the academics. It was rather an *outsider* group, locally based, and using its elected representatives to the full. Its techniques are available to all members of our democracy.

Campaigners of all ages protesting at the statement by Robert Hawley that the nuclear industry would be using the Bay site in the future. April1995.

The Campaigners

Chapter 5

The interviews

This chapter is about the people of the Druridge Bay Campaign, giving them the chance to talk about their involvement in their own words.

I asked each of the interviewees the same questions. Would they tell me about what they did for the campaign; when and how they became involved; a little bit about their background; whether being in the Campaign changed them; and how they perceived my role.

Fiona Hall - writer and political officer

Fiona lives in the inland village of Whittingham, 25 miles from Druridge Bay, in a sweet, flowery stone cottage in an amiable state of disorder. From Manchester originally, her parents were working class Tories. She graduated from Oxford with a degree in Modern Languages, French, spent two years in Botswana, and moved to Northumberland in 1981.

She is a published poet, has taught creative writing classes, and been a part-time supply teacher. She is now full time press officer for a newly-elected Liberal Democrat MP. Her two daughters are aged 15 and 18 at the time of writing. She was chair of the Druridge Bay Campaign from November 1994 to October 1996, and vice-chair for several years. She spoke to me over the telephone

"I'm not from a campaigning kind of family. I got involved in Third World issues when I was at university and then I was in Botswana for two years. As a supporter of Oxfam I lobbied my MP on aid issues. I was interested in environmental issues in a general way, though I didn't belong to any organisation. After coming to Northumberland in 1981, I was very tied up with my young children.

"One day I read a piece in the local paper, doubtless put in from one of your press releases Bridget, with the Campaign's name, address and telephone number. Then I realised that the problem of the potential nuclear power station had been going on for some years. That would be about 1986. I was very shocked. I thought Northumberland the most beautiful place I'd ever lived in. I realised there was a very real threat on my doorstep. I phoned the telephone number in the paper, and became a member.

"Then I started getting the newsletter, and came to the Christmas Fair. You were trying to get VIP supporters at the time. I'd lived near Fleur Adcock, the poet, and I said I'd contact her. That was how I became involved.

"After that, I helped the Campaign in its effort to get Alnwick District Council to be affiliated. Other members and I, in Whittingham, became Whittingham Vale Support Group. We all spoke to different councillors. I went to see Marian Guiry. She was very very hostile and unfriendly. I wasn't used to that. She seemed offended that I'd gone to her house to lobby her about the Druridge Bay Campaign. She had a totally different perspective.

"To her, at 25 miles distance, Druridge Bay was far away. It could have been in Dorset. She couldn't understand why I was making all this fuss when there were lots of local issues, which she would call environmental issues, actually in the village. An old blocked well was one. But I felt Druridge was frighteningly close. Politically, she was an Independent I think, but conservative with a small c, and with a conservative outlook on life.

"I was on Steering Committee first as a member, representing Whittingham Vale Support Group. Then I was vice chair and chair for, let me see, altogether about six years. I was particularly involved with lobbying of MPs at the time of the Energy Conservation Bill, and in some of the work on nuclear insurance. Of course when I was chair, I was responsible for running meetings.

"Steering Committee was very consensual. Everybody put their minds to the problem of the moment, giving contributions from their own point of view.

"One of the strengths of the Campaign was that you and me as chair always worked together. You often rang me, and were always prepared to listen to my comments. You appreciated my outside view, as someone not working for the Campaign, but who knew the issues, the personalities, what was going on.

"Being in the Campaign has had a great influence on my life. It has enabled me to do what I'm doing now. I've worked with you a lot on actions and publicity. When you were ill for three months, I did your job, and learned in more detail how to put out press releases. It was the first time I had done that kind of work.

"Then, because I'd had that experience I offered to do press releases for Lembit Opik when he stood in the Euro elections in Northumbria in 1994. I built on that to work for him in his role as Newcastle councillor. I worked for him in the 1997 general election, and now he's an MP and I'm his full-time press officer, a paid post. I'd had a writing background, an interest in words, a certain literacy. But I'd never have considered doing this as a job.

"It is impossible to exaggerate the influence you have had Bridget. I don't think the Campaign would have been successful if you hadn't been there. That's the bottom line. It's not just a question of continuity, though that's important. You were the driving force behind many of the actions. You always had a vision of where we were going, an overview. To most people in Northumberland, you *are* the Druridge Bay Campaign. You're the face on TV. If I talk to people about the Druridge Bay Campaign, they always say: "Oh but you're not - " and I say: "- Bridget Gubbins!" (We laugh.) It's a tremendous endorsement of your abilities. And the media *like* to have a face to associate with a campaign. It's very much a strength.

"We were very sensitive to the delicate balance between being respectable and challenging, in forcing big men in suits to change their minds. Road protesters get a lot of publicity, but they don't achieve much. They are purely confrontational. They don't engage. At times, we were confrontational, but at other times we put on our suits and were middle aged and respectable. There were these two different styles. We had to choose which was appropriate. You saw that clearly. You resisted the chair when it was needed.

"RMC needed us. They needed an agreement with us, because we were damaging their public image. The CEGB, and the later Nuclear Electric, didn't need to engage with us, though they might have given in on little matters. RMC was a private company in a competitive market, and had its image to consider. I don't think we ever felt the CEGB was watching us. But Tim Stokes (RMC's public relations man) used to phone us up, such as before their AGM, and say: 'Are you thinking of coming to London in the next few days?' I got the feeling that we often spoiled his breakfast.

"You often used to say you were not a super scientific genius. That's the whole point. We needed people like Nigel Mortimer, like Graham Stacy, for their brains, their expertise. But you could put things in laymen's terms. We were all a bit like that. We had to speak for everybody."

Jane Gifford - artist

Jane moved to the North East from Essex in 1970. She is an artist and art lecturer. She helped set up a communal house in Newcastle, and lived there for many years. She is colourful, sensitive, wise and witty. She represented Tyneside Anti-Nuclear Campaign on the DBC Steering Committee, was chair between April 1990 and October 1992, as well as being vice chair for lengthy periods. What follows is a synthesis of a telephone conversation and a later letter which Jane sent to me.

"I was first active in the Torness Alliance. People came from all over the country to the protests, which were large and very well-organised. There were several weekends of confrontation, including the straw bale event. The bales were provided by local farmers, and we all climbed on them, and over the fence, on to the site. This demonstration came only two days after Maggie Thatcher was elected. It was in 1979. Robin Cook was there. He said "It's going to be dreadful!" or words to that effect. And he sounded altogether depressed about the result.

"The nearest I came to death was being in a large hole excavated by a digger. People were hanging from the digger's bucket and trying to stop it. When I looked up, the sun was blotted out as a large body - Don Kent - hurled himself into the fray, nearly squashing me!

"People were dancing round the holes in rings, and moving the stones the contractor was blocking the way with.

“As well as opposing nuclear power at Torness, many protesters saw their lives and actions as being part of a process of change. I know I did. It wasn’t enough just to protest. Our ways of stopping nuclear power had to be about building the world the way we wanted it to be. Non-hierarchical, non-violent, non-exploitative of the world and others.

“When I was involved in the Cheviots waste dump inquiry in Newcastle, our anti-nuclear group performed several media stunts such as tipping a waste paper bin over the inspector’s desk to represent nuclear waste. We also sat on his desk dressed in radiation suits, and were carried off and put in the cells. Another time, we barricaded ourselves into the public gallery, and were going to stay there all night. But they shook the door and the elaborate barricade fell down in one go. So that was twice we were were dragged off.

“Marjorie Mowlam was one of our members. She spoke on TV the day the Cheviots inquiry opened. She picked up a nearby child and held it in her arms while talking to the camera. When we looked at the TV in the evening, she looked like a really concerned mother, talking about the future of children, and the child didn’t even belong to her.

“My father was an electrical engineer, with a history of working in power stations. He was always opposed to nuclear power, so I had his very well-informed viewpoint behind me.

“Tyneside Anti-Nuclear Campaign grew out of the North East Anti-Nuclear Alliance. We set up our office in Newcastle, mainly for the fight against nuclear power at Druridge Bay. Eventually TANC was superseded by the Druridge Bay Campaign itself, an on-the-spot group that included local people, just what Torness had never had.

“You ask what influence being in the Druridge Bay Campaign had on my life. When I joined, I already had ideas about nuclear power and the political process, and I was an environmentalist and ‘peace-nik’. But it was in the Druridge Bay Campaign that any ‘people’ skills and organisational qualities I might possess were practised and honed.

“It was there that I became more centre stage. In TANC for example, really good people like Martin Spence and Marjorie Mowlam had been the organisers. But when they moved on, I felt that the Druridge issue should be stuck with. So yes, I have have gained a lot personally through my involvement with the campaign.

“The Druridge Bay Campaign always acted legally as some of our money came from public funds. So it was a good thing that we never needed to get involved in an illegal direct action. If the situation had demanded it, it is likely that some people would be prepared to make that commitment.

“Having workers was essential to our success. I would urge any group, with urgent work to do, to get staff. They provide continuity and stability. They do the boring things. If I have a cold, I don’t have to go in to the office, and the enthusiasm of volunteers may lead them to activist burnout. Paid workers should pace themselves, and they will do what the group as a whole sees as important.

"Volunteers too are not under any kind of control. If they decided to organise say a snail point-to-point, you can't argue with them. The workers however help to focus the group.

"The Campaign served a purpose with the eighteen years of Conservative government that we have had, which have been so disempowering in every way you can think of. People had an area of action, which was cosmically important, where their actions and their thoughts were seen as important, and could have an influence on people outside. That's what politics should be about. But hundreds and thousands of people were too cynical to try to change things in that era. Their humanity was sapped.

"Being part of the organisation that prevented nuclear power at Druridge Bay (which we did do, make no mistake about it) is probably the most important thing I have done in my life. I'm not agile enough to rescue curly-haired children from under the hooves of bolting horses, and the opportunities for such heroism have been sparse in central Newcastle, but I have done the equivalent. Lives have been saved because of the Druridge Bay Campaign.

"This is my favourite analogy. 'No-one is more important than the earthworm'. I see all the thousands of anti-nuclear activists, Druridge Bay Campaigners and the like, as earthworms. Individually small, but together responsible for the very stuff of life."

Rose Martin - green Conservative

Rose is an older person who was virtually the only active member of the Conservative Party in the Druridge Bay Campaign. As such, we valued and encouraged her. She lives in a village near the sea in Northumberland, and would struggle to meetings despite crippling arthritis. She is reluctant to give herself much credit, and I had to work hard to extract the following from her, over the telephone.

"I was an officer of the Berwick upon Tweed Conservative Association, vice-chair, one of the bigwigs. If I'd been more of an ordinary Conservative, I wouldn't have known anything about the Druridge Bay Campaign.

"The members were talking about who would go into which organisation, partly to see what they were up to. I went on to the Druridge Bay Campaign committee. Then I was struck down with arthritis. It came on very quickly, so really I couldn't help much. I collected money at the fairs, helping the treasurer. I audited the accounts one year. I knew it was right to keep coming, so that you had a Conservative there. It was symbolic.

"I've always been very green. The others in the Conservative Association used to make jokes about it. All I'm interested in is wildlife, animals, the environment, the garden. I don't like big organisations like the CEGB, and I certainly don't like atomic power. I was always against it at Druridge.

"It was funny being the only Conservative on the committee. Some of them, when they knew I was Conservative, didn't trust me. They pulled long faces. But it was better for everybody that I was there."

Nick Scott - ecologist

Nick was the big, bearded warden for Northumberland Wildlife Trust, at Druridge Bay. He always wanted the Druridge Bay Campaign to take on the sand extraction issue, when its main concern was the nuclear power stations proposal. Extrovert and humble by turn, he was one of our most impressive King Canutes. Now he lives in a Buddhist monastery in Sussex, and is the estate ecologist. The following is extracted from a piece he wrote in a Buddhist newsletter.

"A few years ago I read an interview with a Tibetan lama. In it, he was asked what he felt about the current global environmental crisis. He simply replied that the Buddha had said that everything that arises passes away, and that went for the planet too. I found that comment very helpful. For the first time I saw that I did not have to needlessly suffer over the environmental crisis. Do what I could, yes, but I did not have to Save the World.

"I first consciously tried that approach with the sand extraction campaign in Northumberland. The company was digging up sand from the beach to make concrete. They had planning permission, and everyone said it was not possible to stop them. The charity I worked for did not even want to try. But I had to pass the diggers most days, and I found it painful.

"Eventually I decided I had to do something about it, just for my own peace of mind. But I resolved that I was going to do it with as little desire to get it stopped as I could, doing it just because it was the right thing to do. This proved to be one of the most enjoyable things I have done.

"I got the issue adopted by the Druridge Bay Campaign, and we formed a small group. The issue was taken up by *The Journal*, the regional newspaper, which led to a 20,000 signature petition. The master stroke was an idea to use King Canute. We dressed up as Vikings and marched down Yarm high street, filmed by the local TV to deliver a royal proclamation to their head officer.

"Later on we bought a share in the parent company, and we were filmed at their annual general meeting at a posh hotel in London.

"When you set people up in a confrontation, their pride gets in the way. They'll never change their minds. But the concrete company both hated us and were amused by us, because we did it in a nice way.

"Later I was told that was why they changed their minds. When I actually spoke at that AGM, still dressed as King Canute, I said 'Well look - all this bad publicity for just £10,000 worth of sand a year. It's silly'. During the meeting, the chairman defended their position, but afterwards said to the guys running the subsidiary in Yarm 'Why are we doing this?'

"It is the doing which is important, not the result. I find with that perspective I enjoy it, and no longer feel driven, or dwell on the hopelessness of things. And, somehow, I find that I am more effective too."

Ken McDonald - psychologist and countryside worker

Ken has a small business carrying out conservation-minded woodland and countryside work. He is also a qualified psychologist and has a small private counselling practice. He plays a flute in a ceilidh band. He lives in Alnwick, a market town 20 miles north of Morpeth, fifteen miles from Druridge. He is perceptive, original and practical, and is a member of the Radiation Monitoring Group. He talked to me over the telephone.

"Cath my partner and I helped to get the Alnwick Support Group going, back in 1987 and 88. We were going to have a stall in the market place, but it was so expensive that the group made a barrow on wheels, and put a flag on it, leaflets and the petition. We wheeled it around. People were very interested though we did get verbally assaulted by the likes of Councillor Hughie Philipson, who didn't agree with us at all.

"The Alnwick Support Group helped to get Alnwick District Council to affiliate to the Campaign. We sent all the councillors information, and lobbied a few by telephone. Despite this, one councillor stood up at a meeting and solemnly asked 'What is the Druridge Bay Campaign?' Cath rang Councillor Albert Davidson, and for once got a shirty answer. He'd had a bad meeting I think. But the Liberals did support us. You get all sorts of responses when you just ring people up.

"Mostly, I did the radiation monitoring. That got lots of publicity. Paul Crowther was one of the monitoring group. He's a local teacher. His son was about 12 when they were monitoring, and their picture appeared in the local papers. It was good that the children were involved. The Campaign was all about the children. Saving Druridge Bay was for their generation. People would see us when we were out monitoring. Especially at Amble Links. Some would think 'What's this mysterious machine?' It gave us the chance to discuss the issue. Many people already knew. They'd read about it, or seen it on TV.

"What most impressed me about the Druridge Bay Campaign was that it was absolutely not confrontational. A lot of co-operation, creativity and imagination went into its activities. Certainly it was not an argumentative Yes It Is - No It Isn't campaign, sparring like bulls.

"It was not weak either. There is a danger in being too democratic, in becoming loose or imprecise. But somehow, out of the creative space that people were given, there came some extremely good ideas. Its whole philosophy was to do with thoroughness, gentleness and persistence. Quite the opposite of having angry demonstrations.

"If you fight yourself into a corner, confronting people aggressively, your opponents end up being able to dismiss you. You lose sight of the really important issues. But the Druridge campaigners had a lot of good, hard information about nuclear power, without pointing a finger at individual people. It was the issues we attacked, which is much more creative. For example, the nuclear people promised thousands of jobs. So we went to visit other power station sites to find out what happened.*

"We turned our anger into effective schemes. In the end, the Druridge Bay Campaign's case was unanswerable. Also I think it was quite a cohesive force in the community; both reflecting links that were to some extent already there, and strengthening others. Friendships were formed through our common activities and aims, and these have lasted.

"The sand issue was simpler. Eventually, the RMC people's actions became insupportable, when it was public knowledge what they were doing. With the nuclear issue, we have probably all thought at times 'Well maybe they were going to give up anyway', that it was nothing to do with us. But I'm not too sure. I think we certainly managed to stop them while they still thought it was a good idea. I think it is possible that the Druridge Bay Campaign was permeating their thinking. They could see that we could win the arguments before they got to the point of putting in a planning application.

"There was the gentle persistence of the Campaign. The nuclear people couldn't dismiss us as a whole lot of wierdos shouting their heads off. We were not a Rent-a-Mob, where the easiest thing to do is to put it down. We offered alternatives to their proposal. They couldn't just dismiss us.

"We've also built up a good background of experience in effective campaigning, giving us a stronger democratic heritage. This will not be lost. This is one of the strengths of an area like Northumberland.

"And I have to say that a great deal of the direction of the campaign seemed to relate to the personal philosophies of the most active members, like you Bridget.

"In the end, Cllr Hughie Philipson changed his mind about nuclear power. He admitted to you that he had changed his mind. It says something about the maturity of the Campaign that he would tell you that. There is a difference between having a strong position and being confrontational."

* *Details can be found in Generating Pressure. See the bibliography.*

Jonathan Nicholson - planner

Jonathan lives in Newcastle upon Tyne, in an inner-city terrace flat near the University. Rather serious, and very modest, he works as a planning officer with a Northumberland district council. He was chair of the Druridge Bay Campaign between November 1992 and October 1994. He talked to me over the telephone.

"I joined the Green Party in 1984. I went to the founding meeting of the Druridge Bay Campaign in Newcastle, at the miners' hall. I worked in Morpeth at that time, so the Green Party asked me if I'd represent them at Druridge Bay Campaign committee meetings. I came to monthly meetings in Morpeth for three or four years, lapsed and came back again in 1990.

"At first, I came to meetings as an observer. Gradually, I became more and more involved with Druridge Bay, I got to know it, to appreciate it. I feel I didn't contribute much to the Druridge Bay Campaign for the first few years, though I did get involved in the panel that selected people for the two office posts.

"I've been vice chair and chair. I also directly managed one of the summer festivals, and helped manage another in the changeover between the two admin staff. I've helped with development of Campaign policy, with people-management, with supporting and supervising the workers.

"I've gained a lot of confidence while working with the campaign, thanks partly to encouragement and praise from you and other members of the committee.

"I've always looked on the people we've been dealing with, our opponents, as having to do their job. It's a gradual influencing process we've been through, with them.

"I think that the community, as perceived by institutions, is a very powerful force for changing things. It has been one of the successes of the Campaign that we've given the impression we are a very large body of opinion. It is a large body, but it is a disparate body. We've had the effect of seeming to be one body of opinion, the local and regional community. I think we've had a lot of influence nationally too.

"I've gained confidence in the ability of people gradually to encourage systems to evolve in a more tolerant, greener way. So that companies can become less intent on simply making money or realising some sort of corporate aims. To take account of people and their day-to-day lives, their concerns for their environment. I've learned that the community can have a voice, that I can be part of it.

"Now I'm involved in the No Business On The Moor campaign, against Newcastle United's proposed new football stadium in the conservation area. In this campaign, I find that articulate and confident people, who have perhaps a lot of authority in their work environment, are less confident when it comes to campaigning, due to inexperience.

"I have some advantages, as I work in local government. But having been in the DBC, I find I know how to do things in a less angst-ridden, more conciliatory and more humorous way. Some people see institutions as impenetrable, all-powerful entities which they can't influence. They may lack the experience of practical things, the diplomatic way to write letters for example so they don't rub opponents such as developers or the football club people up the wrong way. It's not that we should try to get them on our side, but should get them to co-operate. We need to see them as a group of people rather than as a faceless institution.

"I've seen your role as invaluable Bridget. I feel strongly that you were the driving force, always keeping the publicity bandwagon rolling along, varying it. You may not like me saying this, but it was a spin-doctor role. Always finding a new spin, keeping people interested, the public through the media.

"You always kept the members involved, feeling they had a role to play. And you were very good at identifying the qualities of people, encouraging them to use their abilities for the general good. You made it a fun campaign. I was often sorry if I had to miss events.

"When I used to work at Northumberland County Council, sometimes the other planners would say 'It's that Bridget Gubbins on the phone again'. But that's changed. Over the years you've gained a lot of respect. You're seen as someone who has exerted influence in the region on environmental issues."

Terry and Carole Drummond - retired local residents

Terry and Carole live in a small new detached house on an estate in Ellington village, one mile from Druridge Bay. Terry was born on Tyneside, and served his time in the shipyards, before joining the Royal Navy, then entering the merchant navy. He moved from there to become department manager at the Batchelors Peas factory in Sheffield and Worksop. Carole started off as a clerical worker when she left school, and "worked her way down" to the factory. A keen sportswoman, Carole used to play rounders for England. Terry is 73, and Carole is 53. We chatted together with the tape recorder going round, in the DBC office, before one of our monthly meetings.

Carole: We moved to Northumberland in June 1992. We'd been living here for about a year, trotting up and down the beach. When we saw the sand extraction, we thought: 'Are we the only ones who know about that?' Daft of course. There was a meeting in Morpeth Town Hall, getting to know your council, that sort of thing. Terry and I went along. The Lord Mayor was there, the whole caboodle. Terry got on about sand extraction at Druridge Bay, and kicked up a storm. You know what he's like! (We all laugh.) They all looked a bit taken aback. That was the first time Terry mentioned 'Why don't we all sit on the beach?' That was in the paper a couple of days later. But as we were leaving this meeting, this chap…

Terry: …a doctor-something from Heddon on the Wall. Angus Lunn, a little bloke. Yes he was a councillor. He said 'You want to get in touch with Bridget Gubbins'. I said 'What's she got to do with sand extraction?' He said 'She's the prime mover behind the campaign to get it stopped'.

Carole: A couple of months went by, and we found there was a meeting. Jane Gifford was chairing it. We went. We were very very angry again, at the meeting. It all took off from them.

Terry: Anyway, I rang this Liberal councillor, I can't remember his name. He said 'Don't you know, everybody knows about sand extraction!' Well, how could they? You don't know if you live in Yorkshire. He was right snotty. No it wasn't Alan Beith. It was a councillor. Oh, you know I don't get on with Alan Beith. You know that. So then I went to the Cresswell parish council meeting. I was dis*gust*ed at their attitude. I was disgusted. That councillor! He's a ratbag. He is. Those parish councillors were the ones who were most affected.

Then I came to your meetings. What horrified me, I told Carole this, is that you were talking about appealing to Prince Charles! I could have told them it wasn't worth wasting a stamp. They're the last people I would appeal to, people like that. He's not interested in anything up here anyway. Now there were one or two people around this table, and they were so diplomatic about the things I felt strongly about, that if somebody suggested something that smacked of action, certain individuals would say 'Oh we can't do that. Our remit is this'. But you'll never get anywhere like that. Look at those people protesting about Manchester Airport. It's not the people signing the petitions who are getting the publicity.

Carole: I enjoyed the *doing*. I'm not the sort of person who'll give opinions. Yes, I made the curtains for the sign unveiling! Hm! I'm about as domesticated as a bull in a china shop. I went to London, to RMC's AGM. I was a serf. I love to be in the thick of things. I feel as if I'm *doing* something. And I've written letters, two or three times, to the papers. They were all published. It makes me feel better, even if it doesn't get me anywhere.

Terry: The sign at the bay, by the sand extraction, the hourglass design of sand pouring down, that was Carole's design. It was brilliant. She's got potential she never uses, my wife.

Carole: What I remember Bridget is your unfailing enthusiasm, your smile from ear to ear. Whether you had two people behind you, or a hundred.

Terry: It's true. And there were times when I'd say to Carole 'We're not getting anywhere at all'. But you'd have gone on even if we hadn't. I know you would have. We felt we had to give you support. Yes, I know you were paid for it. But you were alongside in the actions. When we were carrying the banner around the Central Station.

Carole: The undercurrent of encouragement ... the thread of militancy ... you never missed a trick for a bit of free publicity...

Terry: ...very diplomatic talking to TV and Radio...

Carole: ...especially at 6 o'clock in the morning...

Terry: I couldn't have been. I couldn't. We saw you played a pivotal role, no doubt about it. Carole and I have talked about it time and time again.

Carole: Being in the Campaign has made me speak out a bit more. The other day, I heard some people insulting the Manchester Airport protesters. I stuck my two-penn'orth in. Probably before I'd done my bit of protesting, I wouldn't have been so understanding.

Terry: Being in the Campaign has made me *more* aggravated. When everyone was saying 'Oh RMC, they're so good for stopping sand extraction'. I don't understand it! Well, they stopped, I'll give you that. But we should have been compensated! They've ruined the beach. Then to say they were so good! Oh that went through me.

Carole: But it doesn't matter. We got the result we wanted.

Terry: Everybody said it doesn't matter, they've stopped...

Carole: All right. All right.

Terry: Not in my book it isn't!

Jonatha Robinson - sociologist

Born in the USA, she has lived in England for many years. She has two grown daughters. She gained her bachelor's degree in Philosophy and her MA in Education and History in the USA. She was a teacher before qualifying as a social worker. Earnest, honest, very steady, kind and reliable, she was DBC chair from November 1987 to October 1989. What follows is, first, from a telephone conversation, and second, from some notes she sent to me later.

The telephone conversation:

"I represented Northumberland County Council's branch of NALGO on the Steering Committee first, then later on I became chair. I liked to help in practical ways, the organising of the fairs, helping on the day. Sometimes I helped with publicity events too. Cathy my daughter was Postman Pat one day, going round Morpeth to publicise the fair. We had a Clean up the Beach at Druridge event. That was the kind of practical event I liked, rather than remote airy-fairy activities. It demonstrated we were interested in the bay as a whole.

“And I often went up to the Cairn at weekends, to give out leaflets, collect signatures for the petition, talk to people.

“When I was chair, I would go over the various publications we produced, and later had to help prepare for monthly meetings. I had the principle that two years in the chair is long enough. In some organizations, people are chairs for ever and ever. I think someone new should come in every couple of years.

“Yes, being in the Campaign did give me more confidence with the role of a chairman. It also made me think about what was the best way to achieve our aims, in the role of a pressure group, which is different from traditional politics. We were very successful in that we got the local political structure to become allied to us. I think the Druridge Bay Campaign played a useful role.

“It’s not good when a small, dedicated, hardworking group acts as a pressure group, overwhelming others, totally out of proportion to their numbers, because most people can’t be bothered to be active. But we got the elected politicians on our side. We were representative.

“I worked closely with you and Wendy, the admin officer. My conception of the relationship between the elected committee and the paid employees was that the committee made the policies and the employees carried them out. The Druridge Bay Campaign showed me that that was too much of a schematic idea. Obviously you were one of the originators of the Campaign. I don’t know whether you found it a bit difficult, being in the employee role. As it worked out in practice, the categories became a bit blurred.”

The notes:

“Pressure groups are very powerful, their power often out of proportion to the numbers they represent. We may not mind when a group represents a cause which we consider to be ‘right’, but the same opportunity is open to groups which may be the opposite, and how do we deal with this?

“The Druridge Bay Campaign was an example of what I consider to be a ‘good’ pressure group, and while it utilized the advantages a pressure group can have, I was aware of the possibility of it being an undemocratic force itself, or of operating undemocratically.

“The committee, as the democratically elected body representing the various constituencies should make the policies, and everything the Druridge Bay Campaign did should flow from them and be in accord with them. I felt the role of the employees was to implement policy as determined by the committee, to participate bringing the desired ends to fruition.

"I enjoyed the opportunity to make a contribution in an area which meant a lot to me, through the Druridge Bay Campaign. It had the unanticipated side benefits of opportunities for self-development and self-exploration."

Libby Paxton - psychologist

Libby lives in Morpeth in old house overlooking the school playing field, with four young children and psychologist husband. As a child she lived abroad in Malaysia, India, Burma and Sri Lanka. She was educated in a private Catholic convent boarding school. Her degrees are in Psychology and Clinical Psychology. She moved to Morpeth in 1985. As I write this she is chair of the Druridge Bay Campaign. We chatted together in the DBC office.

"At first I volunteered with my children to stick envelopes down, to stick stamps on, because I felt that was all I was capable of doing. I'd always contributed money to campaigns like the Medical Campaign Against Nuclear Weapons and Psychologists for Peace when I was working, but had never been active because of work. Then children came along, and I felt it was much more interesting for them and me to be on an office floor, sticking envelopes down, than in the house.

"Then another Campaign member, Helen, and I took on the organising of a Christmas Fair. It was good working with someone else. We were happy getting all the things together, organising people to run stalls. We didn't know much about the campaigning side. Each year, I learned more about the hazards of running a fair. I've done it every year since 1985.

"After the Chernobyl accident, I began to look at health issues with Toni Stephenson. She was a Quaker, a very kind and compassionate person. We decided that if there was to be a nuclear power station at Druridge, we wanted to know more about the health consequences. This tied up with the nuclear insurance work. If you are going to claim for damage to health, you have to have evidence linking the effects to emissions. Our health research went in parallel with that of the Radiation Monitoring group. I went to one of the Low Level Radiation and Health conferences, in Stirling, in 1988. That was when the first research came out that fathers' sperm could be damaged by exposure to low level radiation, and that this could affect their children. The link between radiation and damage to health has never been proven. The nuclear industry always says 'We don't have to disprove the link. You have to prove there is a link'. They throw the responsibility on to others.

"Toni and I met consultant oncologists and researchers at Newcastle University Department of Oncology. Some cautiously agreed there probably was a link between cancer and radiation, but said that statistically it is difficult to prove. As a psychologist with statistical training I know that. But nuclear power and its effects seemed to be linked to leukaemia clusters.

“So that was another interesting strand to my work with the Campaign. Then, Toni’s husband became ill with cancer. She was taken up with looking after him until he died. Then Toni herself became ill, with leukaemia, and she died. It was so sad. Our work on health seemed to come to an end then. In the middle of all this, my third child was born, followed in 1990 by my fourth.

“My work with the Campaign was a link with sanity. It helped to keep me in touch with the outside world. The most powerful effect it has had on my life is that I am no longer awed by figures of authority. They may seem to be important, but they’re also people, and they can listen and learn. Sometimes you find you know more than them, because you’ve taken the trouble to research an issue. It’s no criticism of them. Politicians for example have many issues to worry about, and their constituents’ concerns can be about anything.

“I think most people are happy to have the politicians take decisions for them. Then they have someone to blame when things go wrong. Being involved in campaigning has helped me to learn that we can be responsible ourselves. That’s very very powerful. What you do might irritate those in authority, but it will have an effect. They still deserve respect for what they do, but it’s more a meeting of minds than that they’re in authority and you’re subservient.

“And also I have learned how the media creates news. You see something on paper, or on the news, and you assume there’s some reality to it. That idea, if I ever had it, has been completely demolished. I’ve seen how we in the Druridge Bay Campaign have helped the media create news.

“People see you Bridget as a figurehead. You can’t escape that. It’s dumped on you. It’s important though, as people do identify a campaign or organisation with particular people. That’s been good for the Druridge Bay Campaign. People have seen you and the Campaign as synonymous. You may not always have liked it. Probably most people don’t even realise that you get paid. But you were the driving force. When things were quiet, nothing much was happening, strong people like you would say ‘We can’t give up now. The threat is still there, the nuclear people haven’t gone away’. Without you, things would have floundered.

“It’s this leadership thing. People do look for strong people to lead them on. That’s how we’re structured as a social group. However democratic a group tries to be, there’ll always be the people who have the ideas, the ability to organise, who find themselves in a position of leadership even if they don’t want to be.

“And you need a mix of people in a campaign. You need the road protesters, and people like the Manchester Airport protesters, who are prepared to go underground, to get the media there. You need as well the supporters, who do the right thing, go to meetings and be polite. You need that mix.

“So you have some success, even minor success. It spurs you on, and it encourages others to join you. Everybody likes to be in something that’s successful. It breeds good feelings, feelings of confidence.

"There was a strong feeling too in the group that was formed, people who didn't really have much in common, who had probably never met up before, that they had a common cause. They were prepared to put themselves out, in all sorts of weathers, going out to actions at the bay, in London. Doing things together binds people. It makes for success.

"When I was organising the Christmas fairs, for example, I could contact people I hadn't spoken to for months, knowing I would get a friendly response. I never got slapped down. If they couldn't do what I asked they would do something different, bring some jumble down, or some old books. They would think at least this stuff would help post a few letters.

"So I was doing the little jobs. I always was glad someone else was at the helm, organising the big things. But the little things feed into the big things. We needed each other. There was always a place for me. I don't think anybody ever felt excluded."

A brief word from the MPs

Alan Beith

> "Although I only saw and dealt with a small number of people who were the face of the Campaign, I was aware of the diversity of support and membership. The sand issue particularly embraced people from right across the political spectrum. My strongest memory is of your dogged persistence.
>
> "Your information was reliable and well researched. I could trust what you sent me. Also, once you had established the interest of the regional media, you were very good at maintaining it.

Jack Thompson

> "The Druridge Campaigners were identified both by me and other people as not aggressive or militant. You were seen to have a well-conducted campaign. If the CEGB had taken more positive actions early on, you would have been able to demonstrate great public outrage.
>
> "The members were from various walks of life. There was a lobby from the mining industry. A number of professional people. It was not a working class group, or an academic group. The Druridge Bay Campaign represented the whole community. It was a community group, though it wasn't set up to be one. It was a side effect of its work.

The role of women

There were many active, lively, interesting women within the Druridge Bay Campaign. I think that this is at the heart of our success. Of course many members were men, some of our greatest. Yet the driving forces were often women, and our way of working was consensual and listening rather than competitive and status-seeking.

In her book about the history of the anti-nuclear movement, *The Burning Question*, Ruth Brandon describes the activities of an American organisation called Women Strike for Peace in 1961. The women suggested that both East and West should immediately destroy the means of launching nuclear missiles, thus reducing the risk of accidental war, and that a committee of women in many nations should ask their governments for a report of progress towards a disarmed world. They were called for questioning by the House Un-American Activities Committee. When the Chairman of the committee used phrases such as "excessive desire for peace" impeding "adequate defense preparations", sapping "national strength", serving "the aggressive plans of world communism", the women would react with uncontrollable laughter.

One of the women's witnesses told the committee: "Our movement is motivated by mothers' love for their children. When they set their breakfast on the table, they see not wheaties and milk, but strontium 90 and iodine 131, and they fear for their health and their lives".

Ruth Brandon says that it was clear that the committee and the women before them lived in parallel worlds which could never meet.

This describes I think the kind of difference at the heart of the Druridge Bay Campaign and our opponents in the UK nuclear industry. However much the officials of the CEGB and government ministers felt they were serving the national or global interest by building nuclear power stations, what we could see was radioactive waste, deadly for tens or hundreds of thousands of years; radioactive cores cemented up on British beaches for at least 135 years; the ever-present risk of accidents; the fear of living next to an outwardly innocent building with inwardly deadly contents.

What motivated us was caring for the future generations, for the life of the planet as a whole, as well as for the lovely beach of which we had become guardians. We used the female skills, not deliberately but because of the way we were. Not usually confrontationally, but when we did, using a touch of humour. Listening to each other, to the opposition, but never flinching from our cause, fiercely protective of what we loved. Not exclusively womanly qualities of course, but different from the dominating authoritarian front of our opponents.

The 1987 beach run.

The Organisation

Chapter 6

In their book *Environmental Groups in Politics*, writers Philip Lowe and Jane Goyder identify various *resources*, needed or used by environmental groups. These are *delay; direct action and sabotage; leadership; expertise; finances; organisation.* Many of these aspects have already been described in earlier chapters. I'll quickly summarise the first four, and then focus in some detail on our finances and organisation.

Delay, direct action, sabotage, leadership

The numerous delays caused both by opponents of the nuclear industry and its own internal difficulties were significant in saving Druridge Bay. Without these delays, the UK could be riddled with nuclear power stations, as is France. In Chapter 1, I have described the various delays which helped to save our bay.

In every preceding chapter there have been descriptions of the Druridge Bay Campaign's *direct actions*, all legal and non-violent. It was never necessary for local people to consider challenging the law. If the nuclear power stations had got to the bulldozer stage, I suspect it is likely that there would have been more powerful direct action, both legal and non-legal, even though the protests, however powerful and emotional, are merely symbolic at that stage. Our success hinged on the proposal being defeated before the planning application was even submitted.

Sabotage occurred only at the time of the first drilling by the CEGB in 1979. This was not endorsed by the Druridge Bay Association.* There is no official knowledge of who was responsible.

The qualities of our *leadership* should come out clearly from the interviews in the previous chapter, and from the comments of some of those most closely involved. Our intensively interactive way of operating meant that there was close day-to-day contact between Steering Committee chairs and the staff. Although I did become the public face of the Campaign, especially during the last few years, the leadership was a joint exercise.

** The Druridge Bay Association was the group formed by local residents of villages close to Druridge, active between 1979 and 1981 only.*
See Chapter 1, The Early Protesters.

Expertise

Expertise was available to us through our members. Other chapters have shown how, if we needed a certain kind of knowledge, we could often call upon them - Nigel Mortimer, with his knowledge of physics and renewable energy, Adrian Smith on Combined Heat and Power, planners such as Jonathan Nicholson or Helen Brownlie, and politicians. Often we would have liked to commission studies, but we couldn't afford to. Either I had to fit in short research projects as part of my work, such as I did on the greenhouse effect, or we asked our members to help us in their spare time, at their own expense. Even Nigel and Helen's report on nuclear under-insurance was done substantially in this way.

Our VIP supporters

One related kind of expertise was our VIP supporters list. We had an impressive long list of over a hundred famous people who had signed a slip supporting our aims. We distributed this list widely, as a way of showing everyone who was interested, and our opponents, the support upon which we could call.

The list consisted of 52 MPs, MEPs, lords and baronesses, and 67 writers, actors and actresses, playwrights, professors, poets, bishops, musicians and others.

We got the idea originally from a Friends of the Earth advertisement in the national papers in 1987. They had collected a list of public figures who were objecting to the building of Sizewell B. We had one of our volunteers go to the library and see how many addresses of those people she could identify in *Who's Who* and similar directories. Then we wrote to them, with a reply slip, asking if they would support us in our objections to nuclear power at Druridge.

Tide Lines, a poetry collection, published by the Druridge Bay Campaign in 1988.

Many did. We added to the list many poets and writers who had contributed to our book *Tide Lines*, an art and poetry anthology about the bay, which had been compiled in 1986 by one of our writer members, Mike Kirkup.

We had also our own northern MPs, many of whom we were able to identify following our Sizewell lobby in 1987. Tony Blair joined our list after his visit in 1989.

We lengthened the list once again when Greenpeace advertised names of scientists in July 1989 who signed up to a statement that a massive increase in nuclear generating capacity was not the answer to the greenhouse effect. In autumn 1989, thanks to good advice from Lord Glenamara, we contacted many lords, baronesses and bishops during the House of Lords phase of the Electricity Privatisation Bill. We asked all those who were sympathetic to be on our list, and many agreed.

This list was of immense value to use. We had to keep it up-to-date, which was a hard job. Every year or two, a volunteer had to check the addresses at the library, and try to find out if anyone had died. Every Christmas, we sent them all a card with a message of appreciation for their support.

We never asked them for money or membership fees. At the back of our minds, we knew that, if we were truly desperate, we might have been able to do so. They were all kind enough to allow us to use their names in our cause, and that was their value to us.

When we wanted help for our sand extraction campaign, Tony Henderson contacted various VIPs at short notice. He was able to publish photographs and comments in *The Journal* from Beryl Bainbridge, Emma Thompson and Juliet Stevenson, expressing their horror about RMC's activities.

We were able to add many of their signatures to both our sand petition and our Sell the Land petition, and we ensured that the media, the government ministers and RMC bosses knew.

Finances

Funding our activities was basic to our work. During the 1980s, before local authorities were hit by capping, this had been easier to obtain, and we had gradually built up a small surplus. We needed this, in case of a planning application and public inquiry, which never in fact happened. By 1991/92, our income had become less than our expenditure. To help us cope, we two members of staff voluntarily reduced our hours from 20 to 16 per week.

Income	*1991/92*	*1993/4*
Local authority funding	£11,100	£10,000
Membership	£1,900	£2,000
Regular fundraising	£2,300	£2,700
	£15,300	£14,700
Outgoing		
Staff costs	£12,700	£12,100
Office costs	£4,600	£4,000
	£17,300	£16,100
Shortfall	£2,000	£1,400

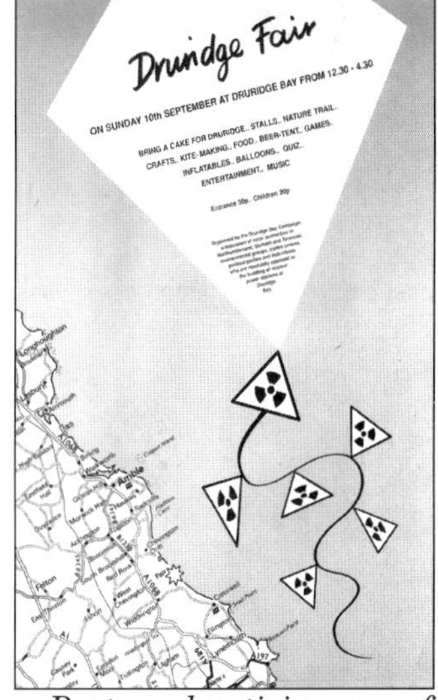

Poster advertising one of the Druridge Bay Campaign's annual fairs.

Almost every year we held a summer event at Druridge, a Christmas fair at Morpeth Town Hall and for many years we held a run on the beach. Every voluntary group knows how to do this sort of thing, and there is not much this book needs to add. It's hard work. It takes a lot of careful and detailed organising. It seems to get harder each year to raise money. We also took stalls to various events organised by other groups, which was a lot of work, often for little return.

Every summer for the last few years, we had an arrangement with the National Trust that we did car-parking duty at their Druridge site. Our volunteers collected the 50 pence entry fee, which we shared 50:50 with the Trust. This brought in between £700 and £1200 income in various years, and enabled us to inform the public about the latest happenings, encourage new members, and get petitions signed.

Office volunteers mailing out a newsletter, 1987. Laura Gubbins, Jane Gifford, Helen Steen, Administrative Officer Wendy Scott, Libby Paxton, George Paxton and Iona Steen.

Funding from local authorities

Every year, a round of applications to the local authorities had to be completed. This often involved putting together a package of financial predictions, justification for our spending, and sometimes attending an interview. It was a time-consuming process, usually co-ordinated between the chair, the treasurer and my co-worker the admin officer.

Undoubtedly, raising money is hard work. Over time, we learned that it became more efficient to split staff time. I concentrated on campaigning, and my co-worker on admin and fundraising, with the members helping with one or the other, or sometimes both.

Why local authorities should fund groups - Cllr Swithenbank

Cllr Swithenbank is the Labour leader of Northumberland County Council, which has given us donations of at least £7000 annually since 1986. He told me why they did so.

> "Very few active groups can carry on for as many years as the Druridge Bay Campaign did. Many years ago, I was chairman of the planning committee. Jack Thompson was leader of the council. (He became an MP in 1983.) Everyone in the Labour group was concerned about nuclear power at Druridge and its impact on the local deep-mining industry. Jack pointed out that as a planning authority, whether dealing directly with a planning application, or commenting on a planning application dealt with by a minister, the county council has a semi-judicial position it has to reserve. How then do ordinary people make their views known? It was on Jack's instigation that the county council funded that public opinion, to help it to function. Without that money coming in, you couldn't have kept going or been so effective. With it, you were able to run a professional campaign, keep up close contact with the media, with premises to function from.
>
> "It is easy for a power company which has access to substantial resources, offices, finance and expertise, to promote their case. How can the little people, people in the community, fight against that?

Our Campaign - Your Campaign

Sustaining a Long Campaign

Our campaign lasted from 1979 to 1997. There were groups within the movement which came and went during this eighteen years.

The greatest strength of all in retaining an active organisation was our federal structure, which was set up in 1986, and lasted until the end. Our steering committee was elected from affiliated groups. Each group decided who it would send to meetings. When that member could no longer serve, the group could put forward another person.

Thus we had a larger resource to draw from than a group of committed individuals.

It may be that a federal structure is not suitable for your campaign. In that case, you'll need to keep attracting new members by the vitality and fun of your activities.

The other essential asset for our eighteen year campaign was our funding, which enable us to run an office and employ two part-time staff. It was seven years after the original announcement before members were in a position to do this. We obtained funding from local authorities. Once we had our office, it was much easier to organise ourselves. Information and records could be stored. We had a convenient meeting place. Staff continuously worked at achieving the campaign's objectives.

Remember

Pace yourselves.

Manage your initial burst of enthusiasm carefully.

Don't lct any individual person take on too much work, even if he or she wants to. Share the jobs.

Any long-running campaign needs a base. If you possibly can, get an office. People know where to find you. You can run your affairs efficiently, store information, and have a regular meeting place.

If possible, employ staff, even if only for a few hours a week. They provide stability and continuity.

"Giving the money to you, representing the community, meant the issue was kept in the public eye, while the county council was totally detached. The pressure was kept up, and why not? Why should it be only the big boys of business with millions of pounds to spend on publicity, on events, on lobbying?

"Without this help, you would have spent so much time collecting donations, and on fundraising activities, that you would not be campaigning, and you would have burned yourselves out.

"That's not to say that councils have money to hand away willy nilly. Councils need to look at the pressure group, what its roots are, where its support is, if it's a representative, community type group. It's not an easy dividing line. We cannot give money to everyone. We have difficult financial circumstances at the moment. But I think if we can't act on behalf of our community, because of the planning reasons I've described, if we don't help, who will?"

Our organisation

Representation on the Steering Committee

Over the years, the number of affiliated groups increased from over thirty at the start in 1984 to about ninety at the height of the campaign, in the mid-80s. By the mid 90s, the number was settling at about fifty. Individual members rose to about 500 in the mid-80s, stabilising at about 300 during the 90s.

The rise and decline reflected the importance of the issues as perceived by the public. After the decision by the Government at the end of 1989, that no more nuclear power stations would be built until at least 1994, some members probably felt the threat had disappeared, or at least was not so immediate. With the start of the sand campaign, new members joined, keeping numbers healthy. There was a strong, dedicated core among the membership, both with the affiliated groups and individual and family members, who stayed faithfully with us, year in and year out.

The membership was represented on the Steering Committee in the following way. The Druridge Bay Campaign was basically set up as a federation of organisations, which were clustered into six sets - trades unions, environmental groups, political party groups, councils, parish councils, and local support groups. Each set elected among itself those to be on Steering Committee, with from four to six places for each set.

Diagram 6.1 shows the structure of the committee. Although this allowed for up to 30 members to be on the committee, there were always fewer than that. 24 would be about average. Far fewer of those members were active and turned up to meetings.

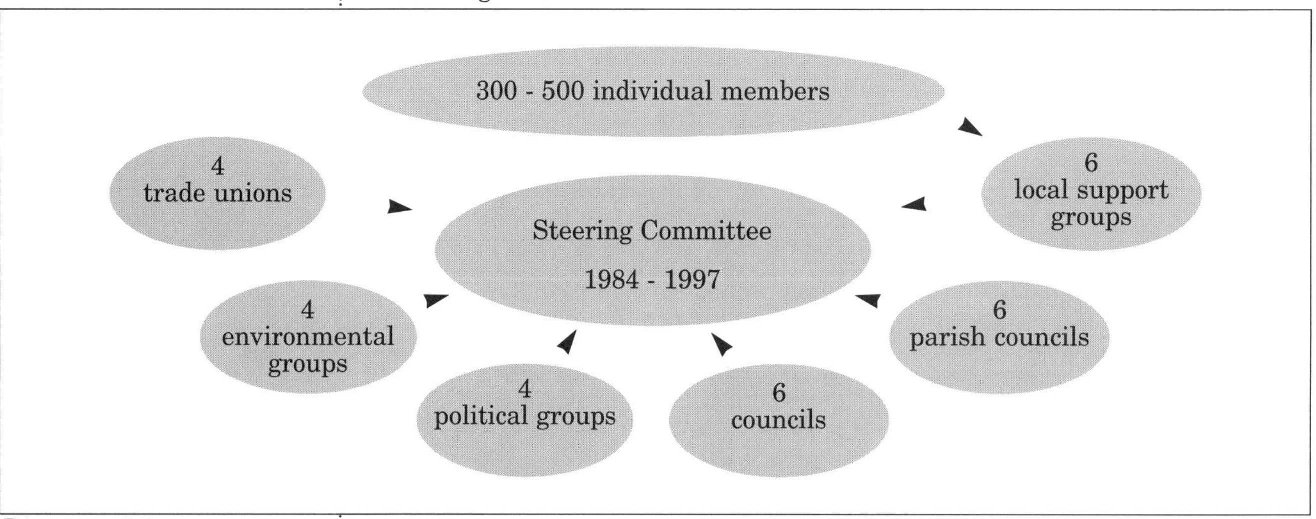

Diagram 6.1

Individual members were represented on the committee via local support groups. Indeed, if there was an enthusiastic member without a local support group, it was very easy for them to form a group, and thus be represented on the committee. All they needed was one or two others to form the group.

The organisation thus had great strengths. The elected groups could change their members, so as people got tired, changed their priorities, or for any reason could not continue, the group could put up a new representative.

The Steering Committee was the central decision-making body, where all authority lay. Members elected their own officers, chair, vice-chair, treasurer and membership secretary.

In practice, there was a generous co-option procedure. If there was ever an enthusiastic group, and the number of places in their set was filled, the Steering Committee would co-opt the group.

Places were allotted to the group rather than to a person. This was a great strength, as groups could change their representatives whenever they needed to.

Like most voluntary groups, it was more a problem trying to keep up the numbers of serving members rather than heavy competition among them to take the places.

In practice, before the AGM, I would ring round the groups, check that they wished to serve for another year, and encourage and persuade them to stand for election. If they did not want to, I would try hard to find another group to fill the gap, to ensure the committee was representative of the membership as a whole.

Over time, the attendance at Steering Committee altered. Gradually, the number of members from groups reduced, and individual members increased.

As attendance began to drop in the early 90s, we encouraged all enthusiastic individual members to attend, even if they were not elected through the formal process. If there had been a matter of constitutional importance to vote on, they could not have voted. However, as we seldom voted, this didn't matter.

The groups which remained formally on the Steering Committee received the minutes and remained supportive, even if they didn't actually attend meetings.

Attendance at Steering Committee Meetings

May	*Total*	*Groups*	*Individual members*	*Workers*
1985	10	8	0	2
1986	9	8	0	1
1987	12	6	4	2
1988	8	4	2	2
1989	11	7	2	2
1990	13	8	3	2
1991	7	3	2	2
1992	6	3	1	2
1993	5	3	1	1
1994	8	3	3	2
1995	10	3	5	2
1996	8	4	2	2
1997	6	2	2	2

Table 6.1

How we made decisions

The Steering Committee made all final decisions. The sub-groups dealt with radiation monitoring, energy and sand, and organised events. They ran their own affairs to a large extent, but would obtain Steering Committee approval for their major decisions. Most of the sub-groups had members on the Steering Committee, and knew pretty well what would be acceptable. My co-worker and I would also be in close touch with all that was going on. We were a link between the groups and the Steering Committee.

A Steering Committee meeting in the Druridge Bay Campaign office. With Jane Gifford, Wendy Scott, Cllr Janet Cann, Gordon Steel and Jonatha Robinson.

We very seldom voted. Our whole ethos was consensual. This made for a happier, non-competitive atmosphere. It was not a deliberate decision. It was just more in our nature.

The only time when we had a real internal election was when we had to choose how the Campaign should continue after the 1989 announcement of no more nuclear power stations until after 1994. Three positions were taken, and feelings were very strong. Should we close down, should we continue in the same way, or should we expand?

Hardly anyone trusted the nuclear industry enough for us go for the first option. The second option was the existing, well-tried way, and it got a fair level of support. The third option gave us more freedom to move into nuclear power and energy work, and included working on sand extraction, but meant taking the risk of making a change. This option got about two thirds of the votes.

The effect of this process caused hurt feelings and rivalries. It was the only time in the thirteen years of the Campaign that there was this antagonism. Jane Gifford, who became Chair afterwards, said that such a process should never happen again. It should be possible to make recommendations to the whole membership via the elected Steering Committee, who as usual would have discussed the issue until everyone was happy about it.

One problem was caused by the fact that I as worker had strong opinion which was different from those of the chair and vice-chair. The chair wanted to close down. The vice-chair wanted the business-as-usual option. I wanted the expanded option. I lobbied for my point of view, and because I was a worker rather than an elected member, caused some aggro. Under Jane's more conciliatory techniques, we would have worked out a different approach to the difficulty.

For thirteen years, then, our decisions were almost always made by discussion and agreement, using our the skills of our chairs, and the willingness of members to listen to each other. Our consensual approach did not mean hours and hours of discussion before decisions could be made. The key to that was good planning ahead of the meetings.

Our Campaign - Your Campaign

A Boring Meeting or Creative Interaction?

What is your idea of a meeting? Is it of pompous chairmen, minutes, points of order, droning speakers, yawning bored members watching the clock and snoozing?

Or is it of a room buzzing with lively alert people, some artistic, some technical, some handy with hammer and nails, some outrageous, some cautious. The co-ordinator or chair is guiding the members, ensuring each item is dealt with. She or he is gently controlling enthusiasms, asking for responses from the shy, and summarising the opinions expressed. The minutes-taker is carefully recording the decisions, and who will do what.

I can't say that all our meetings were as idealistic as my description, but many were. After such a meeting, the group was re-charged for action, and liberated for the fray. Off would go the members to develop the agreed strategy, working towards their goal.

In order for a meeting to be successful, the chair should be clear about the agenda, and what items must be covered. Preparation by relevant members must have been done, so that each meeting moves the campaign forward. There must be a definite closing time. One and a half hours is most people's maximum concentration time. Sometimes a social gathering afterwards brings out more campaigning ideas, and cements friendships.

You can buy books on campaigning techniques, or borrow them from your library, which will help with managing meetings. See the Bibliography.

Remember

Different groups will organise meetings in a style to suit themselves. Yours may be very formal or very informal. You'll learn what suits you by doing it.

You want your meetings to lead towards your goal. They should have clear objectives, and result in well-planned activities. Ensure that they are not merely talking shops.

Allocated tasks should be checked up from one meeting to the next. Were they done? Has something even better turned up in the mean-time?

Socialise at the end, after the business is over.

You want your members to keep coming, so meetings should be fun!

The purpose of meetings

My view of meetings is that they should be fun. They should bring together all the relevant people so that they make can decisions which result in action, and hence progress. I like a clear agenda, with the relevant actions agreed by the previous meeting progressed. Each meeting needs to conclude with clearly delineated action by named members.

When compiling the agenda ready for my chair, I always went through the minutes of the previous meeting carefully, checked that we've all done what we said we would, and tried to think of any new items that need attention. I would then go through the agenda with my chair, so that she had no unwelcome surprises, and encouraged the key people we needed to attend.

The minutes taker has always been our admin person. This job is of crucial importance. She would record every decision clearly, naming who is to do which action. Sometimes statements of principle would be made, where the wording would need to be very accurate. Examples are what could be publicly stated about our radiation monitoring knowledge following a nuclear incident, or about a sensitive issue like large windfarms.

The minutes served us as working documents. Once carefully agreed, they were available in case of people remembering decisions differently, or, much more often, to remind us all of what we said we would do.

Despite all this care, minutes have a very time-limited use. Although they may seem very clear at the time, when looking over those of previous years in preparation for writing this book, I found that many concerns which were on our minds have since been forgotten. They are not the basis upon which history could be written.

A meeting should liberate energies so that people can go off and prepare the next stage of the campaign. As a worker, I loved the advice, support and interaction our meetings engendered.

I do find myself at times at meetings other than our Druridge Bay Campaign ones where I begin to fall asleep or am tempted to throw paper pellets at droning speakers. Ours were not like that. We were all excited about the issues, and wanted to get the details right. Good planning was essential, and each meeting was a step to further development of our campaign.

The role of the chair

Some of our chairs liked to be called Chairman, most preferred Chair or Chairperson. They all knew the importance of everyone being listened to, even when as always happens, some people's contributions are not precisely to the point. They had to learn the skills of controlling those of us who become over-enthusiastic about our points of view, and needed to be kept in order. Kindness, firmness at times, friendliness, a good overview of the DBC strategy and of where the meeting needed to lead, were the important qualities.

The new chair had often served a period as vice-chair, thus gaining experience in a supportive role. Any new nervous chair always had me by her side, ready with the necessary encouragement or piece of information. Soon she would be controlling my own enthusiams, guiding, advising.

The choice of chair is of extreme importance, and as the Campaign's senior worker I always gave this matter a lot of attention. A good working relationship between the chair and me was essential for the Campaign's resulting public image which had to be carefully managed, and for the work that could be achieved. Our chairs had a two-year time-limit, though they could become vice-chairs, and later be re-elected. Just before the time to elect the chair, my closest advisors and I would talk through who we could encourage to put themselves forward for nomination. This was always managed amicably, but was necessary.

Our Campaign - Your Campaign

When People Don't Come to Meetings

This is a perennial difficulty, especially with a long-drawn-out campaign. In constrast to my "Meetings should be fun" message, I know well that over time members may take on other commitments. They move, the women become pregnant, someone in their family becomes ill. They may simply burn out. The issue has used up their creative energy.

What can you do? There are no easy answers, but here are some of the things we tried.

When attendance was clearly dropping, we would send out a friendly letter with an agenda, to arrive about a week before the next meeting. In the letter, we would discuss the urgent decisions that must be made, and why we needed help. Such a letter is more likely to attract interest than a sparse list of agenda items, and it usually resulted in more people turning up.

I learned it was a good idea to telephone the people we needed for particular agenda items, to check they had not forgotten to put the date in their diaries.

If members can't or don't want to come, I tried not to show disappointment. I would tell them we were all grateful for what they've done in the past, and be as understanding as possible about their current situation.

Remember

Try to find out if there are particular reasons for non-attendance. It could be the wrong night for many. If people have problems with baby-sitting, then maybe the children can come too. Perhaps the meeting is too early or too late. Or maybe it is too far away from home.

Be grateful. People do appreciate thanks for every task, however small, however simple. If members feel needed, they're more likely to remain active.

The cause needs everyone, even the inactive supporters. People only have a certain amount of time and energy to spare. Accept the inevitable, and keep up your positive friendly attitude.

As being chair was a hard and time-consuming job, it was more a matter of persuading a suitable candidate than competition among those keen for the post. But it was diplomatic management behind the scenes which resulted in the series of first class excellent chairs with whom I worked.

Thus through a combination of a democratic system and good management, we had an excellent committee, and any member who wanted to become more actively involved had the chance to do so.

Our public identity

The picture we portrayed of ourselves to the general public was agreed by the membership. Basically, we were non-party-political and behaved within the law. Although in the case of nuclear power, particularly in the early days, we were fighting against a right-wing government policy, we tried to bring all viewpoints on board. Members, and the public, needed only to oppose the nuclear stations at Druridge Bay, not necessarily be opposed to nuclear power.

As our membership represented every imaginable point of view, left to right, wholly rational to wholly emotional, only certain people would be authorised to make public statements on behalf of the campaign. This would be the chair, the vice-chair or me as publicity officer. If the media wanted a comment on any controversial topic, we would confer. With experience, I came to know what I could say without needing always to have these conferences. As any inaccurate public statement always comes back to haunt the speaker, often in print, there is an automatic restraint.

We always knew that our public identity had to have broad appeal across the political spectrum, but also among the local population. We tried to obtain a balance between radical thinking and acceptable but attention-attracting action. I asked two people from the Morpeth "establishment" how they and their friends perceived our campaign.

Alex Swailes is a retired head teacher, and leading light in the local operatic society, with deep roots in Northumberland. He lives with his wife, also a retired head teacher, on a smallholding in a Northumbrian village. He wrote:

> "Yours was a 'canny' campaign. The sort of folk like myself and family, whom you kept remarkably well-informed, were encouraged by, first of all the intelligent and strong arguments* which you constantly advanced, and which made absolute sense, and secondly by your energy and planning.
>
> "I remember when a group monitored the radiation levels in gardens within certain radii of the bay. Mine was one of them. I am certain that the idea of being able to check in future years, with all the implications and consequences of that, made someone somewhere say 'We'd be best out of that area. They've done their homework too well'."

Sheila King is a local magistrate, who lives with her retired gynaecologist husband in a detached house in a leafy Morpeth street.

> "I fear I have been one of the many who have been a bit ignorant of the details and facts, who have had a lukewarm interest in the campaign, but were glad that some people were protesting.
>
> "A few people thought you were odd-bods, but were glad of the result. Others were inclined to feel that we would have to have the power station somewhere.
>
> "I did admire your courage, tenacity, and your belief in what you were doing, as did many I have spoken to. The dignified way you conducted yourselves was admirable, and your persistence and dedication paid off."

* *For more details of the arguments used by the Druridge Bay Campaign, refer to Generating Pressure. See bibliography.*

Links with other campaigning groups

As Jack Thompson our MP has pointed out, our links with other groups were a great strength. Just as we had a network of members and supporters in the North East and a national VIP list, we were linked with other anti-nuclear groups across the UK.

We exchanged newsletters, visited each other on occasions, and learned from each other's experiences. This happened in the days before Internet communication and video-conferencing. It was all done by post or telephone, or meetings and conferences. It's already beginning to seem old-fashioned.

We also had regular contact with groups campaigning against nuclear power in the USA, France, Austria and Slovakia.

In 1995, I was invited to Oldenburg University in Germany, to talk about anti-nuclear groups in the UK, which I did from the perspective of the Druridge Bay Campaign. They wanted to know how such groups network.

Diagram 6.2 shows how we related to the other networks. The marginal notes give details about the groups on the diagram as they were in 1995.

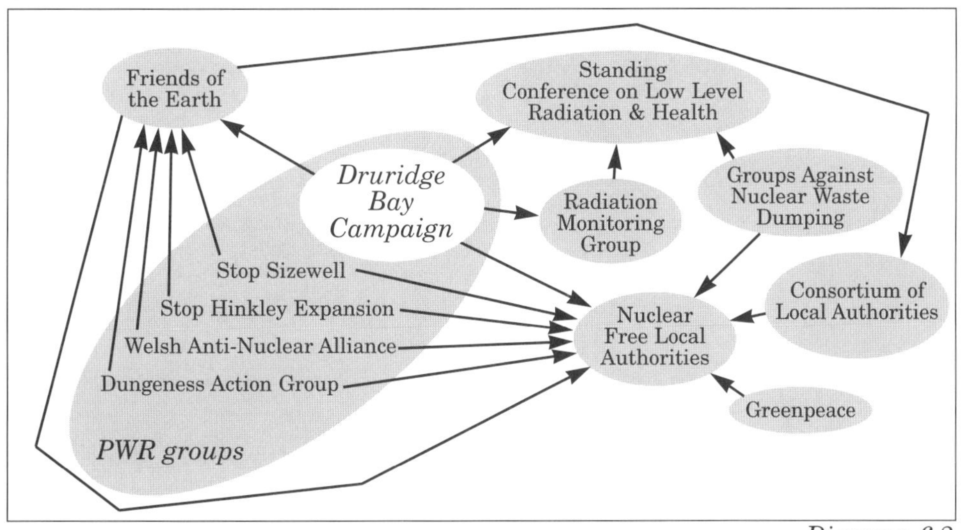

Diagram 6.2

What webs were spun! Contacts endlessly coming together, and interacting for brief periods, then loosened or lost. The common thread was concern for the planet, and the need to expose the danger of nuclear power.

Friends of the Earth
Campaigning on nuclear power and waste. 250 local groups and 60 Energy Activist groups.

Greenpeace
Campaigning on nuclear power, reprocessing and solar energy. 220 local groups.

Nuclear Free Local Authorities
Campaigning on nuclear power, re-processing and waste. 100 - 120 local councils across the UK.

Consortium of Local Authorities
Campaigning on nuclear power (particularly on the economic aspects). 20 local councils in South Wales and South West England.

PWR Network
Campaigning to stop the building of new nuclear power stations. Five local networks.

Standing Conference on Low Level Radiation and Health
50 radiation monitoring groups, nuclear power campaigns and health groups. Hundreds of individuals.

Groups against nuclear dumping
Various local networks at different times. Overlaps with other anti-nuclear groups.

Our membership scheme

The Druridge Bay Campaign started out as a federation of groups. The annual membership fees were set at £50 for local authorities and other public bodies; £20 for regional organizations and those with over 100 members, and £10 for organizations with under 100 members.

These amounts remained fairly constant. We had to balance the orginal enthusiasm of the early campaign with the reality of the long timescale, and the general feeling of financial depression in the late 80s. Individual members paid between £8 and £2. For this, they received newsletters three to four times a year, which showed every way in which they could become more involved, and all about our fairs, activities and lobbying.

Evolution of the groups

The DBC's overall activities centred on the Steering Committee, which was the constant factor in the comings and going of groups, over thirteen years.

Diagram 6.3 shows how the various groups related to the centre. At times they would spin off relatively independently, as the Sand Group and the Energy Group did, and then gradually come back to the centre after their output was diverted, or their main work was done.

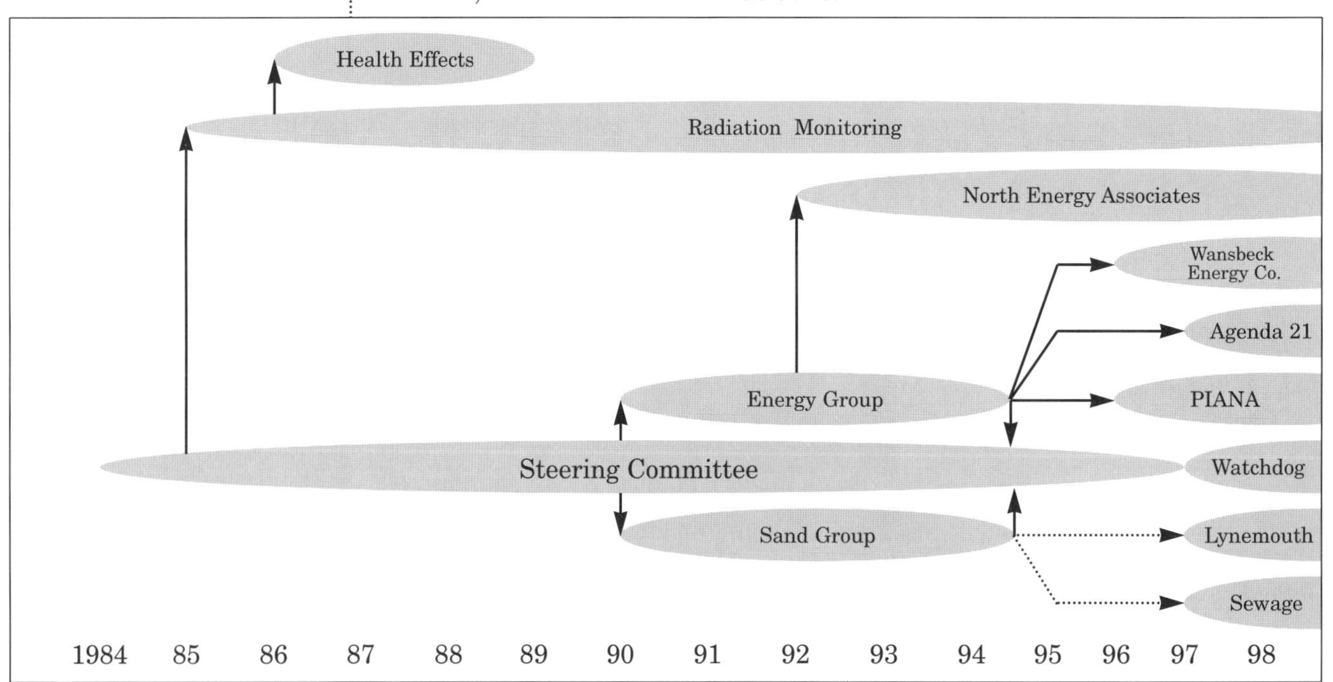

Diagram 6.3

The Radiation Monitoring Group got on with its monitoring programme, only reporting to Steering Committee from time to time. Its remit of measuring background radiation at fixed points, and of checking for unusual emissions, was fairly unvaried. Libby Paxton and Toni Stephenson's work on health effects of radiation was linked to this group, but it only lasted for a short time for reasons explained earlier.

The Energy Group's work threw off two organizations, one of which is a new pressure group, PIANA, and one of which is an ongoing renewables consultancy, North Energy Associates. Its ideas fed into the Wansbeck Energy Company, and into Northumberland's Agenda 21 Energy Group.

Now that the DBC's main aims are achieved, we are returning to the status of a voluntary group, without office and staff, but with an alert membership which will campaign on other environmental issues associated with Druridge Bay. Principally, we will remain ready to tackle the return of the nuclear threat. The land has been drilled, and proved suitable. Nuclear power station sites are few and far between. The global and national energy situation may change. We are keeping our records and membership alive.

Philippa Young of Tyne Tees TV interviews Druridge Bay Campaign chair, Libby Paxton, about an engineers' report stating that erosion caused by sand extration was irreversible. March 1997.

Protest and the Media

Chapter 7

Media stunts for the whole community

I greatly admire the tree-protestors and the airport tunnellers. Their style and commitment are superb. They achieved a level of awareness-raising of historic importance, even if the bypasses are built, the runway constructed. Their methods are those of people who reject many of the extremes of materialistic society, as I do.

Not all groups of people are comfortable with those styles of protest. Our campaign had to reflect the views of the whole spectrum of a regional population. Some of our members would do more outrageous actions, some the amusing ones, and others would be happy organising fairs. We had to pace our energies too, over many many years. Most people had to keep jobs or find jobs, and look after their families. We were a locally-rooted campaign, unlike the footloose road-protestors who could move from one site to another. Our techniques had to be accessible to many.

Our media stunts were not as dramatic as those of the headline gathering Newbury by-pass protestors, or as daring as those of the underground tunnellers. Our relationship with the media was nevertheless of fundamental importance, and showed what relatively mainstream folk can achieve.

The media as a power for good

Without any doubt, the media in the North East have been an enormous power for good. By reporting on our campaigns, they have helped to bring about our successes. This is not to say that they have always sided with us. They have always had to report the issues objectively, but at the same time reflect the views and concerns of the local people.

The Druridge Bay Campaign was the principal route through which local concern about the nuclear power stations proposal, and about sand extraction at the bay, was expressed.

Communicating in two directions

We communicated in two different directions through the local media. Firstly, we informed decision-makers in local and national government, and in the Ready Mixed Concrete group, of what we wanted to achieve. Secondly, we informed the public of the latest state of play. Hundreds or thousands of people probably followed our cause with sympathy, others we assumed we would gradually bring round, and others probably disagreed or were indifferent.

We knew that the North East public took an interest by the ready way in which the media followed our stories. We knew that the decision-makers read our newspaper coverage, as they would be supplied with newspaper cuttings. Certain companies provide a cuttings service, which selects topics on whatever issue is required, for relevant bodies. For example, at North Energy Associates, we receive the British Wind Energy Association's cuttings service every fortnight. We get every pro- and anti-windfarm mention in the national and local papers, including the letters pages. This is how I know the sort of service that is received by government departments, or a company such as RMC.

Thus, issuing a press release, getting a letter printed on the letters page, or organising an action which would be reported by local media, were the surest ways of being seen and heard. In terms of time spent, and influence gained, communicating through the media is the simplest and most effective of all methods of reaching both target audiences.

An example of how we communicated in both directions is when pressuring energy minister Tim Eggar to sell the land. We got ourselves on TV and in the local papers by demonstrating outside Morpeth post office with our banner and a giant postcard which we sent to him. Thus we reached our public, building and maintaining our support base. At the same time, we reached the decision-makers directly by the postcard itself, and indirectly via our media coverage. This simple action took only a morning to prepare, and the efforts of a dozen or so volunteers turning out for an hour.

The same procedure happened shortly after that, when the 40,000 signature petition was taken to London, with a send-off in the Central Station. Often an action such as this, informing both our own North East public and the minister, would be planned at a meeting a week or two beforehand, with last-minute ringing round to find a willing piper and volunteers to come to the station to carry the banners. Simple, effective actions like this would get as much media coverage as large events which take hours of organising.

How did we know the media would come?

We could never tell accurately which events or issues the media would cover. It was always a gamble. Some actions which we thought fascinating would result in very little coverage. Others would attract TV, to our suprise. Sometimes BBC would come, sometimes Tyne Tees. Again, we never quite knew why. To a large

Our Campaign - Your Campaign

How to Start Building up Press Contacts

Let's assume you have never contacted the press before. Where do you start? How do you build up a network of friendly newspeople?

First, study the local and regional papers to find out which reporters cover activities in your area and your kind of story.

Get the newspapers' main phone numbers, ring them and ask for a particular reporter or the newsdesk. Tell them about your new campaign and ask if they would like to be kept informed about what you are doing. To whom should you address your press release? Tell them you are new to campaigning and ask their advice. (They'll have a story out of you in no time.) Once you've made the contact, you've got friends.

Approach the local TV and radio stations in the same way.

National newspapers are much harder to interest, but again check them to see which reporters cover your kind of story. There is nothing to stop you phoning the newspaper and asking for the reporter by name.

The busier and more high-profile the media, the more exceptional your story or campaign must be. Sometimes, when they speak to you, the national or TV reporters give off a sense of their self-importance, their bustle and their deadlines, which makes your story feel insignificant. At other times, they like your story and then they are extremely helpful and polite, even ingratiating, until they get what they want.

Most reporters however are friendly and considerate. They like people and they like stories, which is why they are in their job. They get the best stories out of people by being kind and encouraging, and their contact list is their most important asset.

Remember

They need you and you need them.

It's a subtle balance.

With practice you will learn who to phone and how far to push.

extent, it depended on what other items were competing for attention on the day. We had to plan in the hope that we would be covered, but be prepared for disappointment.

One disappointment was our House of Commons meeting in December 1994, which we had organised with Alan Beith, arranging for speakers, including our own on nuclear under-insurance, to brief MPs. We had felt confident that this would attract TV, and had a good visual display of members with enlarged £5 notes on banners, representing the amount of compensation the average member of the public would get following a nuclear accident. It didn't attract TV, though it did get coverage in *The Journal*. Lots of members had travelled to London for this event. It was successful in terms of contacts made and experience gained in lobbying by our members, but not as a media event. You take a chance, but you don't always succeed.

To cover for the worst eventuality, no coverage at all, I always had my little compact camera in my pocket. Sometimes I would arrange for one of our members to take photos. The one-hour processing service in Morpeth came in handy. I could get the films developed and to the local newspapers to meet deadlines. These had a high chance of being used. As the free papers have very low budgets for photographers, they in particular would often use my pictures. Examples of two simple actions which brought out no reporters were the April Fool Green Duffer award to RMC's chairman, and the Halloween action of scaring away the digger. My own pictures were used by local papers, after no reporters turned up.

Combining all these techniques meant that virtually every action we ran got some cover. We would get perhaps one or two newspapers, and in the case of the more spectacular events, maybe that plus one television station and radio. At the key moments such as the great successes, we would get both TV stations competing to do the best coverage.

Most effective in terms of public attention were picture stories in the papers, or TV coverage. In between times, there were many opportunities to send out comments as written press releases, or letters to the letters pages, which kept the issues alive.

A summary of the number of press releases issued is shown in Table 7.1 (below). The lower number in later years is balanced by the fact that by this time, the media regularly contacted me first, or we would hatch up stories together.

I have nine bulging ring files of cuttings of newspaper coverage we initiated over the years since 1983. We could not afford newspaper cuttings services of course, so there will be quite a few which we never tracked down.

DBC Press Releases

Year	Releases	Year	Releases
1985	47	1991	16
1986	37	1992	15
1987	49	1993	20
1988	36	1994	11
1989	29	1995	14
1990	15	1996	20
		TOTAL	309

DBC Media Coverage

Newspaper cover at estimated 3 per press release=	927
TV appearances per year (guestimate)=	4
Radio commentaries per year (guestimate)=	6

Table 7.1

Our Campaign - Your Campaign

Your Press Release

The simplest and most powerful way to communicate with your opponents, your supporters and the general public is through the media. You attract media interest through the press release. It must be clear and interesting.

It should be on your identifiable headed notepaper and must have the date, the words 'Press Release' and a heading summarising its content. It should be on one side of a sheet of A4 if possible.

Don't agonise too much over the heading. Whatever you put the sub-editors will invent a new one.

On the opening paragraph, you need to say *what* you are doing, *who* is doing it, *where* the action is taking place, *when* it is happening and *why* you are doing it. These key words are the five Ws of journalism.

The press release does not always have to be about an event. One of your expert supporters may want to express an opinion. You may be sending a letter to your opponent, or have received one. You may be feeling miserable, delighted or outraged by a new development. The possibilities are endless.

It is useful to include a quote. Study how the newspapers use quotes and copy the style. You'll quickly learn that people seldom talk exactly as their words appear in the press. Reporters tidy up the quotes, without (in theory) changing the meaning of what has been said. You can do the same. Contact your chairperson or member to be quoted, take notes and turn the words into a neat couple of sentences. Or do it other way around, by preparing the quote and then checking that the person would like to say those words.

Being able to write a press release at very short notice is one of your advantages over your opponents and also over councils or organisations who support you. Of course what you write must be accurate and should be agreed with your chairperson, but you don't have to get every word double-checked by a long chain of command.

It is essential to include the phone number of contact persons at the end of the press release, who between them should be available round the clock. They should be trusted to answer any press queries without being tempted into making outrageous statements which will later embarrass you.

The press releases can be hand delivered, posted, faxed or sent by e-mail. You need to check when the newspaper deadlines are, especially for the weeklies. For my non-urgent press releases, I found getting them all out by Monday midday caught all the local weeklies' deadlines as well as being generally useful for the dailies. In other cases they would be timed to the event and to which particular media I was targeting.

Remember

Having a quick efficient means of contacting the media is one of the strongest weapons in your armoury. Devise your system and use it well.

We know they received our media messages

RMC always knew about our events because the press would ring them up. Tim Stokes, their public relations executive, told us that it was often quite late when they found out what we were up to, so there wasn't a lot of time to come up with a response. When King Canute and his court paraded through the streets of Yarm, Tim had come up to Cleveland from London to be there. When we asked him if he had been sent up, he said he wanted to come. It was part of his job. He told us he knew of everything we managed to get in the local press via his cuttings service. Thus, on the many occasions when we had no direct contact with RMC, details of our public statements, our letters, our marches, all reached headquarters.

In the next chapter, I report how Rex Melville from Magnox Electric told us that his chairman, John Collier, knew all about the Druridge Bay Campaign. Considering that we had very little direct contact with him, he can only have known the details via our media coverage, and his cuttings service. So whereas writing or communicating directly with one's opponents is part of the role of the pressure group, informing the media has a much more powerful impact. The opponents know that thousands of people beside themselves are being informed.

An academic view of media and environmental groups

In their book *Environmental Groups in Politics*, Philip Lowe and Jane Goyder make the following comments.

> "Good contacts with the media are vital if a group is to generate support for its aims. They can also be an important campaigning weapon for enviromental groups in putting pressure on civil servants, ministers and parliamentarians.
>
> "The media have not simply been passive recorders of environmental events, but active agents, investigating issues, giving prominence to the views of environmentalists and conducting their own campaigns."

The writers point out three main objectives for environmental groups to achieve via the media. These are

- to maintain support, among their own activists and membership, and to bring in new recruits
- to influence an impending decision by those in power
- to improve the climate of opinion through long-term educational and propaganda campaigns.

Our Campaign - Your Campaign

When the Media Don't Turn Up

You will nearly always get some media coverage if your cause has popular appeal and if your event has some of the following characteristics:

- your press release has a good story line
- it's a 'first time' action
- you have a VIP coming
- you've prepared good visual effects

You can improve your chances by informing as many media people as possible; from daily, weekly and free papers and local TV and radio. If you think your event is very brilliant and original, you may want to inform national papers too.

Only inform TV and radio for your more spectacular events. They need the strongest possible story lines and you don't want to bore them.

It is worth phoning the newsdesks the day before, to check that they have received your press release. It is helpful to know in advance if TV people are planning to come.

If all this fails and no-one turns up, don't despair. Ensure that one of your members is ready with a camera. Ask your group to line up theatrically, faces to the camera and children to the forefront, and take your own pictures. As well as group pictures, choose one or two key people and take closer-up pictures showing clearly what you are doing. Make sure that the slogans on banners can be read. Note down everyone's names, from left to right and the ages of the children.

Rush your film to a one-hour processing shop and while waiting, telephone your friendly reporters. Ask if they would like to see your pictures and offer to personally deliver them. You have a good chance of your local and free papers using them.

Remember

A well planned event will almost always lead to some publicity.

The media need you as much as you need them.

Bearing these comments in mind, I turned the tables on some of those reporters who have frequently interviewed me, and asked them for their views on the Druridge Bay Campaign's effectiveness. I also asked them to give advice to groups seeking media coverage.

Adrian Pitches, BBC TV Look North's environment reporter

I interviewed him after he'd interviewed me, out at the bay, on the day when we erected a plaque near the former digging site, commemorating the end of sand extraction. A keen birdwatcher, he had his binoculars out too, because there was a rare Temnick's Stint on one of the ponds.

"I've been with Look North as the environment reporter between 1989 and 1991. Then I was off for a spell, before coming back north. I remember many of your stunts, with King Canute, your actions at the sand extraction site. I've also been out a number of times to Druridge to do stories on the nuclear issue. You used pegs like the radiation monitoring programme and Chernobyl, with the Cairn in the backdrop.

"You've managed to keep the nuclear and sand issues going along hand in hand. The sand digging was more of a visual story, simply because we can see it going on. The nuclear power station was a less conspicuous threat, with a field which may one day have a power station, but it's not been as obvious as seeing a digger down on the beach. It was a more difficult story to portray.

"Of course I am interested in environmental issues, but I try to divorce that interest from my reporting. I have to retain my impartiality as a BBC journalist, to reflect both sides whatever my feelings might be. But certainly my interest in Druridge Bay - I come here to do birdwatching - has meant that I've always been keen to do stories when there was a new development.

"There have been times when you've staged events, and we have decided it's not necessarily anything new. Perhaps it was an anniversary you were marking, and we decided we were not coming out. But whenever I could, and whenever there was a genuine news peg, I've been keen to come.

"I think the Druridge stories were important ones. So many people from Tyneside and beyond use the bay as an amenity, an asset they like to enjoy. It's not just a story about a limited group of people, but a story that resonates for many others. That's why it's important to the BBC too. Clearly, if we can put out a story that appeals to a large audience, it achieves our aims better than if it appeals only to a minority.

"You certainly managed to garner a good level of public support. You kept the profile up commendably, considering you're a relatively small group with limited resources and no doubt limited time. You've got your message across very well, continually banging on about the twin issues of the bay. And to a degree you've had a sympathetic media. *The Journal,* the local weeklies, other broadcasters have all been keen to report the campaign. You were pushing on an open door, but you had to keep pushing.

Our Campaign - Your Campaign

An Event at Short Notice

You may suddenly find that your opponent is putting in the dreaded planning application, or the House of Commons is debating a topic of relevance to you, or a VIP is coming to your town. You have two days notice, what do you do?

This is when you need all your carefully acquired resources:

- Your contacts book. You must phone round quickly to decide on your action with key committee members and then gather people to help you. Very often you will need people who are available in the daytime. Members who are prepared to bring young children are especially important.
- Your printing or photocopying facilities. It is likely that you'll need to produce a briefing document, a poster or a leaflet.
- Your press contacts. As soon as you have planned what you will do, inform them. Quickly write a press release, with date, time, place and one or more person's phone number. Phone the newsdesks. Make sure that the contact persons between them are available round the clock.
- Your banners, flags and placards.

We often had to act extremely quickly. One time we were told that Walter Marshall, chairman of the CEGB, was flying north from Hartlepool nuclear power station to Torness by helicopter, more or less over Druridge Bay. After a few phone calls, half a dozen of our members and *The Journal* photographer were on their way to the Bay. We marked out one of our slogans DRURIDGE? NO! on giant letters on the sand and dug out the words. The photographer guided us where to do it, so that he could get the elevation he needed, from the top of a high sand dune.

It didn't matter whether or not Walter Marshall did see the message in reality. He or his staff would certainly have seen the newspaper coverage, as would the public at large.

Remember

A simple, well timed action can be just as effective as a costly or complex media event planned far in advance.

"You got the support of a network of people who you'll probably never know, people who have seen you on TV, and read your comments in the press. The media spotlight moved your profile along, and helped to generate local goodwill.

"Your campaign did lead to the end of sand extraction. RMC is a big company with its own corporate objectives. The reason it decided to stop when it did may well have been political. It may have seen the writing on the wall, that there may be a change of government. That a new government would be far more sympathetic to your concerns, and to those of the Labour-controlled county council. But they're also aware that companies need green PR these days. It's something they have to come to terms with. When they realised they had another sand extraction site about to come on stream at Wooperton, and that other sites they were prospecting elsewhere around the county would be included in the next minerals local plan, they realised it would be very good PR for them to come up with this dramatic move. And it would satisfy you.

"But if there hadn't been the alternative supplies of sand, and they have the permission at Druridge to go on well into the next century, I don't think they would have stopped, whatever your protestations. When you come down to it, it's harsh economics that dominate.

"What tips can I offer to other campaigns? It helps to have a photogenic attractive area to protect. It would be an uphill struggle if you have an unattractive area which not many people visit.

"The sand extraction situation was very unusual, if not unique in the UK. It's certainly unusual for a beach to be demolished like that. You had all the ingredients for an interesting story.

"At the same time, there's the element of timing. If a group phones up every week, eventually the reporters would get fed up, and say 'Leave us alone, we've done your story.' However if you *ration* the way you do these things, say doing something new every couple of months, and have a good reason for coming back to us, you're more likely each time to get coverage.

"It's a multi-faceted thing. You have to have a campaign which resonates with the media who are reporting it. You have to have something important to protect, and you have to say interesting things about it. If you have all those factors on board, you're probably ultimately - *ultimately* - going to have a successful campaign. Which indeed you did."

Barbara Henderson, Radio Newcastle's Northumberland reporter

I interviewed her at her home near Morpeth. Friendly and relaxed, expecting a new baby in a couple of months, she has followed our stories for years. She has interviewed us at Druridge, and visited us in our homes or the DBC office.

"What you did particularly well was that you were always available at the drop of a hat, which for radio and other media is the essential thing. You have to able to respond to moves on the national scene. You were always prepared to be interviewed on national issues, from the perspective of Druridge Bay. That was nice.

"Also your own protests were very well organised. You always thought ahead about the timings, about what would look good on TV, what would sound good. You always had the right people there, ready to be interviewed, all lined up. You made our job very easy.

“You were also good at keeping the sand and nuclear issues separated. You didn’t fuddle them.

“For a radio reporter, the important thing groups need to keep in mind is sound. Druridge Bay is a good subject. Even if I’m interviewing you in your office I could always go out and get seaside sounds, so that it sounded like we did the interview at Druridge Bay. I do have pre-recorded sounds if I need them. But I liked doing interviews on the dunes, or with the sand digger in the background - that sounded really good.

“From the point of view of radio, we have to paint a picture using the noise, so anything you can do that lends itself to a nice noisy background rather than a person speaking in an office with a dead sound around it - that’s what I want.

“Also you were clearly in command of your subject. When we spoke to you, we always felt confident you could answer any question put to you by a layperson. You were not just people getting cross about something in your own back yard who didn’t know the issues. I felt you knew what you were talking about, you had gone into the subject in some depth. We could carry out quite detailed interviews, which came across well.

“As well as knowing the topic, the people we interview need to be able to speak coherently, which you did. Fiona always did. There are people we have to go to because of their position who we dread interviewing. They run out before the end of their sentence, or their accent is very thick. They just don’t sound good at all. So simply having a good speaker is important.

“And once we got to know you, and knew we could rely on a good interview, that helped to get us out the next time.

“You also kept up a good level of public support. You kept the pot boiling, kept the stories going. It was a continuous live issue. We are aware when people are following an issue. We get a response. People may ring up, and ask how they can get in touch with someone on the programme. Or they will say, I heard what you said and I don’t agree with it. It’s not so much from our records that I can tell you this, but from my feelings about the reaction of the listeners.

“Then my editor would encourage me. If I said the Druridge Bay Campaign is doing such-and-such, he would say ‘Oh yes fine. Do that one.’ It was always considered a hot issue.

“I think you certainly had influence. For example, if I rang RMC or a planning officer at County Hall, they were very aware of your existence and what you were saying about the issues. Not only aware of you, but of the last thing you had said. You were making your mark with them. I can’t say whether or not you eventually affected their decisions, but certainly they were aware of you and would refer to you.

“When RMC turned to Ingram, and the new pressure group started there, I got the impression that they turned to you, that they could learn from you.

"On the nuclear issue, people have very set views. I always know what side somebody is on. You Druridge campaigners put your arguments across very forcefully. I remember the one I did with you about nuclear insurance. That was a national issue that made a lot of people raise their eyebrows, an issue they were not aware of. People should have known about it, but they didn't. You were able to make people question it at quite a high level.

"Tips for other campaigns? They must think in terms of what will *sound* good. Not that you have an important point to make, but how it will get across so that people will actually listen to it, not say 'Oh this is very dull' and switch off. You have to come up with the tricks, the rallies, the press conferences, having regular speakers, being prepared to co-operate with us, responding to things as they happen. To give and take a bit."

Tony Henderson, *The Journal* environment reporter

The Journal *is the North East regional morning daily paper. It has a circulation of 60,000, and 80,000 on Saturday, when Tony Henderson* has his own Environment Page. If I had to give a prize to one reporter of the many excellent ones I came to know, it would be to Tony. We chatted in a bar at the newspaper office.*

"I would like to think that *The Journal*'s coverage really helped to stop sand extraction. Each copy of the paper is read by three to four people, that means 200,000 every day. People can read things once and then forget it. But if a topic is in time and time again, if it's persistent, then it takes root in people's minds.

"And if a paper is giving a topic persistently high profile coverage, radio and TV think it's important. They tend to feed off the papers. It snowballs.

"The big companies like RMC can ignore individual pressure groups. But in these PR-conscious days, they hate the constant drip, drip, drip of bad publicity. Once the penny drops that a newspaper is going to be persistent in its campaign, they know it's only a matter of time before they have to do something. The sheer relentless role of publicity plays its part.

"Of course the campaign group has to produce the substance for the stories. The flow of stuff was very good. Particularly the AGM action, that was great. And the pensioners who sat in front of the digger. Even putting up new signs. Anything that made a picture. And the papers give the issue the oxygen of publicity. It doesn't leave the company any room for manoeuvre.

"You would feed me ideas, and I could suggest things to you. It was a joint thing. Obviously the DBC was the main source, but I could look for other things which didn't involve you. A newspaper which runs a campaign, as *The Journal* did on sand extraction, will pick up stories from any arena. I would say to myself

* *Tony Henderson is not related to Barbara Henderson*

‘What’s worrying people about this activity? Erosion!’ So I’d go to the Country Park warden. He’d mention sand martins, so next I’d go to the wildlife trust. The National Park would comment. The Tourist Board. It takes on a life of its own. People start writing in to the letters page.

“Do I enjoy my influence? If I’m writing about about a legitimate concern, if I’m concerned about it, it’s a big plus. We like to achieve results. It’s rare that a reporter can do that. Every one of us likes to do positive stories, but it’s not always possible.

“There are only two or three times where I can personally look back and say ‘That was a major success’. Newspapers are often knocked for being negative, for looking for sensation, for intruding into people’s lives. It’s nice to do something where everyone would agree on objectives, for the environment, the community, for ordinary people who feel powerless against bigger forces. Sometimes it can be done.

“If you do make enough noise, if you are persistent, small groups of people can have an effect against very big firms. It’s difficult for ordinary people on the ground to get through to these big organizations. How do you get past the secretary? How do you get to the managing director? It’s obviously easy for newspapers to do it. Using newspapers is a very important weapon in the armoury of groups who have a genuine cause for concern.

“You ask what influence I think the Druridge Bay Campaign had on ending the nuclear threat to the bay? I think it was absolutely essential. If the Druridge Bay Campaign hadn’t taken it up, who would have? You kept up that consistent target. Despite fighting sand extraction in parallel, the nuclear thing was never allowed to drop out of sight. You always said ‘Yes, sand extraction is important, but the nuclear power threat was the original one, and it’s still there’. Although *The Journal* concentrated on the sand issue for a year or so, we still sometimes did nuclear power stories.

“Immediately RMC made their first statement that sand extraction would eventually stop, at the end of 1993, at *The Journal* we said ‘Right, that one’s down. Now the nuclear ogre is still in the background’. If the Druridge Bay Campaign had not kept going on the nuclear issue, it might never have been resolved, the land might never have been sold.

“I know a lot of commentators have said that stopping the nuclear power stations building programme was nothing to do with local campaigns. It was because the nuclear industry was privatised. The city people wouldn’t buy it. The Government said it was putting no money into new nuclear power stations. There could have been no nuclear power station at Druridge whether you had existed or not. These points have some truth. But they’re all pieces of a jigsaw. All parts that add up to a greater whole. The unease, the groundswell of opposition to nuclear power among the population has been a contributory factor. Bound to have been.

“Financial matters, yes they came into play, and what was to be done with nuclear waste, the decommissioning costs. Finally people realised that nuclear power wasn’t going to turn the lights on for nothing, which was promised in the 50s.

“Grassroots pressure contributed. It always makes politicians uneasy. If anything, it keeps the issue in the public eye. The topic is consistently troublesome. So when politicians have to consider it, in financial terms, or productivity terms, or dangerous waste terms, they’re constantly aware that people are watching them. It’s in their mind. It’s not something they can deal with in a small dark room and no-one’s going to realise what’s happening. If an issue is consistently high on the agenda, that counts for a lot.

“Even a local group, acting in a local area, counts. You were part of the network of groups round the country. The overall force would be weaker if each voice hadn’t combined its strength. It’s like the bundle of reeds that symbolised the Roman Republic. It’s easy to snap one, but you can’t snap the whole bundle.

“The politicians begin to think ‘Shouldn’t we be looking at nuclear power more analytically instead of blundering on?’ The biggest surprise to me was the NIREX decision, not to allow the underground rock laboratory. Just sheer persistent questioning from Cumbrians Opposed to a Radioactive Environment, a small but effective group, from Cumbria County Council, from the National Park. They gave relentless pressure, so that in the end, the Government said ‘We just can’t do it.’ Every five years the politicians know they have to stand for re-election.

“The media is the way the local groups get their views out. Their coverage is essential. Local newspapers must act in a thorough, professional way, and radio and TV follow. There is a danger that some newspapers may do it in a superficial, exaggerated way. But it’s the duty of a local paper to get the tone right. To report thoroughly, responsibly and intelligently. To give both sides. To give balance. Every time I did an RMC story, I went to poor old Chris Leese, their estates manager. ‘Sorry, I’m back again.’ To give him his due, I knew he was doing his job. And he knew I was just doing mine. In the end, relationships were fairly cordial.

“*The Journal* did take a position, that sand extraction was ‘A Bad Thing’. Our leader writers showed that, and the SAVE OUR BAY logo. But at the same time we had to be balanced. Not everybody who reads the paper takes the side of the pressure group. Some will think nuclear power is the best thing since sliced bread. They think pressure groups are ex-hippies, fringe loonies, mental, open-toed sandals. Often people would approach me and say ‘Everybody lives in a house, everybody wants to drive on a road, everybody needs sand. Who the hell uses that windswept beach anyway?’ It’s a large constituency who need to be persuaded. They won’t be if they read something that’s not balanced. People don’t like to be hectored or lectured to. If people have leanings the other way, at least they’ll sit down and read the story because it has both sides. They can come to the story fresh. They see Druridge Bay Campaign says this, the company says that. We give them the chance to say ‘What do you think?’

"Sometimes I would give the company the stage. I would tell them 'You can say what you like'. They would think 'Gosh, what *do* we say?' And sometimes they would say the wrong thing. 'It's none of your business. Go away'.

"You ask why it was hard for you to get things in the national papers? They are so London-based, with an enormous southern and south-eastern bias. Things which happen in the North East or Scotland are seen as remote, they're not interested. The Sunday heavies are full of stories about the tube, Hampstead dinner parties, what wine you drink with this or that. They never get off their backsides and come up to the North East. The heavies are dominated by big sweep, broad brush topics, Northern Ireland, Europe, BSE. It's not often localised causes get in.

"Plus the tabloids are not reflective of real life at all. They reflect a crazy world where soap operas are the real world. The stories are about TV.

Bridget Gubbins at Druridge Bay with The Journal's *petitions against sand extraction, before taking them to London.*

"Local newspapers serve and reflect the local community. That's their strength.

"What tips can I offer local environmentalists to help them be effective with the media? The first thing is to form a group, and give yourself a name. To decide what is your target, what you are concerned about. What do you plan to do about it? What do you hope to achieve? You must get a very clear idea about your target.

"Once you have that, you are ready to get in touch with all branches of the media, local, weekly, daily and regional newspapers, TV and radio. There are two ways. You can write to the editor, or news editor. Follow the letter up with a call. You ask to speak to the editor or news editor. Ask 'Did you get my letter? Are you interested? Do you want to talk about it?' Make sure they have the names and contact numbers. Any newspaper worth its salt will follow that up.

"It is a big help if you can get one or two journalists who will follow the story long term, if you can develop a relationship and keep in close touch. Give them as much information as possible.

"You shouldn't worry about bothering us if you ring up. Many people are naturally shy. People sometimes ring me up and say 'Sorry to bother you'. But sometimes things happen and I say to them 'Why didn't you tell me?' They reply 'I didn't like to bother you. I didn't think it was important enough'. Every journalist would rather hear than not hear. We get lots of calls with which we have a lot of sympathy. If they say 'We're planting trees', well it's great. It makes a real contribution. But I can't do 50 tree planting stories in a year, with 50 photos. So not everything's going to make it, but a good proportion will.

"It's best to approach the editor or news editor first. They're the ones who decide what's going to be covered. But there's no hard and fast rule. If you know a reporter, you can ring them and they can go to the news editor and say 'I've got this story. I want to report it'.

"You can use press releases and faxes, and follow them up with a phone call. If you phone first, I am likely to say 'Great! Can you send me a fax?'

"We welcome stunts. Newspapers and especially TV have a constant hunger for pictures. Visual things are important. King Canute - that was great visual stuff. Not just people standing with their arms folded on a beach. We need something that will grab attention.

"Newspapers aren't doing their job if they don't serve the community, and don't reflect its fears, concerns and hopes. Local people and local campaigners should realise their newspaper is there to be used. It's their platform. It's their shop window."

Vince Gledhill, *Evening Chronicle* reporter

Vince Gledhill is the Northumberland reporter for the North East regional evening newspaper. He has reported the Druridge issue for nearly 20 years. He wrote this short piece for me, in response to my letter.

"Publicity was always seen as a crucial weapon in the battle that the Druridge Bay Campaign set out to win. But publicity is an unstable weapon liable to backfire. Over-the-top actions can in the short term capture headlines, but in the long term can also damage the legitimacy of a campaign group and cloud the serious message it may want to put across.

"For almost 20 years, the Druridge Bay campaigners succeeded in that most tricky of balancing acts. The attention-grabbing escapades were sometimes enjoyable events in their own right, such as family galas and fun runs. Unfortunately, while they were popular with participants, their news value was limited, particularly for the larger daily newspapers where column inches are at a premium and equally worthy news stories have to compete for the same space.

"Similarly the more often the same event is repeated, the less chance it has to catch the attention of journalists. So the task for the DBC was to keep its name and its causes in the headlines by coming up with a variety of stories. It was a task DBC managed through a range of serious and non-serious events. They ranged from meetings with government ministers in London to present hard

Our Campaign - Your Campaign

Preparing Theatrical Actions

Everyone needs to be very clear what is expected of them, when preparing dramatic actions. At our planning meeting, we would agree who would carry the banners, who would wheel the pushchairs, who would talk to the press, who would bring the camera. Exact time and place details must be worked out. It's a good idea to ensure that every participant has this in writing.

If the action has to be planned at short notice and there's no time for a planning meeting, key members or staff will need to work out the details by discussion on the phone and then circulate written arrangements to all concerned.

The police must be informed if street or roads are the site of the action. We always found ours to be helpful.

At the event, as our campaign's employee, I was often bustling around rather like a stage director, making sure things worked visually, that everyone knew their cue, organising people for photocalls, making myself helpful to the media.

There always has to be an element of improvisation and flexibility. The media people know what they want and they would organise us themselves.

Remember

Be as organised as possible, but be flexible on the day and ready for the event not to go exactly as planned.

Campaigning is an art not a science.

data to back the emotional arguments, to someone dressing as King Canute and trying to hold back the waves at Druridge Bay to highlight the progressive intrusion of the sea following commercial sand extraction.

"The trick did not lie in whether one way of pushing the DBC case was better than another. Speaking as a reporter with easily jaded news editors to keep happy, the different tactics used by the DBC allowed me to repeat what was essentially a singular message for nearly 20 years, because it was delivered in such a variety of ways.

"Certainly, DBC managed to use the media as effectively as many a highly paid public relations agency could, but how far that played a part in the organisation realising its twin ambitions of no nuclear power station at Druridge and an end to commercial sand extraction is impossible to say.

"It may be that commercial imperatives simply coincided with the aims of the DBC, but it could equally be that the high profile of the DBC and the sincerity of its campaign delayed what might otherwise have been a walkover by the nuclear industry just long enough for the economic arguments to swing against it."

Terry Hackett, *Morpeth Herald* editor

Back in 1979, Terry spent three days at public meetings about the nuclear power station at Ashington Technical College. He wrote a detailed report about this, which I took out of my cuttings file when I went to the Morpeth Herald office to talk to him.

"That cutting certainly takes me back. I was district reporter for the *Morpeth Gazette* at that time. It's hard to think it's been going on that long. Yes, I've reported the Druridge story on and off for all those years. I'm sure a lot of people in 1979 felt that the nuclear power stations were a *fait accompli*. That there was not much chance that the little people, the objectors, could do anything against the power of the CEGB. To come to the end of the road, for the campaign to be won the way it was, was something little short of miraculous.

"The *Gazette* newspapers did have an editorial position opposing the nuclear power stations. Back in 1979, it was not quite as forthright as it is now, but nevertheless it was a stance of opposition.

"I was always convinced personally that if there has to be a wrong site for a nuclear development, it had to be Druridge Bay. I don't know where there are any right sites (we laugh) but anybody who's lived in Northumberland all their life as I have - a lot of my childhood was spent playing at the bay - must have been devastated to think nuclear power there was a real prospect. It was bad enough having acres of opencast coal backing on to the bay. But at least once you got over the dunes, the beach was totally unspoiled.

"To think that people would have been denied the use of the bay, as they would have been, was an appalling prospect.

"I don't know whether we can rest assured that nothing like this will ever rear its ugly head again. We know all too well that some things like this never go away completely. You must feel fairly confident, but who's to know that there won't be some other horror visited on us?

"A lot of people who campaign don't realise how much use the media can be to them. They think we may be opposed to them, when in fact we are often prepared to support them. The important thing for any campaign is to be able to keep the pressure on. It was a lesson the Druridge Bay Campaign learned fast. There can be little doubt that public pressure, stemming from constant exposure in the newspapers, and on radio and televison, contributed significantly towards your success.

“What reporters value most of all is having an easy point of contact. Any news editor in the North East knows your name as being the person to contact about anything to do with Druridge Bay. You always seemed to be there. Other campaigns can draw a lot of lessons from the Druridge Bay Campaign in how to use the media.

“Northumberland owes a great debt of gratitude to the long list of those who have fought so hard against the nightmare prospect of a nuclear power station at a major beauty spot and the continual damage wreaked by sand extraction.”

We couldn’t have done it without them

The reporting by the media of our activities was absolutely fundamental to our success. No doubt much pressure is effective behind closed doors. But an otherwise powerless group of local people, such as we were, would remain almost ineffective without what Tony Henderson called “the oxygen of publicity”. Through media cover, our views could be communicated in two directions, to a potentially sympathetic electorate, and to the decision-makers.

Our local media thus have helped save Druridge Bay, both in stopping the iniquitous effect of sand extraction on the beach, and in the long term removal of the nuclear threat. They claim that their reporting was objective, and I am sure it was. Both we and our opponents were given the chance to express their views. At the same time, the editorial stance often supported us. What the reporters did was give us a platform. Because we were doing good things, and doing them imaginatively, we were able to carry them with us.

I don’t know if media in other parts of Britain are as good as ours, as true and reflective of local concerns, as uninfluenced by the agendas of those who control them. I take my hat off to the *Morpeth Herald*, the *News Post Leader*, the *Northumberland Gazette*, the *Northumberland Herald and Post*, *The Journal*, *The Chronicle*, Radio Newcastle, BBC Look North, and Tyne Tees news teams. We couldn’t have done it without them.

Bridget Gubbins, Bill Gubbins, Libby Paxton, Terry Drummond and Fiona Hall celebrate. 2 December 1996.

Who Saved Druridge?

Chapter 8

It is very difficult for any pressure group to assess the effect of its activities. There are always so many players - those whom the group opposes, the media, local politicians and council officials, MPs and civil servants, private and influential individuals, the vague force of public opinion.

So how much were the two great "successes" of the Druridge Bay Campaign, at the end of 1996, due to our activities?

How much was due to circumstances outside our control, or to other players?

Would the same results have happened anyway?

These are such difficult questions that I have asked people who observed the proceedings for their views. Some of these people are allies or campaign members, and some are our opponents. The first set of interviews address the nuclear issue, the second set both nuclear and sand, and the last two interviews are from Ready Mixed Concrete representatives on the sand issue.

Crispin Aubrey, writer and anti-nuclear campaigner

Crispin was one of the most active members of Stop Hinkley Expansion, the Druridge Bay Campaign's sister organisation in Somerset. Hinkley already had two nuclear power stations, a Magnox and an AGR, when it became the CEGB's preferred site for the second PWR. A writer and journalist, Crispin has published books about nuclear power, and currently edits the magazine of the British Wind Energy Association. This is his reply to my letter asking what he thinks stopped the nuclear power programme from expanding, and the role of anti-nuclear groups like ours.

"I think it was a combination of forces which came together at the same time in the late 1980s to fatally undermine the nuclear industry.

"One element was the anti-nuclear movement itself, in which Stop Hinkley Expansion and the Druridge Bay Campaign played their part. The movement had been attacking the industry right across Europe from the mid-1970s. This contributed to the extremely bad image which nuclear power had developed in public consciousness, and which the media has generally supported. This has undoubtedly had an effect on the way decision-makers and politicians think about the nuclear industry, however much they may claim not to be influenced.

"The second element was the industry's own failures, especially Chernobyl. Its effect was Europe-wide. People in Britain could hear about the cloud passing overhead, they could read about the sheep in Wales, and they could see that the origin of all this was a power station over 1500 miles away. It meant that, in a crowded island like ours, nobody was free from the danger. It revived all the ongoing concerns, like the disposal of nuclear waste, and leukaemia clusters.

"The third element was privatisation. The Conservative government, such staunch supporters of nuclear power, suddenly said that it would have to stand on its own two feet. They must have realised that this was going to be impossible, but ideology apparently overran their traditional love for the magic atom. The result was the exposure of the economic failings of nuclear power.

"This brings us back to the anti-nuclear movement. Potential investors, looking at privatisation in 1988/89 could see the opposition around the country, and they knew that building a new power station was going to be difficult. The Hinkley inquiry was then going on. Instead of the expected time of three months, it actually took 14 months. Once nuclear power was dropped from the privatisation of the electricity industry, and a moratorium declared on public investment in new power stations, the game was up."

Professor Ian Fells, University of Newcastle

Professor Fells is renowned in the North East for favouring nuclear power. On various occasions, he and Druridge Bay Campaigners have put forward opposing viewpoints. I wrote to him asking what influence he thinks the Druridge Bay Campaign had on stopping nuclear power at Druridge, and if he thought we were acting against the national interest. Here is an excerpt from his short reply.

"As I have often said, a nuclear power station was very low in their (CEGB, Nuclear Electric, Magnox) order of priorities. Despite being a green field site close to the sea, it is not an ideal spot as far as electricity generation is concerned. But it was certainly a factor in their thinking that if they ever did want to go ahead with a station at Druridge Bay they would have to fight a very energetic protest group at the public inquiry.

"I do not think you acted against the public interest, the siting of a nuclear power station anywhere must be subject to the most rigorous examinations."

Rex Melville, retired nuclear company executive

Rex Melville was with the CEGB, following privatisation he became company secretary of Nuclear Electric, and finally company secretary of Magnox. I had a telephone conversation with him in May 1997 during which I took notes, which I typed up and sent to him. He made some adjustments, and the following is selected from that version.

BG. What were the main reasons for the selling of the land at Druridge?

"The Druridge Bay site was acquired by the CEGB for a potential nuclear power station. It had been in the Company's portfolio for a long time, during which there have been many changes on the nuclear power front. A major influence was the Government's White Paper on the future of nuclear power, which eventually resulted in a moratorium on further nuclear power stations, after which Nuclear Electric stated it would shelve plans to build Sizewell C (December 1995).

"There were other factors influencing the Druridge Bay site. The majority of the demand for electricity is in the south of the country. Constructing large generating plant in the north would require electricity to be transmitted to its market through the National Grid. The north-south links are already working to capacity."

BG. Was this also true in the early days?

"It may have been."

BG. How aware were you of the opposition at Druridge?

"We have always listened to and understood the views of the DBC, as we have done with all the pressure groups and campaigners who have expressed an interest or an opposition to our plans. Almost every nuclear site has been the subject of vociferous and often constructive campaigns. For our part, we have tried to accommodate their views. We needed Sizewell B for electricity demand and economic purposes.

"The work you did was praiseworthy. You promoted your cause. We did not ride roughshod over your views, we took them into account. There was no hurry to build a nuclear power station at Druridge Bay. So the campaign never reached a stage of head-on confrontation where the bulldozers moved in. Your campaign appeared to be well-managed, well-thought out and conducted in a civil manner. Some campaigns were more hostile.

"I joined Nuclear Electric in 1990, when John Collier was appointed the first Chairman. He was a great champion of nuclear power, a wonderful man, who worked hard to promote the merits of nuclear power but respected the views of others in the process. He had great respect for the Druridge Bay Campaign.

BG. How did he? We never met him. We may have had the odd letter from him.

"He was very well aware of local opposition to the development of a nuclear power station in Druridge Bay.

"Anti-nuclear campaigners have very strong feelings against nuclear power as a technology and whatever rational arguments and justification we put forward, they will never be convinced otherwise."

BG. That includes me.

"I respect that. But we think that nuclear technology is needed; certainly in the long term on economic, environmental and fuel diversity terms. Also to protect rapidly depleting fossil fuel reserves which will be needed for domestic consumption. Our safety record is excellent. It has always been our top priority. There has never been in the UK a major life-threatening incident at our power stations which has endangered our staff or the public at large."

BG. How do you feel about your career in the nuclear industry, since the 1960s? Are you disappointed that there are not more nuclear power stations?

"My long career with the CEGB started in 1963. In the 50s and 60s there was very little economic, environmental or political opposition to the Magnox stations, the UK's first nuclear power programme. Then the AGR programme of the 60s and 70s started, and there began to be opposition on safety and environmental grounds. This opposition increased in the late 70s with Three Mile Island, and in the 80s with Chernobyl. Safety was always our top priority, but we re-doubled our emphasis.

"In the mid to late 70s, the CEGB was advocating that the UK should build a programme of PWR power stations. But a political decision was taken by Tony Benn, the Minister of Energy, that the second programme should be the AGR power stations. If we had built PWRs from the late 70s, as France did, and built a whole programme of them, we may well have had a significant proportion of nuclear capacity on the system today.

BG. Could there have been one at Druridge?

"There may well have been."

Dr Nigel Mortimer, energy analyst and researcher

Nigel has been a member of the Druridge Bay Campaign since the early 80s. A physicist, he was a research associate at Sunderland Polytechnic's Renewable Energy Centre, before running his own Resources Research Unit at Sheffield Hallam University. Fundamentally opposed to nuclear power, he has been our closest and longest-standing advisor. He provided information on alternative energy scenarios for the region, and has done research criticising the CEGB's electricity demand forecasts for the North East, upon which they originally based their case for building nuclear power stations at Druridge. He also contributed substantially to our work on nuclear under-insurance. The following is taken from a live interview which I taped.

BG. What was the role of the Druridge Bay Campaign in stopping nuclear power stations at Druridge?

"The Druridge Bay Campaign did an excellent job of exposing the fundamentally flawed concept of nuclear power at Druridge. It was the weakest possible choice for such a development, a greenfield site in a beautiful area. The Campaign sensitised local opinion, and that sensitivity became a key issue. It became difficult for the CEGB. The site was the easiest one to withdraw from. The strategic arguments were weak, in face of concerted public opinion. The financial issues came later. By the mid 1990s, it was easier to withdraw than to continue.

"The CEGB at first must have thought Druridge would be a soft target, that the public would welcome it, there was local unemployment and they could offer jobs. But it wasn't a soft target because of the Druridge Bay Campaign and its persistence.

"Druridge was a weak choice because there was no pro-nuclear feeling locally. If there is already a nuclear power station, there will always be people who'll say another is a good thing. But Druridge is in a rural area. People saw it as industrial, as an intrusion, and as a threat to the coal industry - those two things combined.

"All the CEGB thought was that they needed a site with stable geology, cooling water, a good connection to the National Grid. They didn't think of the difficulty of getting that proposal through. They thought 'We can build them wherever we choose'. The one thing that assisted the Druridge Bay Campaign was CEGB arrogance.

"The Druridge Bay Campaign put forward sound arguments. The CEGB said that the North East needed a nuclear power station, playing on the fact that old power stations in the region would have to be closed eventually and replaced. They tried to scaremonger people into accepting nuclear power stations or they wouldn't have electricity.

"Everybody knew in the early 80s what power cuts were. We'd had many in the 70s. The CEGB said 'With nuclear power you won't have any problems'.

"The strongest thing the Druridge Bay Campaign did was to rubbish that case. There are other means of ensuring supply. Energy conservation and improved energy efficiency can make inroads into demand. There was plenty of local coal, which can be used more cleanly and efficiently. And there are renewables. People could see these were the answer to any real problems. The hearts and minds argument appealed to people.

"And everybody knows there is a grid. The North East is not separate from the rest of the country. In reality we know areas aren't self sufficient. If that was the case you'd shut down London tomorrow.

"Back in the early 80s, the forecasts by the CEGB of rising demand were totally ridiculous. There is no other word for them. They were total extrapolations on past trends. There was no chance of the trends continuing. You only have to look at the difference between their forecasts and what happened. Subsequent changes in the coal industry and the energy industry have meant that we've managed without nuclear power, certainly in the North East.

"The CEGB's original argument was incredibly weak, but they were a nationalised industry. If the electricity industry hadn't been privatised, the fight would still be on.

"If it had come to a public inquiry at Druridge Bay, there is no guarantee the anti-nuclear case would have won, as it didn't at Sizewell. National need could have over-ruled it. But it would have been an interesting test case as there were nuclear power stations on all the other PWR sites, where there was a local argument in favour of development.

"Nobody should ever underestimate the ability of the Druridge Bay Campaign to sensitise local opinion, and to organise it into a coherent set of arguments. It played a crucial role.

"By itself, the Campaign would not have amounted to anything. But when all the factors were taken into account, the Campaign created an environment where, when faced with financial problems like Nuclear Electric and now Magnox obviously are, if they're looking to get rid of one of the proposals, then it became the easiest one to get rid of. It became more trouble than it was worth."

Fred Barker, research and policy analyst

Fred Barker co-ordinated the submissions to the Government's nuclear review in 1994 and during nuclear power privatisation in 1995-96 for the Consortium of Local Authorities. COLA is a group of local authorities in South Wales and the south west of England, who opposed the building of a PWR at Hinkley in Somerset. Hinkley was one of the "family" of PWR sites to which Druridge was to belong, and of which Sizewell B was the first and only one constructed.

The following is taken from a detailed letter Fred wrote to me, in answer to my questions as to who stopped the nuclear power programme. His letter emphasises the national context. The content within brackets is written by me.

"There were four main factors which stopped the nuclear power station building programme. The most important was Tory Government energy policy. The second related to the views in the City. The third entailed the strongly expressed views of other major players in the electricity industry, in particular the Office of Electricity Regulation and the CBI. The fourth was the detailed, research-based Nuclear Review submissions of groups such as COLA and the Nuclear Free Local Authorities.

"First, there was Tory Government energy policy.

> 'The aim of the Government's energy policy is to ensure secure, diverse and sustainable supplies of energy in forms that people and businesses want, and at competitive prices.
>
> 'Security and diversity of supply are best achieved through the operation of competitive and open markets.'
>
> *From the White Paper,* The Prospects for Coal, *March 1993.*

(The conclusion to be drawn from this is that government subsidies for the building and operating of nuclear power stations were unlikely to be available. The industry must be able to stand on its own feet.)

"Second, views in the City, as expressed by the Government's own consultants, Barclays de Zoete Wedd were as follows.

> 'We doubt that the banks would be content to rely on the creditworthiness of Nuclear Electric and any overseas partners without explicit Government underwriting of regulatory risk.'
>
> *Report by Barclays de Zoete Wedd to the DTI, December 1994.*

(Essentially, banks would not finance new nuclear power stations without substantial government underwriting, which it was not likely to give.)

"Third, there were the views of major players such as OFFER, the electricity regulator, and the CBI.

'Many commentators suggest that Nuclear Electric's forecasts may be optimistic and may significantly understate the level of subsidy required.'

OFFER submission to the DTI's Nuclear Review, October 1994.

'The need for intervention to ensure fuel diversity has shifted a long way since the privatisation of the electricity supply industry. Although there are differing views, the CBI does not find conclusive arguments, under current market conditions, for supporting new nuclear plant on diversity grounds.'

CBI submission to the DTI's Nuclear Review, September 1994.

"Fourth, there were the research based Nuclear Review submissions of COLA and other bodies.

"COLA's investment appraisal illustrated the enormous scale of Government support likely to be required for Sizewell C: this was equivalent to a total financial subsidy in the range of £3.6 - £4.5 billion. It also concluded that new nuclear plant falls far short of passing the Government's criterion for support and market intervention - that there should be strong environmental or strategic benefits.

"The Nuclear Free Local Authorities group opposed Nuclear Electric's position that nuclear generation will be essential to the country's long term energy mix if the Government is to avoid increases in carbon dioxide emissions. It argued that measures consistent with current government policy could achieve carbon dioxide reductions, such as additional support for energy efficiency, renewables and taxation of road fuels."

Cllr Ian Swithenbank, leader of Northumberland County Council

Cllr Swithenbank has not been directly involved with the Druridge Bay Campaign. We have only met him twice or thrice during the eleven years in which the council has given us annual donations. The following is taken from the transcripts of our taped conversation in May 1997.

BG. What was the Druridge Bay Campaign's role, relative to the County Council's role, in stopping sand extraction?

"Obviously the public pressure by the Druridge Bay Campaign over sand extraction would concern any large company that has to think of its reputation as well as its profits. And that pressure led them to the point where they came to talk to us realistically. They came to my office at County Hall. I told them we can't buy out their planning permission, but surely it's now in their interest to look at other options. Where do we go from here? They said they could go on to the year 2042. All they have to do is shovel the sand up from the beach, but if there was sand available elsewhere, of a reasonable quality, at a reasonable price, perhaps they could find another site.

"Their intention at first was to obtain planning permissions, and then withdraw. It's always difficult. It takes time. There are lots of processes to be followed. They came one day and said these options aren't yet resolved, but they were prepared to make an announcement that they were coming off Druridge Bay. I was delighted. We called a press meeting at fairly short notice.

"The Druridge Bay Campaign was a big help certainly. I think we'd have probably got there eventually, but we'd have been several years down the line from a decision without it. For a firm to move when they didn't have to, when they didn't have a planning permission for the alternative grades of sand they needed, for a site that could well be suitable but has not yet gone through the planning process! - I was rather taken aback, but I was delighted.

"I think the announcement about the selling of the land by Magnox a few days before helped. If they were already thinking of stopping, that would encourage them that they were doing the right thing. They knew all your attentions would be focussed on them after that. And if a big powerful company like Magnox responds to a campaign like yours, RMC would respect that. The whole new attitude of running business ethically was coming to the fore. The Druridge Bay sand issue's time had come. It was tremendous for the campaigners to have two successes coming together."

BG. How do you see the roles of the county council and the Druridge Bay Campaign on the nuclear power issue?

"It is very easy at the time of success to say that the Druridge Bay Campaign, or me, or individuals, were responsible for the outcome. It was a long haul, by a lot of individuals. It cost a lot, and it produced success, but it didn't come easily. We must have funded the Druridge Bay Campaign to almost £100,000 over the years.

"Our problem was that if we at the county council had gone into all the detailed arguments about nuclear power at Druridge, before we had had the opportunity to comment on a planning application, we would have appeared to be biased, and this would later have invalidated our position. By giving the money to you, as a community group, to enable you to express your position, we were totally detached. You were able to raise economic issues related to nuclear power and coal, its role in the local economy and the local environment, even matters such as nuclear insurance.

"You had your role to play. We had to reserve our position, to be able to respond to a particular application, not to be biased."

Jack Thompson MP for Wansbeck

Jack, like Alan Beith, has been a Campaign supporter since the early 80s. This is part of a live interview in the DBC office, which I taped. Some of the interview appears in Chapter 4.

"The county council worked as hard as it could to stop the sand extraction, to recover the situation left by the government inspector after the inquiries in the 1960s. The success was a combination of the efforts of the legal and professional people at County Hall and the grassroots campaigners.

"It's always a good idea not to show a totally negative case. The county council tried to show that there could be other places where sand might be extracted with minimum environmental problems to other people. The company needed a commercially acceptable and dignified retreat. The sand company cares only about cost and quality of materials. If they can calculate that there is no more cost in a new place, and the quality is as good, they can say to themselves 'Let's accede at Druridge, and get the hassle off our backs'.

"The nuclear issue was the same. You always tried to show there was an alternative. Blyth could be re-furbished. There are clean coal systems. It put the nuclear power people in the position of arguing against an alternative.

"The economics of nuclear power, the Chernobyl accident, and the arguments of the environmentalists, plus possibly the anticipated Labour government, all helped in the final decision by Magnox to sell the land at Druridge."

Alan Beith MP for Berwick upon Tweed

Alan has been mentioned numerous times throughout this book. He has done everthing he can to oppose nuclear power and sand extraction at Druridge since 1979. Liz Carruthers, my co-worker, and I visited him at his house in Berwick. Liz took notes while we chatted. Some of the interview appears in Chapter 4. Here are more excerpts.

“It was privatisation of the electricity industry that stopped nuclear power. It was the death knell for the industry. It forced costs out into the open.

“But there was always the risk in the early days that the engine might have got too far down the track. If the CEGB had got a planning application in for nuclear power station at Druridge ahead of the collapse of nuclear power, then we might not have been able to stop it. I always felt that if we could hold on for long enough, then we would be safe.

“The collapse became certain in the late 1980s, and it was just a matter of how long before it happened. With the Thatcherite view that we need nuclear power to combat global warming, the Druridge Bay Campaign could never afford to let up. The nuclear companies also came to realise that it was better to build more power stations where there were existing sites. They knew the reasons against Druridge Bay, but it was vital that our area was not allowed to move up the queue.

“The Druridge Bay Campaign was of crucial importance in stopping sand extraction. Why else should RMC stop? It was extremely embarrassing for them. The Government would not assist in revocation of the original permission. The county council found a solution, but would they have done so if RMC had not faced hostile public opinion, which influenced RMC? I think not.

“The Campaign were quite right to co-operate with the opposition to RMC in the Ingram Valley. It could have been difficult if the company had got away with playing one situation against the other.

“If the Druridge Bay Campaign had flagged, RMC would have carried on. You got under their skin. You put rather subtle pressure on the company, while still talking sensibly to them.”

Chris Leese, Estates Manager, Northern Aggregates

Chris Leese is an earnest, matter-of-fact young Yorkshireman, direct in his speech and manner, sincere in his apparent love of his work, including extracting sand from the beach, and with a certain wistful sensitivity. He and Terry Drummond had some furious encounters. The following are extracts from his reply to my letter.

"Clearly you were effective in raising the profile of what had, up until your organisation's involvement, been a relatively non-controversial activity. I think you used the press particularly well, and were successful in maintaining the profile of your campaign.

"What I did feel was unfortunate was that certain members (a very few) of the Campaign personalised the issue (I do not include you in this incidentally) because we are after all human! What this did do for myself and some of my colleagues was to create a greater resolve on occasions, and even a siege mentality.

"I feel this was probably counter productive for you. There may have been a danger, had the issue become more generally personalised, that you might have lost a certain amount of sympathy and support, although you will have to judge for yourself whether this actually happened.

"I suspect you probably recognised this potential and took appropriate steps. (Actually I would be quite interested to know if this is correct.)

"One incident that stands out in my mind was having to try to evict Mr Drummond from his deck chair at the end of our access ramp, where he had threatened to repose until we stopped digging sand - quite a bizarre scenario in its own right! Having unsuccessfully tried to reason with him, I was walking back to my car in none too good a humour, to be confronted by a very old man waving a walking stick, and holding on to quite a large dog.

"'Here we go again', I thought, and tried as best as I could to ignore said gentleman. However our paths converged. The old boy looked up at me and I cringed, expecting another onslaught.

" 'It's a pity you can't demand all your sand back, laddie', he said. 'Because if you could, half the houses in Morpeth would fall down, and that would teach the so and so's'. (Actually, he didn't say so and so's!!) I returned to my car with a smile, and faith in human nature restored. Perhaps our message was getting through to at least *some* people!

"Those are a few comments which reflect my side of the story. I'd be quite interested to see your book; an autographed copy perhaps? I think at least I deserve that!"

Tim Stokes, Public Relations Executive, Ready Mixed Concrete group

Tim Stokes came to our office, with Stewart Vale from Northern Aggregates, the subsidiary company which had been removing the sand. They came on the day when we unveiled the plaque at Druridge, commemorating the end of sand extraction, in May 1997. Members Joan Meredith and Rosie Snowdon took notes. Tim Stokes went over my writing up of the notes and amended them. And I input selections from his amendments.

BG. How much influence did the Druridge Bay Campaign have on RMC?

"RMC is a multinational company and the world's leading supplier of ready mixed concrete. Northern Aggregates Limited is based in the North East of England. It sees it as part of its role to speak to local people and to build good working relationships with communities close to its quarry sites. We have quarry liaison committees where local people can air their views, and opinions can be exchanged.

"The company saw the Druridge Bay Campaign as an extension of this process. It wanted to take on board your views and those of other interested parties.

"There is a growing public awareness of the environment, and of the need for industry to improve its performance. Recent examples have been the Newbury bypass protests, Brent Spar, and Manchester Airport.

"We have progressively improved our environmental performance, and continually review and update our policies. We have to make money of course, but we have moved forward. There is pressure from campaigning groups like you, from changing legislation, and from our own sense of responsibility to local communities and society in general.

"Historically, the aggregates industry may have been perceived as a rather macho-type world, tending to pursue its own interests and objectives. If this was so, it has changed. Inevitably, as the new generation of young people move into positions of responsibility, they will apply new experiences and principles.

BG. Would you have come to the same decision without the activities of the Druridge Bay Campaign?

"You maintained a focussed and sustained campaign. Comments by Alan Beith and others were taken on board, but it was the work of the Campaign that ensured Druridge Bay was kept on the agenda. This led to the dialogue and the increased understanding between the company and the County Council.

"You *created* the debate."

So were the successes owing to the Druridge Bay Campaign?

Thinking over all the comments I have recorded here, and the many conversations I have had over the last few months, here are my views.

Nuclear power stations

The nuclear issue is long-standing and complex. It began in the 50s, and for Druridge at least, ended only in 1996. Gradually during its first thirty years, the civil nuclear industry gained in power and confidence, until it was generating between 14 and 20% of our electricity.

In 1965 a decision by a Labour government to go for the AGR design of nuclear power station caused such a slowdown of the nuclear power programme that it helped save the UK from being as riddled with nuclear power as France.

The industry was still optimistically growing in 1978, when the first announcement that Druridge was a suitable site for nuclear power stations was made. For the next two decades, people in Northumberland and Tyneside never let the issue die. We carried on the protest and the awareness raising that has contributed to the unpopularity everywhere of this method of generating electricity.

The Chernobyl accident increased awareness of the dangers. The nuclear power stations' final death-knell sounded when the Conservative government tried to privatise them, and found them so uneconomic that they could not be sold. Eventually, Nuclear Electric was privatised in summer 1996, after a pledge that the privatised company would build no new nuclear power stations. Nuclear Electric was split into two parts, British Energy, which was privatised and held the newer nuclear power stations, and Magnox Electric which held the older unprivatisable Magnox stations plus other properties including the land at Druridge.

The Druridge Bay Campaign was the North East region's contribution to the national anti-nuclear movement, which attacked the nuclear industry at every opportunity, and on every front. In particular, it was attacked during the prolonged Sizewell Inquiry, during the privatisation of electricity procedure, during the Hinkley public inquiry, during the government's nuclear review, and during nuclear privatisation.

We focussed on acting locally, and supporting the national anti-nuclear movement. We ensured that the Central Electricity Generating Board, later Nuclear Electric and finally Magnox Electric, knew that they would get huge difficulties if they put in a planning application. Ultimately, we were responsible for ensuring that Magnox Electric sold their Druridge property.

We in the Druridge Bay Campaign weren't solely responsible for saving Druridge Bay from nuclear power stations, but we played our part. Indirectly we probably contributed to the swing of public opinion against nuclear power in the country, helping to save other innocent beaches. It is significant and satisfying to know that we did those things.

Sand extraction

The sand extraction issue is different. We had a much more total and direct influence. Commercial digging of sand had been troubling people locally prior to public inquiries in the 1960s, at which the government inspector granted ill-thought out permissions. If the local authorities in Northumberland had used the relevant legal methods open to them to stop extraction, they would have been liable to high levels of compensation which they couldn't afford.

The technique which was available to stop sand extraction was to embarrass and shame the company. This is what the Druridge Bay Campaign did. With countless actions, by tying in the idea of King Canute who tried to keep the sea at bay, and with the support of the local media, the company in the end decided that the profits from extraction were not worth the hassle. Discussions with the county council had been ongoing too. The cessation was not entirely due to us. Nevertheless, as Northumberland County Council leader Ian Swithenbank has admitted, RMC would undoubtedly have gone on for many more years. They had the legal right to do so, and it was a cheap and profitable part of their operation.

But they did stop, and it was largely due to us. As RMC's own public relations executive has admitted, we *created* the debate.

* * *

I have given space to many viewpoints in this book, my own, those of Druridge Bay Campaign members, and those whom we opposed. I would like Jane Gifford to have the last word.

> "The Druridge Bay Campaign was like a contemporary Scheherazade, the heroine of the Arabian Nights. She saved herself by delaying her execution until the Sultan changed his mind.
>
> "The Druridge Bay Campaign guaranteed that a nuclear power station would always be passionately opposed for as long as necessary. This bought time in which eighteen years of accidents, technological and political change, and increased environmental awareness propelled public opinion in our direction.
>
> "We were always right. We just had to wait for the others to catch up!"

End words

I would like everyone who has read this book to go to Druridge Bay;
to climb up from the landward side to the crest of the dunes;
to meet the great, open space of wind and water and sand and sky
the elements;

to gaze out to sea, misty and bitter grey, or blue and quivering silver;
to dream, mindlessly, while the fearsome grandeur of the water rolls, the wind blusters and deafens;

to let the eyes rove northwards
where the crescent of sand sweeps away towards the headland
and the other bays beyond leap towards the Scottish border,
the breathtaking, gasping spaces.

And to look westward, inland,
the far-off opencast heaps
the ponds and pools reflecting blue nearby
the cosmetic surgery of the coal mining industry
the smoothed mounds, the fences
the ruin of an ancient hospital, which survived on an island of coal
the hamlet of farm and cottages, prettivated, titivated, a little forlorn.

And to look south, at the rather dull fields
planted with barley and leys of grass, with tame sheep grazing.

In those fields could have been big square buildings, pylons, wires, transformers, car parks, widened roads, signs.
And in the deep and shining centre
the power that concentrates and seduces, bribes with endless promises,
weekly sending its load of gleaming poisons along the country roads and railway lines
to the polluted sea on the other side of the land;
the poisons that will be deadly for longer than humankind has lived on this earth.

There is the farm, where the digger truck parked at night
that hacked away daily at the beach and the dunes.
The digger has gone now.
The farmer will find other ways of making a living, as he has always had to do.
He will buy back the land he sold to the power people.

On the skyline are tiny smoking cigarette chimneys standing over the woodlands,
Alcan, the power station that burns the coal from under the sea;
a reminder that the land and sea over which the eyes rove is lying on beds of coal.

It is not the most beautiful of British landscapes.
It doesn't appear on many scenic calendars,
but it has a place in history for what it has not become.

I would like everyone who goes there to stand on the crest of the dunes,
and gaze;
to remember the small people, who did humble things;
who stood up to the diggers and to the vague and distant powers, who wrote letters, collected signatures, stood at the car park, organised fairs, ran on the beach, signed petitions, loved, wept and prayed for their land, who sang and danced and laughed for it.

They have made a legend.
They helped the course of history in Northumberland to be different
from what the giant powers wanted it to be.
They drove those powers from their bay.

Chronology - Druridge Bay Nuclear Power Stations

Dec '78	CEGB announces Druridge may be site for nuclear power station.
Mar '83	Founding of Cairn at Druridge by Mid-Northumberland Friends of the Earth.
Jan '84	Druridge Bay Campaign established as federation of groups opposed to nuclear power stations at Druridge.
May '84	CEGB starts detailed test drilling at Druridge.
Dec '84	CEGB buys land at Druridge, enough for two nuclear power stations.
Apr '86	Druridge Bay Campaign sets up office and employs staff.
Nov '89	*Government announcement: nuclear power will not be privatised, and no more nuclear power stations until after a review in 1994.*
Apr '91	Letter from Nuclear Electric says they still consider Druridge Bay a suitable site.
Nov '91	Frank Dobson, shadow energy spokesperson, says a Labour government would insist on Nuclear Electric selling the land at Druridge.
Dec '91	Publication of Druridge Bay Campaign's second book, *Generating Pressure*.
Jan '92	Consultants North Energy Associates founded by DBC supporters, to promote alternatives to nuclear power.
Dec '93	Alan Beith agrees to introduce Energy Conservation Bill, as asked by Druridge Bay Campaign's Energy Group.
Apr '94	Government stops Alan Beith's Energy Conservation Bill.
Jul '94	Druridge Bay Campaign launches its "Sell the Land" campaign.
Oct '94	Energy Group launches its nuclear under-insurance campaign.
Apr '95	*The Journal* runs front page story and interview with Robert Hawley, Chief Executive of Nuclear Electric, "WE WILL BUILD AT DRURIDGE".
May '95	The profitable part of Nuclear Electric will be privatised. Druridge land will go to Magnox Electric, not to be privatised.
Jul '95	Druridge Bay Campaign launches "Sell the Land" petition.
Jan '96	Druridge Bay Campaigners send giant postcard to Tim Eggar, asking him to "Sell the Land".
Feb '96	40,000 star studded signature petition goes to Tim Eggar, saying they don't want nuclear power stations at Druridge, and asking him to sell the land.
27 Nov '96	Magnox issued a statement. They would sell the land.
	The Druridge Bay Campaign had finally achieved its goal. There would never be nuclear power stations at Druridge Bay.
14 Dec '96	Druridge Bay Campaign holds its Celebration Party.

Chronology - Sand Extraction at Druridge Bay

DBC agrees to widen remit into other threats to Druridge Bay besides the nuclear power proposal. This opens the way for the sand campaign.	*Mar '90*
Lorry protest at Druridge.	*Nov '90*
Alan Beith speaks in House of Commons adjournment debate. Environment Minister Tim Yeo refuses to help.	*Dec '90*
12,000 signature petition gathered by Northumberland Wildlife Trust delivered to Castle Morpeth Borough Council.	*Mar '91*
King Canute attempts to hold back the sea at Druridge.	*Mar '91*
John Cummings MP for Easington backs Druridge Bay Campaigners in the House of Commons Environment Select Committee.	*Dec '91*
Alan Beith unveils new sign at sand extraction site at Druridge.	*May '92*
Public Inquiry at Powburn picketed, where Druridge Campaigners expose RMC as not being concerned about the environment.	*Sept '92*
King Canute and serfs go to Northern Aggregates headquarters in Cleveland.	*Oct '92*
Alan Beith and Jack Thompson speak about Druridge sand extraction in House of Commons debate on coastal protection.	*Dec '92*
The Journal takes on sand campaign, and publishes petition.	*26 Apr '93*
King Canute, courtiers and serfs go to RMC's AGM in London.	*May '93*
Terry and Carole Drummond sit in front of digger at beach.	*May '93*
Storms cause breach in dunes at sand extraction site.	*Sept '93*
King Canute and serfs go to London to present 20,000 signature petition. Alan Beith goes with campaigners to see Environment Minister Tony Baldry.	*22 Nov '93*
The first stage in sand victory. After secret talks between Northumberland County Council and RMC, a breakthrough is announced. Extraction will stop when RMC has alternative sites.	*22 Nov '93*
New sand sign unveiled at Druridge, saying How Long RMC? - On same day, two members attend RMC's AGM in London.	*Apr '94*
Storms flood through dunes, and extraction continues.	*Jan '95*
King Canute and court march through Morpeth streets, then erect new Greedy RMC sign. It is three years since RMC said they would stop.	*Nov '96*
Nuclear land sale announcement made. Local newspaper editorials attacks RMC because they still extract sand. Media attention focussed on Druridge.	*28 Nov '96*
Campaigners dash from Druridge Bay to County Hall, where RMC announce they will stop sand extraction, immediately.	*12 Dec '96*
Druridge Bay Campaign Celebration Party, for the two victories.	*14 Dec '96*

Bibliography and some recommended reading

Pressure Groups

Alderman, Geoffrey, *Pressure Groups and Government in Great Britain* (Longman, 1984)

Baggott, Rob, *Pressure groups today* (Manchester University Press, 1995)

Ball, Alan & Millard, Frances, *Pressure Politics in Industrial Societies* (Macmillan, 1986)

Grant, Wyn, *Pressure Groups, Politics and Democracy in Britain* (Harvester Wheatsheaf, 1994)

Jordan, Grant & Richardson, J J, *Government and Pressure Groups in Britain* (Clarendon Press, 1987)

Lowe, Philip & Goyder, Jane, *Environmental Groups in Politics* (George Allen & Unwin, 1983)

Campaigns

Brandon, Ruth, *The Burning Question: the anti-nuclear movement since 1945* (Heinemann, 1987)

Bryant, Barbara & Thompson, M Denton-, *Twyford Down, roads, campaigning and environmental law* (E & FN Spon, 1995)

Gubbins, Bridget, *Generating Pressure: the campaign against nuclear power at Druridge Bay* (Earthright Publications, 1991)

Kirkup, Mike, *Tidelines* (Druridge Bay Campaign, 1988)

Merrick, *Battle for the Trees* (Godhaven Ink, 1996)

Practical campaigning

Bird, Polly, *How to Run a Local Campaign* (Northcote House, 1989)

Campaigners' Guide to Local Plans (Council for the Protection of Rural England, 1992)

Campaigners' Guide to Road Proposals (Council for the Protection of Rural England, 1993)

Campaigners' Guide to Minerals (Council for the Protection of Rural England, 1996)

Energy-conscious Planning: the case for action (Council for the Protection of Rural England, 1991)

Harding, Thomas, *The Video Activist Handbook* (Pluto Press, 1997)

Lattimer, Mark, *The Campaigning Handbook* (Directory for Social Change, 1994)

Mackenzie, Craig, *The Shareholder Action Handbook* (New Consumer, 1993)

Road Raging: top tips for wrecking roadbuilding (Road Alert, 1997)

Nuclear power

Bertell, Rosalie, *No Immediate Danger* (Women's Press, 1985)

Brownlie, Helen, Mortimer, Dr Nigel, *Nuclear Under-Insurance: a Hidden Subsidy* (Druridge Bay Campaign, 1994)

Brownlie, Helen, Mortimer, Dr Nigel & Gubbins, Bridget, *Under-Insurance: a Nuclear Liability* (Druridge Bay Campaign, 1995)

Bolter, Harold, *Inside Sellafield* (Quartet, 199?)

Caufield, Catherine, *Multiple Exposures* (Secker and Warburg, 1989)

Hall, Jeremy, *Real Lives, Half Lives* (Penguin, 1996)

May, John, *The Greenpeace Book of the Nuclear Age: the hidden history, the human cost* (Victor Gollanz, 1990)

Patterson, Walter, *Nuclear Power* (Penguin, 1983)

Roche, Adi, *Children of Chernobyl* (Harper Collins, 1996)

Glossary of Reactor Types

Magnox reactors

"Magnox" is the alloy used as fuel cladding in the first-generation British gas-cooled reactors, which are therefore called Magnox reactors. Examples are Sizewell A, Hinkley A, Oldbury and Wylfa. They have a graphite core, and are carbon dioxide-cooled. They were gradually increased in capacity from 50MW to about 800 MW, but were expensive to build, produced little heat output per unit volume of the reactor, and often seriously overran their construction time,

Advanced Gas-cooled Reactors (AGRs)

These are the second-generation of British nuclear power stations. They have a graphite core, and are carbon-dioxide cooled. Examples are Hartlepool, Torness and Hinkley B. They were of approximately 600 MW theoretical capacity, and often built as twin-reactors. Like the Magnox stations, they often overran their construction time by years, and had numerous difficulties in operation. Eventually, the CEGB decided that further nuclear power stations should be of the PWR type, typically built in France and the USA.

Pressurised Water Reactors (PWRs)

These were to have been the third generation of British nuclear power stations, and Druridge was to have been the site of one of them. Only one was constructed, at Sizewell in Suffolk, completed in 1995. They are large, water-cooled reactors with a theoretical capacity of 1200 MW. The CEGB obtained planning permission for a PWR at Hinkley, in 1990 after a public inquiry, and applied for planning permission in 1993 for a twin reactor, ie a 2400 MW nuclear power station, to be known as Sizewell C. None of these stations will now be built.

Steam Generating Heavy Water Reactors (SGHWRs)

One of various reactor designs developed by the Atomic Energy Authority, a 100 MW model of which was built at Winfrith in Dorset. No commercial reactor was built. Winfrith at one time was a suggested site for the PWR.

Fast Reactors

Fast "breeder" reactors are designed to breed more fissile nuclei than they consume. They were the nuclear planners' dream, in that theoretically they would supply a potentially endless source of energy. However they are cooled with sodium, which explodes in contact with water. The technology is expensive and dangerous, and its development has been dropped by most countries of the world, including the UK.

List of Illustrations

Photographs

Photographs credited 'subject' were supplied by the subject and the photographer is not known.

Drawings etc

Diagrams

All diagrams were redrawn by Jon Nott from originals by Bridget Gubbins.

Tables

Index